DATE DUE

Silicon Valley Fever

SILICON VALLEY FEVER

GROWTH OF HIGH-TECHNOLOGY CULTURE

Everett M. Rogers   &   Judith K. Larsen

STANFORD UNIVERSITY   COGNOS ASSOCIATES

Basic Books, Inc., Publishers

NEW YORK

The authors gratefully acknowledge Peter Ciotti for permission to adapt portions of "Revenge of the Nerds," which appeared in *California* (July 1982).

Library of Congress Cataloging in Publication Data

Rogers, Everett M.
  Silicon Valley fever.

  Includes bibliographical references and index.
  1. Microelectronics industry—California—Santa Clara
County—History. 2. Semiconductor industry—California—
Santa Clara County—History. 3. High-technology
industries—California—Santa Clara County—History.
I. Larsen, Judith K. II. Title.
HD9696.A3U593 1984   338.4'76213817'0979473   83-45257
ISBN 0-465-07821-4

Dedicated to the spirit of

Frederick E. Terman,

who first saw the vision of

Silicon Valley

In the interest of protecting the privacy of individuals whose real identities are not central to the true story told here, certain names and other descriptive details have been altered.

CONTENTS

ACKNOWLEDGEMENTS   IX

PART I
BEGINNINGS

1: *The Apple Story*   3
2: *The Rise of Silicon Valley*   25

PART II
THE CULTURE OF HIGH TECHNOLOGY

3: *Catching the Silicon Valley Fever*   43
4: *Venture Capital*   62
5: *Networks*   79
6: *Winning at the Game: Intel*   96
7: *Losing: Companies That Don't Make It*   122
8: *Working*   137
9: *Lifestyles*   155
10: *Goodies*   168
11: *Problems in Paradise*   184

PART III
THE TOMORROW OF SILICON VALLEY

12: *Growing Competition: The Japanese*   205

13: *The Spread of "Silicon Valleys"*   230

14: *The Impact of Silicon Valley*   252

NOTES   277

INDEX   293

ACKNOWLEDGEMENTS

ONE SUNDAY MORNING two years ago, a half-filled plane left San Francisco for Pittsburgh. Coincidentally, as we'd known each other previously, we both happened to be on that plane. Of course our conversation turned to the topic of current interest—Silicon Valley. We discussed our impressions of the high-tech life that was developing around us in California. By the time our plane landed at the Greater Pittsburgh International Airport, we had an outline for a book. This volume is the result of what began as a routine, cross-country flight.

Local newspapers can be a rich source of data for social scientists. We found the *San Jose Mercury News* to be especially valuable, along with the *Peninsula Times-Tribune,* the *San Francisco Chronicle,* and the *Palo Alto Weekly.* Articles in these and other papers and magazines often alerted us to new developments in the fast-changing Silicon Valley scene. We followed up these leads and many others with personal interviews, usually tape recorded, with such key individuals as the late Frederick E. Terman, William Hewlett, Robert N. Noyce, Jerry Sanders, Lester Hogan, Marcian E. Hoff, Jr., and approximately a hundred others. The entrepreneurs of Silicon Valley have solid self-concepts and perhaps this encouraged them to talk openly with us about their experiences. We found them to be unusually helpful and cooperative.

Special thanks go to Nick Larsen, an engineer, entrepreneur, and a keen observer of Silicon Valley, who supplied countless stories about less-publicized events. Howard Bogert, a veteran of the Silicon Valley semiconductor industry, was a special friend. Sincere thanks go to Jeff Davis, an engineering student at Stanford University, who helped us learn a great deal about entrepreneurship, and to Robert Byers, Director of News and Publications at Stanford University, who shared his files and his special knowledge about Silicon Valley. The staff of the University Archives in the Stanford University Library also deserve mention for their helpfulness. Martin Kessler, our publisher, provided us with encouragement. Finally, Julia Burnett helped us convert ideas into words.

Perhaps our deepest gratitude goes to the hundreds of Silicon Valley people we interviewed who explained their experiences and observations. They were generous with their time and contributed much to our understanding of Silicon Valley life.

Just as some people in Silicon Valley are jogging bores or computer bores, we have been "Silicon Valley bores" to our families, friends, and colleagues for the past couple of years. We apologize for our intense involvement in this topic. But we can't promise any further lessening of our interest in the culture of high technology. It is the future.

EVERETT M. ROGERS
Stanford, California

JUDITH K. LARSEN
Los Altos, California

PART I

BEGINNINGS

THE HISTORY of Silicon Valley is short, consisting of no more than three decades. We begin this book with the epic story of Apple Computer Inc., because it captures all the pieces of the typical Silicon Valley success story.

1

The Apple Story

THE program chairperson for the 1976 national conference of county and local government officials must have had a sadistic streak to have scheduled the conference's first session in the main ballroom of Atlanta's Peachtree Plaza Hotel at the ungodly hour of 8:00 A.M. The printed program listed Ted Nelson as the first speaker, on the topic of "Computer Lib" (Nelson had authored a book by this title). One might wonder just how many local government officials this subject would pull out of their hotel beds that early in the morning.

Ted Nelson looked very boyish and somewhat preppy in a Harvard school tie and a blazer. He began by turning up the volume of a tape recorder, so that the theme from "2001: A Space Odyssey" blasted the audience. His first slide showed the sun rising over a big rock. The second, a close-up, showed an Altair 8800 microcomputer on the rock. Next was Ted Nelson in a monkey mask, standing on the rock and holding the little computer triumphantly over his head. His presentation went on from there. Nelson shouted that for too long computers had been the sole possession of superior-acting professionals in

air-conditioned computer centers.¹ Now, said Nelson, microcomputers like the Altair are easily available, sold by retail
stores like the chain of Byte Shops then springing up around the
United States. He ended with the "2001" theme, again turned up
to rock concert volume, while yelling "Demystify computers!
COMPUTERS BELONG TO ALL MANKIND!"—revolutionary
phrases about giving computer power to the people. The audience was silent for a few seconds—shocked.

Then they stood up and applauded for five minutes.

The Computer Kids

Back in 1976, Ted Nelson was one of a small set of precocious
"computer nerds" who were about to shock the computer establishment: Harry Garland and Roger Melen of Cromemco; Adam
Osborne of Osborne Computer; Bill Gates of Microsoft; Ed Roberts of Altair; and Nolan Bushnell of Atari. And to become most
famous of all, Steven P. Jobs and Stephan G. Wozniak, who were
then founding Apple Computer Inc., in Silicon Valley. About the
time that Ted Nelson was speaking in Atlanta, this crew of microcomputer revolutionaries were in their twenties, products of having grown up during the radical 1960s. Then, most of the set still
preferred jeans and workshirts to three-piece suits. Now, when
they are mostly multimillionaires and their companies are listed
on Wall Street, they appear in public in Brooks Brothers pin-
stripes.

Until the mid-1970s when the microcomputer burst on the
American scene, computers were owned and operated by the establishment—government, big corporations, and other large institutions. These big computers (called mainframe computers because they are so large that the electronic equipment must be
mounted on a fixed frame) are mainly used for data-crunching:
accounting, record keeping, research, data analysis, banking, and
airline ticketing. But thanks to the invention of the microprocessor by Ted Hoff at Intel in 1971, it soon was possible to produce

a very small computer, one that would sell for only a few thousand dollars, or less. At that price, millions of Americans might find some useful tasks for their very own computer. Because they were built around a microprocessor, these small computers were dubbed "microcomputers." They have set off a revolution in miniature, moving computing power into the hands of the people. Just as Ted Nelson wanted.

At first, in 1975, these microcomputers were only a hobbyist's plaything. The Altair 8800[2] could be ordered by mail or purchased at retail computer stores. The salesmen were bright teenagers who treated their customers with a horribly superior air and talked to them in obtuse computer jargon. The Altair kit cost about $400, but a user had to spend another $2,000 or so for peripheral equipment. About 2,000 Altair 8800s went out the door in 1975, mostly to engineers, scientists, or computer programmers. The only problem was once you got home with your personal computer it couldn't do anything very useful. And the number of hobbyists willing to spend a few thousand dollars for a computer that didn't do much was pretty limited.

But then the home computer market took off, thanks especially to Apple Computer, Tandy Corporation's Radio Shack, and Commodore. These companies realized that if software programs were available, thousands—even millions—of microcomputers would be sold. It wasn't the big mainframe computer companies like IBM and CDC (Control Data Corporation) and Burroughs that pioneered in launching the personal computer, or even the DECs (Digital Equipment Corporation) or Data Generals (two minicomputer firms). In fact, the two leading manufacturers of home computers did not begin with much financial strength. Radio Shack invested a grand total of $150,000 in tooling, engineering, and software to get its first successful TRS-80 Model I to market.[3]

Apple started out in Steve Jobs's garage in Los Altos, California, and was produced mainly because Jobs and his partner Steve Wozniak wanted an Altair but couldn't afford to buy one.[4] The Apple Computer story is prototypical of Silicon Valley entrepreneurial success.

Jobs and Woz (a nickname, pronounced "Wahz") are true children of Silicon Valley. Growing up in its high-voltage environ-

ment was a natural preparation for their electronic life. Jobs and
Wozniak met twenty years ago, when they were in grade school,
in a friend's garage. As later events showed, garages were to play
an important role in their lives. Jobs was impressed with Wozniak, who had built a computer which had just won first prize in
a Bay Area science fair. Wozniak had been interested in computers since his childhood when his father, an electronics engineer
at Lockheed Missiles and Space Company in Sunnyvale, helped
him design logic circuits. During his grade school days in Sunnyvale, Wozniak worked with such intense concentration that he
often didn't look up when someone spoke to him. His mother got
his attention by rapping him sharply on top of his skull.[5] By any
measure Wozniak was precocious, and showed signs early of the
technical genius he was to become. He was the smartest student
at Homestead High School in Santa Clara, scoring a perfect 800
on the mathematics entrance exam for college. Some of his class-
mates remember him as being quiet and withdrawn, but brilliant.
In short, he was the stereotype of the computer genius, or "nerd,"
as the type is called.

Wozniak enrolled at the University of Colorado, then at De
Anza College in Cupertino, and finally at the University of California, Berkeley. He wasn't very happy at any of these schools.
In 1972 he dropped out of Berkeley to go to work at Hewlett-Packard. Meanwhile Jobs enrolled at Reed College in Portland, Oregon, but dropped out during the first semester to search
for a guru in India. When Jobs returned, he joined Atari, the video
games company. This brought Jobs and Wozniak together again
back in Silicon Valley where they began collaborating, as a
hobby, designing a computer circuit board. It would become the
Apple.

They also collaborated in a mischevious bit of electronic
wizardry that almost got them in serious trouble. In 1971, Wozniak read an *Esquire* article about a "phreak" (for phone freak)
named Cap'n Crunch who seized long-distance telephone lines
with a "blue box" that allowed him to make illegal toll calls. Woz
and Jobs started manufacturing blue boxes and peddling them in
Wozniak's Berkeley dormitory. Selling the gadgets wasn't illegal,
but using them was. Eventually Woz and Jobs were apprehended
by the highway patrol while using a blue box on a roadside tele-

phone when their car had broken down. They were able to talk their way out of that jam because the policemen didn't know what the blue box was for.[6] Some years later, Apple hired Cap'n Crunch to design an automatic dialing mechanism for their microcomputer. With his unorthodox brilliance, Crunch also designed a program for an Apple II to make 150,000 calls to toll-free "800" numbers, to harass the telephone company.[7]

Wozniak's offbeat sense of humor also came out in other ways. He ran a Dial-A-Joke service from his home answering machine specializing in Polish and Italian ethnic jokes. He averaged 2,000 calls a day. One call from a young baby sitter, Alice Robertson, led to a lengthy conversation. Always shy around women, it took Woz another five phone calls before they finally met in person in 1973. They got married but later divorced. Wozniak had never cared much for money, and when Apple made him rich he gave $50 million of his company stock to his ex-wife, plus other stock to her family, to his relatives, and to a few friends. Today all of them are fairly wealthy.[8]

Wozniak's second wife is Candi Clark, a former Olympic kayaker and Berkeley business administration graduate, who met Woz at Apple, where she worked. Presently they live in seclusion in the Santa Cruz Mountains, some miles southwest of Silicon Valley. Woz went back to Berkeley and finished his B.S. degree in computer science in 1983.

Wozniak then returned to Apple Computer Inc., as a computer designer. Jobs has received the public recognition for the company's success. Woz says that it doesn't really matter: "Steve's great and I'm not a competitive person, and I don't care who's at the top because I . . . still have my whole life."[9] There was a division of labor between Jobs and Wozniak in the early history of Apple's success: Woz was the brilliant technician, while Jobs created the infrastructure of the company. His silver tongue and aggressive manner equipped him beautifully to deal with venture capitalists, government officials, and media reporters. Modesty is not one of Jobs's shortcomings, and he admits to demoralizing some of his employees with harsh judgments. He occasionally walks into one of Apple's R&D (research and development) labs, looks over a worker's project, and announces, "This is a piece of shit."[10] If the individual is cowed by Jobs's pushy approach and does not defend his work, the Apple mogul is likely to think him incompetent. By his own admission, Jobs needs to learn more about managing people. In fact, Apple could not have succeeded had Jobs not brought in some top managers to run the company for him.

Nevertheless, one can't entirely blame a 28 year-old self-made multimillionaire for feeling self-confident.[11] And if Woz would be credited with being an electronic superstar in designing the Apple II, Jobs would be recognized for building a company around their computer.

The Birth of Apple I

The story of how the Apple computer was born illustrates many aspects common to high-technology entrepreneurial adventures in Silicon Valley: Someone frustrated by a particular problem decides to do something about it, and in the process creates a new product that many people want to buy. Surprised by success at first, the entrepreneur forms a new company, and after overcoming many difficulties, may attain huge financial success. It's a special kind of dream. The sudden exhilaration of achieving entrepreneurial fame has a heady effect on the instant businessman, not unlike the consequences of sudden success for professional athletes, movie stars, and rock musicians.

To build the Apple I, Woz and Jobs "liberated" some electronics parts from Hewlett-Packard and Atari, where they worked.[12] When Wozniak was designing the Apple I, he definitely thought in low cost terms. He didn't use the Intel 8080, the leading microprocessor available, as the heart of his machine because it cost $270 in single quantity. It also was inaccessible, because electronics distributors told Woz that he would have to set up an account and be registered as a company. Wozniak said, "Then Chuck Peddle[13] came out with the 6502 [a microprocessor] and announced they were going to sell it over the counter at WESCON [a big annual computer show on the West Coast]. So a few friends of mine went down to WESCON and $20 went over the table and microprocessors came back. . . . So for twenty bucks you could get a microprocessor. That put me in business."[14]

When the Apple I was shown at the Home Brew Computer Club (an association of several hundred computerphiles which met on the Stanford University campus) it was an immediate hit, and Jobs's and Wozniak's friends suddenly wanted one. Said Jobs: "So we were spending all of our time helping them build their computers. It was taking up our weekends, our nights, everything. So I sold my Volkswagen, Woz sold his calculator, and we got 1,300 bucks together. We paid a friend of mine to lay out a printed circuit board for this computer. . . . We figured we could make a hundred of them and sell them for $50 each, which would leave us with a $2,500 profit with which we could go and get our VW and calculator back."[15] It took sixty hours for Wozniak and Jobs to assemble their first Apple, but with the help of the printed circuit board, they cut this construction time to only six hours per computer. Without intending to do so, Wozniak and Jobs had launched the microcomputer industry in response to consumer demand.

Jobs took one of his computer boards to The Byte Shop, a local retail computer store, in June 1976. He said, "They ordered 50 of them. Jesus! Dollar signs! But they threw in a new twist. They said they wanted them fully assembled. At that time, there was no computer you could buy fully assembled. They were all kits."[16] Then Jobs pulled one of his better coups. Never bashful, he acted the big executive when he contacted several electronics suppliers, demanding the standard terms they gave to major firms like Hewlett-Packard. "We convinced them to give us about $25,000 worth of parts on net 30 days credit. Now we didn't even know what net 30 days credit was. We took all these boxes of parts home. We built 100 boards, and we took 50 down to The Byte Shop and we were paid cash. We paid the suppliers in 29 days, which started our attention to cash flow."[17]

The partners assembled the computers in Jobs's parents' garage, which was now filled with plastic-packaged semiconductor chips and printed circuit boards. Jobs tied up his parents' phone for hours while he wheeled and dealed for a lawyer's services and for a public relations firm to design some advertising. The

Wozniak-Jobs partnership was always a little short of capital, so Jobs had to convince the lawyer to provide his services on a pay-later basis. Regis McKenna, president of a local public relations firm said no to Jobs's proposition three times, but finally acquiesced. And McKenna gave free services too, to be paid later.[18]

The Apple garage was getting crowded with electronics, and Jobs-Wozniak decided they were outgrowing their shoestring operation. Jobs said: "Sometime about the fall of 1976, I realized that the market was growing faster than we could grow. We needed some more money."[19]

Apple and its contemporaries helped create a new kind of business enterprise in America—retail computer stores. These local businesses sprang up to fill a public need. The first computer stores just sort of happened when some enterprising individual got the idea that money could be made by retailing microcomputers. Ted Heiser is usually credited with starting the first computer store in Los Angeles in June 1975. Heiser had a daytime job, so his store was only open on nights and weekends. The first full-time computer store in the world was launched at 1063 El Camino Real West in Mountain View, right in the heart of Silicon Valley. Co-owners Boyd W. Wilson and Paul Terrell called it The Byte Shop. It opened in December 1975 and sold the Altair 8800, books like Ted Nelson's *Computer Lib,* computer t-shirts, and magazines and manuals about microcomputers.[20]

Wilson remembers when Job and Wozniak came in to sell him their Apple circuit boards in June 1976. They recall that The Byte Shop ordered 50 Apples, but Wilson thinks it was more like 25 or so. Both parties agree that Wilson urged Jobs and Woz to enclose their Apple circuit board in a case, and thus produce a functioning microcomputer. Wilson knew that his customers wanted complete units, not just components or kits. So he gave the Apple co-founders a big push toward starting their own company. They were resistant at first. Jobs said, "We didn't want to go into business."[21] Later when Jobs came into The Byte Shop again, Wilson showed him an Apple circuit board encased in a tacky-looking wood box: "That persuaded Jobs that he had to manufacture Apple computers complete with a good-looking case," says Wilson.[22]

In its early days the success of Apple and The Byte Shop was closely linked because now the computer store had a hot product to sell. Within two years Wilson's Byte Shop had become a chain of seventy-five stores. They collapsed a few years later from cash flow problems. The Byte Shop and Apple eventually went separate ways, and now Wilson sells Cromemco and Fortune computers in one store, called The Original Byte Shop.

Computer stores are here to stay. The ten largest U.S. cities each have at least 200 sales outlets, and there are over 13,000 computer stores worldwide. An additional 17,000 stores sell computers along with other products. Recently, The Original Byte Shop moved a few blocks north to 1545 El Camino Real West, a better location. The old building, where Apple got its start, is now an adult bookstore. A sign in the window says: "Couples Welcome."

Nolan Bushnell Laughed

When Jobs and Wozniak, the reluctant entrepreneurs, realized the Apple computer was a viable product that people would buy, they went to their bosses at Atari and Hewlett-Packard with it. Jobs tried to convince Nolan Bushnell, founder of Atari and creator of Pong, the first video game, that microcomputers had a bright future. But computers were not in Atari's product line, and Bushnell laughed at Jobs.

In 1983, in a talk he gave at an engineers' banquet in Sunnyvale, California, Bushnell recalled this event: "Let's say that you work for a big company. You go in to your manager and say, 'I've got an idea for a product that I know has a $10 million market out there.' The manager says 'Ha ha. Ten million dollar market? We're a $10 million company.' You say 'Hmm. Ten million dollars seems okay to me.' . . . This new product area is . . . a personal computer! [Wild audience applause at Bushnell's expense]. We all knew that profits were in mainframes and minicomputers. That was in 1975. So new small companies can grow in the cracks of the market. Pretty soon, they grow up and walk with the big boys. Now that $10 million dollar business that Atari turned down . . . . See, I never said we were perfect." In 1982 microcomputer sales topped $5.4 billion.

Next, Wozniak went to his supervisor at Hewlett-Packard, proposing that the Apple computer be produced at H-P. He tried on three different occasions. But H-P officials pointed out that Woz didn't have a college degree, nor the formal qualifications for computer design. Jobs and Wozniak can take a certain pleasure out of the fact that both Atari and Hewlett-Packard are now, after a belated start, heavily into the microcomputer game. And trying hard to catch up with Apple, an industry leader.[23]

The U.S. public was ready and waiting to buy Apple computers as Jobs's and Wozniak's early experiences in the Homebrew Computer Club, at The Byte Shop, and with their garage production operations, had taught them. The buying public did not ask whether their microcomputer came from a reputable firm that could provide service, maintenance, and user training. Consumers wanted to buy a microcomputer so badly they were unwilling to wait four or five years until highly regarded firms like IBM entered the microcomputer field. Apple identified a niche and filled it, growing at an almost reckless pace during its early life so as to achieve a substantial market share. And Apple invested heavily in advertising, hoping to hold this ground when IBM entered the microcomputer field.

When Jobs and Wozniak went to their respective supervisors at Atari and H-P to invite these established firms to take over their prototype Apple computer, their bosses may have been quite correct in laughing. The estimated size of the microcomputer market in 1976 looked too small to these large firms, but to a start-up like Apple this potential market was very attractive. Later, to the surprise of established computer firms, the microcomputer market just grew and grew. No one, not even Jobs and Woz, could have guessed how large this market would become.

In the fall of 1976, Jobs finally decided that they ought to found their own company, but Wozniak remained adamantly opposed. So Jobs phoned a number of Woz's relatives and got them to pressure him into agreeing. Jobs and Woz were working in their garage one day in 1976 when Don Valentine, a local venture capitalist, drove up in his spiffy Mercedes. Valentine had been recommended by McKenna and by Nolan Bushnell, Jobs's ex-boss at Atari, as someone who could help them raise capital. Valentine's reaction to Jobs's appearance (cut off jeans, sandals, shoulder-length hair, and a Ho Chi Minh beard) expressed later to McKenna was "Why did you send me to this renegade from the human race?"[24] Valentine didn't give them money, but he did refer them to Armas C. "Mark" Markkula, Jr., former marketing manager at Intel.

Shortly thereafter, Markkula drove up to the Apple garage in his Corvette. At 38, he was already a millionaire and retired from Intel. Markkula asked to see their business plan. Jobs and Wozniak looked at each other; they didn't know what a business plan was. Markkula explained that a detailed prospectus was essential for raising venture capital.

Then he sat down with Jobs and Wozniak for the next two weeks. Working day and night they produced a business plan for Apple Computer Inc. Markkula put up $91,000 of his own money, and helped secure a $250,000 line of credit at the Bank of America. The three of them took the Apple business plan to venture capitalists that Markkula knew and raised another $600,000. We'll talk more about venture capitalists and their great influence on Silicon Valley start-up firms in chapter 4.

Apple's capital problems were solved. Jobs and Wozniak made Markkula their third full partner, thus gaining his marketing ability and business sense. He recommended that Apple hire 33-year-old Michael Scott, Director of Manufacturing at National Semiconductor, as president of Apple. Scott was a hard-nosed production expert, just what Apple needed. He agreed to come on board at a pay cut of 50 percent. At this stage Markkula was chairman, Jobs was vice-chairman, and Wozniak was vice-president for R&D.

It was time to move out of the garage, and to begin producing the Apple II.

Prior to 1977, computers were heavy, square metal boxes, complicated, intimidating, and difficult to use. The Apple II was to change all that. Wozniak designed a computer that was so sophisticated that it actually was simple. As a result of the Apple II's simplicity, it was remarkably easy (1) to program and (2) to manufacture. The Apple II weighed only twelve pounds, and went together with just ten screws. The outer case was a pastel adobe grey with the six-color Apple logo (an apple with a bite out of it) mounted above the keyboard. The outside appearance

Call It Apple

A problem facing the founders of every start-up is what to call their new firm. Often they want to convey an image of high-technology and of microelectronics, but they don't want to be too specific as they may later decide to add different product lines. An astute observer of the Silicon Valley scene, Michael Malone, formerly a reporter for the *San Jose Mercury News,* detects three eras in naming new companies:

1. Until 1960, local firms usually took their titles from the names of their founders: (Bill) Hewlett-(Dave) Packard, Varian (brothers) Corporation, and (Sherman) Fairchild Semiconductor. In this period there was little to distinguish the names of Silicon Valley firms from grocery stores or roofing companies or any other kind of business.
2. With the founding of Signetics Corporation in 1961, named for "signal network electronics," a spate of puns on "electronics" and "technology" began with firms called "teks," "techs," "tecks," and "ecks"; Intel (for "integrated electronics"); Avantek (for "avante-garde technology"); and Zilog (for Z, the last word, in integrated logic). Acurex Corporation of Mountain View fed the following stipulations into a computer: the name must have six letters arranged vowel/consonant/vowel, start with "A," and be both technical sounding but vague enough to be unrestrictive. Of the various names spit out by the computer (some of them obscene), "Acurex" was the winner.
3. After 1975, new firms switched from using space-age names to more mellow titles implying honesty, truth, and health: Coherent, Verbatim, North Star, and Tandem, for example. Apple Computer Inc. is a good representative of this era. When founder Steve Jobs returned from India he had had a bout with dysentery and became a vegetarian. He decided that people were architected to be fruit eaters and he became especially hooked on apples. He ate a lot of them, becoming a fruitarian for a while. When his new firm was getting underway in the garage in 1976, the U.S. Securities and Exchange Commission required that a form be completed with a company name. Jobs suggested "Apple Computer" because the transposition of the two words would be an intriguing name with high public impact. It also conveyed the friendly, organic image that Jobs wanted. Other employees suggested "double xx" names like "Matrix Technology, Inc." One day Jobs told them: "Come up with a better name than Apple by 5 P.M. [when the SEC form had to be mailed] or that's it." No one did, so the company was named "Apple Computer Inc." "At least that got us ahead of Atari in the telephone book," says Jobs.[25]

was carefully designed by Jobs and a friend at Atari to convey a nonthreatening impression of friendliness to the user. Inside was a neat little package of Wozniak's wizardry: a compact power supply, a single circuit board that contained the microprocessor and other semiconductor chips, and a connection for the keyboard. It looked awfully simple to the uninitiated, but each of these components represented a brilliant bit of complicated design.

The first big victory in creating the Apple II was making the power supply. Jobs specified that this part be less than four inches high, so that the computer could have a wide, low appearance. Until 1976 all microcomputers used a linear transformer that was about half the size of a loaf of bread. Worse, these power supplies gave off a lot of heat, so a fan was required to cool the insides of the computer. The fan made a hum when the computer was operating, an unfriendly sound. Woz got help from an electrical engineer named Rod Holt, who had been working for Atari. Holt called himself a second-string quarterback at Atari because he worked as a back-up to the chief engineer, a weekend motorcycle racer who often showed up on Monday mornings in bandages or a sling.[26] On those occasions, Holt would fill in, but otherwise he had lots of time on his hands. So when Jobs phoned him in the fall of 1976 with an offer of a job at Apple, Holt was interested.

But when he met Jobs he was rather taken aback. Jobs was then 21, had a beard and uncut hair, no shoes, and didn't bathe.[27] Further, the existing prototype model of the Apple didn't work reliably, and it violated FCC regulations regarding radiation emissions.[28] Holt decided that Apple needed an experienced engineer. So he went to work on the power supply problem. He came up with a switching power supply that took regular household current and rapidly switched on and off, thus eliminating the heating problem. Further, it was about as big as a box of Animal Crackers, so it fit Jobs's size requirements. Best of all, it was fail-safe because it shut down if anything went wrong. One problem solved—or so it seemed.

However getting Wozniak to accept Holt's power supply was another matter. He didn't trust it, and frequently blamed Holt's design when anything went wrong with the prototype of the Apple II computer. Gradually, Holt became the take-charge guy when Woz lost interest in designing components for the Apple

II. Wozniak would come up with a brilliant solution to a design problem, but then his attention would wander when the gadget only needed a final two percent of effort to debug it. In came Holt to finish up.[29] Today, Rod Holt is a star at Apple Computer, with the special title of Apple Fellow, and a license to pursue research on any hot idea that he wants.

As 1976 came to an end, the Apple II was taking shape. One of Wozniak's greatest feats took place in a few brilliant days during the week after Christmas. He pulled off the equivalent of an entire year's work in designing the Apple II's floppy disk controllers. Until then the only way to load programs into a microcomputer was with magnetic tape and a cassette recorder, a very slow process. A floppy disk looks much like a 45 r.p.m. record and represents an efficient means of storing computer programs and inputting them to the machine. Existing disk controllers required thirty to sixty integrated circuits. But Woz devised a way to do it with just eight. Holt regards Wozniak's solution to the disk controller as a supreme accomplishment, yet it is so subtle that few designers, even at Apple, fully understand it.[30]

Woz was also an artist in designing the printed circuit board for the Apple II. The board is a piece of green plastic on which thin lines of copper are etched as substitutes for insulated electrical wires. Semiconductor chips encased in small plastic packages are plugged into the board to form the basic circuitry of the computer. Woz worked until 2 A.M. every night for several weeks laying out the circuit board. He could have turned the actual construction over to a technician, but Wozniak, the craftsman, wanted to do it himself. That's when he noticed that he could practically eliminate feedthroughs (small holes in the circuit board which pass a line of solder through to the other side). Woz reduced the number of feedthroughs from fifty to three. Not that the feedthroughs are a technical disadvantage. "I just wanted to minimize feedthroughs," said Wozniak. "It's totally aesthetic. Nobody even knows I did it. But I know, and it's just aesthetically perfect to me."[31]

Wozniak is like that. He can work like a fiend and complete superb original projects from time to time if he gets interested in them. But if he doesn't regard some design task as fun, he simply doesn't do it. So managing Woz while he designed the Apple II took all of Jobs's persuasive skills; Holt says "Jobs would pull every trick in the book. He pulled the scorned lover act, he pulled the enthusiast act, he would bring in people from computer clubs who agreed with him." Eventually, Woz might give in. Often he didn't. If some project didn't interest Wozniak, he'd promise to get it done by, say, next Monday. But on Monday, he wouldn't show up at all. On Tuesday, he'd say "I'll have it for you tomorrow." This would go on and on. Holt says, "I don't think Wozniak was ever in control of his mind. His mind just did what it damn well felt like."[32]

Apple's success is due to much more than just Wozniak and Jobs. Important members of the cast are the thousands of software programmers around the country who created useful programs to run on the Apple II.[33] At no cost to the company, Apple suddenly had a whole cafeteria of complementary programs and auxiliary equipment that the purchaser of an Apple computer could utilize. This meant that the actual utility of an Apple was much greater than that of its chief competitors, which had fewer programs. Thus Apple's success was part of a rather widespread technological movement, rather than just a consequence of Jobs-Wozniak (although they must be credited with building a friendly computer that was easy to program). When the hobbyist market for microcomputers dried up in 1978, dozens of little computer firms collapsed.[34] But not Apple, thanks to its cadre of free-lance programmers who had designed accounting, word processing, spelling, teaching, graphics, and a host of other programs. By 1983 over 15,000 programs were available for the Apple computer; 95 percent of them were developed by independent software programmers. The top selling word-processing program is WordStar, which sells for $495 and today has about 300,000 users.[35] (An untold number of pirate copies of WordStar are also being used.)

Most software programs run on BASIC (the Beginners' All-Purpose Symbolic Instruction Code), an easy-to-learn programming language that resembles normal English. Microsoft BASIC-8 was created by Bill Gates and Paul Allen for microcomputer use in 1975 when Gates was a sophomore at Harvard. They formed the Microsoft company to market BASIC. It now runs on several million computers. The availability of BASIC language gave a big boost to Apple (the coincidental timing was perfect) and vice versa.

From the beginning, Jobs realized the importance of software: "I absolutely think there is a technology race, but when someone fired the gun, most of the people went running in the wrong direction. They are running after 16 bits and they are running after more memory. I don't think that is the race at all. I think the race is a software-technology race."[36]

In April 1977 Apple decided to give the first public showing of their product at the West Coast Computer Faire in San Francisco. Their dozen or so employees worked all night to finish five Apple II's. At the time these were the only functioning Apple II's in the world.[37] Whew! Thousands of people came by the Apple display at the Faire to look, try out the new machine, and fill out an order form.

Almost immediately the sales of the Apple II started to go through the roof. During 1977 (Apple's fiscal year ends in September), sales were $2.5 million. The next year, $15 million. Then $70 million in 1979; $117 million in 1980; $335 million in 1981; and $583 million in 1982. Even by Silicon Valley standards, that rate of growth is almost unbelievable. The 1982 sales figures put Apple in the *Fortune* 500, marking the first time that a new company had qualified for this select club in only five years.

In order to acquire the huge amounts of capital needed for growth, Apple "went public" with its first stock offering on December 12, 1980. It was a special event on Wall Street, which had never seen anything quite like it. The 4,600,000 shares that were sold at $22 each brought in $101 million and made instant millionaires out of Jobs ($165 million); Markkula ($154 million); Wozniak ($88 million); and Scott ($62 million). Together they owned 40 percent of Apple. The venture capitalists who previously had taken a chance on Apple also got a rich return: $243 for every $1 invested. Arthur Rock, a San Francisco-based venture capitalist, had purchased 640,000 shares at 9 cents a share in 1978. Less than three years later, his $57,600 investment was worth $14 million and the Midas-like reputation of the already legendary Arthur Rock took another leap.

One of the ways in which Apple fought off its competitors was by creating a high level of public awareness via advertising. In summer 1981 Apple launched its first national advertising campaign for home computers. The ads showed Dick Cavett urging parents to buy an Apple for their children's education. The name Apple was easy for the public to remember and although the ad blitz was expensive, the company became favorably positioned in the public eye.

In 1981, when IBM announced that it was entering the microcomputer market, many observers predicted hard times ahead for small, start-up companies that had pioneered the microcomputer business. But the response by Apple Computer was to run a full-page ad nationally that proclaimed: "Welcome IBM!" The publicity thus generated served to legitimize the microcomputer for the American public. Indeed, Apple's sales have continued to increase since the beginning of competition from IBM, and Apple's market share has held at around 26 percent, although IBM has rapidly gained (at the expense of other microcomputer firms) to a similar market share. In 1982 Apple sold 33,000 computers each month, the majority of which were Apple IIs, a model still being sold for the fifth straight year. That's a long time in the computer industry, where technology changes almost daily.

Jobs and Woz knew that in order to avoid being acquired or to keep from being destroyed by competition that would grab its market share, Apple would have to grow very rapidly. Such growth is difficult to control and the problem, as Markkula noted, would be to keep the race car on the track. For a while in 1981, when the Apple III came out prematurely and had many problems, it seemed the race car was out of control.

The Disaster of Apple III

Release of the Apple III was a long-awaited event by computer users and by investors. In just about every sense, it was a disaster. After such a string of incredible victories, maybe it was about time for Apple Computer Inc., to return to reality—with a very loud thud.

The Apple III was designed with three times the memory and twice the column width (80 characters instead of 40) of its little brother, the Apple II. When the Apple III was released in mid-1981 it cost $4,500, compared to $2,500 for the Apple II. All the software programs for the Apple II would also run on the Apple III, but its greater power and capacity allowed many other uses. So far so good.

But from the first, problems surrounded the Apple III. The company announced the new machine about a year before it was finally ready for sale, creating expectations. Then many of the first Apple IIIs that were shipped didn't work.

The Apple III was born with a host of pesky technical problems of the kind that can occur when a new product is rushed into mass production without adequate testing. A glaring problem was that the semiconductor chips didn't fit securely in their sockets on the printed circuit board, so they fell out during shipment. The company halted further production for several months to correct this problem. In addition, adequate software programs were not ready for the new computer. And to further complicate the situation, IBM was weighing in with its personal computer at about this time.

In the midst of this mess, Mike Scott, the no-nonsense president of Apple, fired forty employees on February 25, 1981. Perhaps many of the problems surrounding the launching of Apple III wouldn't have happened if Woz had been involved in designing it, but he was out of action suffering from a spell of temporary amnesia, a result of a crash in his plane. Jobs was described as "sick at heart," feeling that the mass firing was like the captain shooting off the bow of his own ship.[38] Yet Jobs felt he had to back up his company president.

However within a month Scott was asked to step down to a lesser post in the company. Soon thereafter he quit, firing off a bitter public letter in which he charged that Apple had degenerated into a bunch of "yes-men" whose "cover-your-ass" attitudes were exceeded only by their "foolhardy plans."[39] Mark Markkula stepped into the breach as company president, the Apple III was reissued, and the price of Apple stock began to recover.[40]

The disaster of Apple III is an example of "the adolescent

transition," the point in a high-technology company's rapid growth when it must change from an engineering to an administrative style. Problems of the transition occur when an entrepreneurial firm grows so fast that its infrastructure can't keep pace with the tremendous number of new employees who enter the company unsocialized to its culture. Bringing a firm's organizational structure along at a rate commensurate with its burgeoning sales is no easy matter, as the case of Apple suggests. It is entirely possible for a new firm to grow itself to death.

Looking back ruefully at Apple's adolescent transition, Jobs said, "One of Apple's greatest assets is having made more mistakes than anyone else in the industry. We've recently added a whole new group to our list. So we feel we're far ahead of the competition."[41]

In 1983 Apple avoided the mistakes of its launching of the Apple III when it brought out a sophisticated office machine, the Lisa, named after Steve Jobs's daughter.[42] Working in high secrecy, a close-knit team of 300 engineers and programmers, tucked away in a special building behind The Good Earth restaurant in Cupertino, spent over three years and $50 million in designing the Lisa. "We are betting our company on the strategic decisions we made on Lisa," Jobs claimed dramatically.[43] The unique aspect of the new computer was that it could be controlled by a "mouse," a palm-sized device that moves the cursor on the Lisa's screen when it is rolled along a desktop. The Lisa is a kind of electronic workspace that maps what office workers have previously done on their desks by sorting papers, writing, and reading. A user can type a business letter on one part of the screen, shove it to a corner, draw a graph, and then make some spreadsheet calculations. Shifts among these activities are controlled by icons, little drawings of a calculator, a clipboard, a trashcan, etc., across the bottom of the computer screen. By using the mouse and the icons, the typical office worker finds the Lisa such a friendly computer that one can learn to use it in about twenty minutes.[44] As such, the Lisa represents the first big technical improvement in microcomputers since Woz built the Apple II back in 1976. The dramatic announcement of Lisa by Steve Jobs at the 1983 Apple stockholders' meeting thus launched the second generation of microcomputers.

Whether many purchasers will pay $10,000 for the Lisa remains to be seen. Ominously, IBM announced that it soon would have a mouse for its computer.

The Apple Empire

During the 1980s, Apple Computer Inc. became a worldwide operation. In addition to its central operations in Silicon Valley, Apple has plants in Singapore; Cork, Ireland; and in Carrollton, Texas (outside of Dallas). By 1983 Apple had 3,500 employees. Assembling the silicon chips on the printed circuit boards takes lots of labor and Apple subcontracts this work out to "board-stuffing" companies like General Technology Corporation (GTC) in San Jose. Their business for Apple began in 1976 when Steve Jobs walked in the door of GTC and offered a contract to GTC President Richard Olson. At that time GTC had 30 board-stuffers and could only complete 100 circuit boards a day.

By 1983 GTC had 450 employees. Many are women who are black, Spanish-speaking, or members of other minority groups. They start working at minimum wage and are trained to insert the pronged chips into the circuit boards. The work is boring and the chances of upward mobility are dim for board-stuffers. Each employee signs a checklist after completing a board to indicate responsibility for the work. Then the circuit board is tested, any mistakes are corrected, and out the door go the "guts" of another Apple computer.

A board may go to Apple's Singapore assembly plant, where it joins the plastic case, the keyboard, and other components to be mounted on an aluminum base plate. It all fits together with ten screws, just as Woz designed it in 1976. The Chinese workers in Singapore, along with their counterparts in Ireland, Texas, and Silicon Valley, had assembled about three-quarters of a million Apple computers by early 1983. About 30 percent were sold outside the United States.

So the sun never sets on Apple Computer Inc. if one counts the suppliers, the assembly plants, the computer retail stores, and of course the users of Apple computers.

In early 1983 Jobs claimed that Apple had created 300 millionaires among its employees. Jobs, of course, is one of them. In fact, many, many times a millionaire. Jobs's equity in Apple was worth $284 million in mid-1983.[45] According to an analysis by *Forbes* magazine in 1982, the 28-year-old Jobs was the youngest of the 400 richest individuals in the U.S. Not bad for a young guy whose company began in a garage.

Fame as well as riches have come Jobs's way. On February 15, 1982, he appeared on the cover of *Time* magazine. The cover photograph showed Jobs wearing his familiar denim work shirt, even though he had bought a house in posh Los Gatos (albeit unfurnished). Today he still likes to ride his motorcycle to work, even though he now owns a Mercedes.

Jobs said that when he was young, he had the impression that an individual couldn't change the world. It was too big and complicated and powerful. But his recent experience in Apple Computer gave him ecstatic feelings; he said, "You can poke the world here and have an impact on society over there."[46] Such a sense of efficacy is one of the great thrills of life for many entrepreneurs.

Once an individual realizes this feeling of power over the future, he's hard to stop. Jobs gave an Apple computer to each of the 10,400 California schools in 1983. That's quite a batch of computers, worth $10 million. But with a tax deduction, the cost to Apple was "only" one million dollars. Next Jobs says he'll try to convince the federal government to give him a tax break so that he can give an Apple to every school in America.

Jobs speaks in powerful analogies. For example, he says that "Fairchild Semiconductor was like a ripe dandelion; you blow on it and the seeds of entrepreneurship spread on the wind."[47] And when asked in an interview about Japanese competition in microcomputers, Jobs said: "The first wave came and it sort of flopped up on the shore like a dead fish. The second wave is due this spring . . . they are going to flop up on the shore like dead fish."[48] To Jobs, the two main problems facing Japanese computer companies are software and distribution. These are two of Apple's special advantages, of course.

Why were Steve Jobs and Steve Wozniak so successful? Certainly they were at the right place at the right time; that much is luck, and derives in part from the circumstance that they were both born and grew up in Silicon Valley. Woz is certainly a com-

puter genius, and Jobs had the moxie to launch a company around
their microcomputer. But otherwise we don't see much that would
especially mark these two young individuals for instant wealth.
Mythology and the media now attribute them with almost super-
natural powers. We don't think so. Jobs and Woz are just two
young men who happened to stumble into a pot of gold.

The Apple story contains the main elements of Silicon Valley
success: entrepreneurial spirit; venture capital; personal networks of information exchange; social inequalities represented
by Third World women board stuffers; and highly competitive
workstyles of (often uncredentialed) technologists. Each of these
elements will be detailed in a later chapter.

But first, we must tell what came before Apple in Silicon
Valley.

2

The Rise of
Silicon Valley

"When we set out to create a community of technical scholars in Silicon Valley, there wasn't much here and the rest
of the world looked awfully big. Now a lot of the rest of the
world is here."

Frederick E. Terman*

"Silicon has become the crude oil of industry progress."

Jerry Sanders, president
Advanced Micro Devices, 1980

MANY AMERICANS probably have only a hazy idea of where
Silicon Valley is, what it does, and how it affects us. Unless you
know what to look for, Silicon Valley is practically invisible.

Just as Manchester and the Saar Valley and Pittsburgh were
once the centers for industrial progress, the microelectronics industry also has a heartland. Silicon Valley is located in a thirty-
by ten-mile strip between San Francisco and San Jose, California.
Now the Valley is famous, but it didn't even have a name for its
first twenty years. It was referred to, somewhat clumsily, as "the
West Coast electronics industry," or "Palo Alto," or as "Santa
Clara County." But Silicon Valley didn't need a name in those
days because the industry was still small and unknown.

Then in 1971 Don C. Hoefler, editor of a weekly scoop sheet
about the semiconductor industry, *Microelectronics News,*

*In Gene Bylinsky, "California's Great Breeding Ground for Industry," *Fortune,* June 1974.

coined the name "Silicon Valley."[1] It was cute and it made sense. Semiconductor chips, made of silicon, are the fundamental product of the local high-technology industries and although the area isn't a valley in a strict geographical sense, most of the firms are located on level ground bounded on opposite sides by a range of hills and by San Francisco Bay. So with a little imagination it is a valley.

The name stuck and became widely used. Increasingly the media carried news about Silicon Valley—wondrous electronics products, instant millionaires, and brand new industries like microcomputers and bioengineering. Silicon Valley articles began to appear regularly in *Fortune, Time,* and *Business Week.* The American public thus became increasingly aware of Silicon Valley as did Europeans and the Japanese. In fact, so many Japanese tourists came to visit that in 1981 a map of the area was published in their language showing the major firms' locations, as well as hotels and restaurants.

Welcome to Silicon Valley

A trip by auto through Silicon Valley would logically start at Stanford University, whose campus includes the Stanford Research Park, home of Hewlett-Packard and dozens of the other early firms in the area (Figure 2.1). The Silicon Valley complex started at Stanford (some call it the most successful "firm" in the Valley), and driving south toward San Jose one essentially tracks through a year-by-year history of Silicon Valley's development. In Palo Alto, one notices several high-rise office buildings, home of the venture capital firms that provide funds for the entrepreneur-engineers who start the hundreds of "spin-off" firms, founded on the basis of technological innovations developed at another company.

Next we come to Mountain View, home of Fairchild Semiconductor, itself a progenitor of many spin-off firms. A few miles further down the Valley is the main concentration of semiconduc-

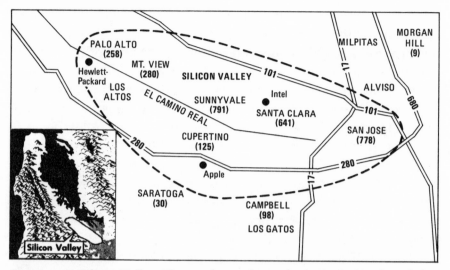

Figure 2.1. Silicon Valley. The number under each city is the number of electronics firms identified by Richard Schmieder in *Rich's Guide to Santa Clara County's Silicon Valley* (Palo Alto: Rich Enterprises, 1982). Total: 3,010, comprising 2,736 individual firms and 264 affiliates.

tor firms in Sunnyvale, Cupertino, and Santa Clara. This is the heart of Silicon Valley today. Intel is headquartered in Santa Clara; nearby is AMD (Advanced Micro Devices), and the Wagonwheel Bar, an early watering hole for semiconductor engineers. To the right in the low mountains lies Los Altos Hills, a favorite residence of the new millionaires. Nearby, in Cupertino, is Apple and other of the newer "start-ups."

At the lower end of Silicon Valley is San Jose, the fast-growing, rambling city which is home to the minorities that compose the majority of skilled manual workers in Silicon Valley firms—Mexicans, Filipinos, Vietnamese. They reside mainly in "South County" in order to escape the exorbitant housing values of the "North County" communities, where most of the engineers and managers live. As one crosses the city limits from Santa Clara, Sunnyvale, and Cupertino into San Jose, socioeconomic status drops noticeably. Traffic, smog from auto emission, and crime are worse. There are social problems, even in paradise.

Although San Jose is mainly a bedroom community for Silicon Valley, recently microelectronics firms are finding space there and in adjacent suburban towns like Milipitas and Alviso. These plants are generally younger and smaller than their counterparts in the heart of the Valley a few miles north. The newer plants are in the southern fringe of the high-technology complex because Silicon Valley has run out of land. Many of the newest manufacturing plants aren't even in California—they are in Texas, Colorado, Oregon, or even in Malaysia, the Philippines, or Mexico due to cheap labor and affordable housing. However the companies' R&D facilities are still in Silicon Valley, even if the new production facilities are being built elsewhere.

Almost all of Silicon Valley lies in Santa Clara County, which in 1950 was the prune capital of America. The county had only 800 manufacturing employees then and half of them worked in canneries and food processing plants. Today the fruit trees have all but disappeared.

Silicon Valley is the birthplace of pocket calculators, video games, home computers, cordless telephones, laser technology, microprocessors, and digital watches. Just about everything that's new in electronics in recent years has come out of Silicon Valley. In the American Electronics Association 1,111 of the firms (about 62 percent) are in California. Massachusetts is second, with only 112 firms. AEA headquarters are located, appropriately, in Palo Alto.

Silicon Valley represents Olympic-style capitalism. Its economic achievement is indicated by the fact that it has become the nation's ninth-largest manufacturing center, with sales of over $40 billion annually. About 40,000 new jobs are created here each year, most of them somehow related to information technology. Silicon Valley is an almost perfect example of an "information society," in which a majority of the workforce engages in gathering, processing, or distributing information, or in making information technology. The local economy is the fastest-growing and wealthiest in the United States, with a median family income of over $30,000 in Santa Clara County. From 1970 to 1980, San Jose jumped from being the 29th to the 18th largest city in the United States, making it the fastest-growing city in the nation. A high-technology complex like Silicon Valley is also a center for an intellectual elite. There are over 6,000 Ph.D.s in this small area, one of every six doctorates in California, the state with the greatest concentration of such highly educated individuals in America.

Joe Riley, a former electronics executive who helped found the posh Decathlon Club (whose annual membership dues are $1,500) said, "There are 220,000 people working within 12 minutes of this club. Of these, 80,000 are college-educated and 75,000 are workaholics."[2] Or, as one electronics executive told us: "Our credo is work hard, play hard, and don't worry about the difference between work and play. There isn't any." A distinctive lifestyle and workstyle is found in Silicon Valley. Engineers put in fifteen-hour days and seven-day weeks and many plan to retire as millionaires in ten years.

A Palo Alto investment firm, Thompson Tuckman Anderson Inc., determined there are 15,280 millionaires residing between Los Altos Hills and Atherton (in the northern third of Silicon Valley).[3] Not all of these wealthy folk made their money in high technology, but nevertheless Silicon Valley represents the greatest concentration of new wealth in the United States.

Presently the electronics industry accounts for $100 billion in annual sales. By the end of the 1980s it will reach $400 billion and become the world's fourth largest industry (after steel, autos, and chemicals). It will also be the only one of these industries that is high technology.

What exactly does "high technology" mean? A high-tech industry is characterized by: (1) highly skilled employees, many of whom are scientists and engineers; (2) a fast rate of growth; (3) a high ratio of R&D expenditures to sales; and (4) a worldwide market for its products. Not only is the technology very advanced, but it is also continuously changing, at a much faster rate of progress than other industries. Electronics is not the only high-tech industry today; genetic engineering is another, as are aerospace, pharmaceuticals, and instrumentation. Within electronics some sectors—like computers and semiconductors—are based on a technology that is advancing the most rapidly. So microelectronics is the highest of high-tech.

Most people are mystified by microelectronics, especially semiconductors. The microscopic size of semiconductors, seldom seen by consumers, adds to their mystery. And Intel, Fairchild, and AMD, the firms that produce these tiny bits of information technology, may be big in Silicon Valley, but they are largely unknown to the rest of the world.

The Birth of Electronics in Palo Alto

A critical event in electronics history took place in the summer of 1912 in a small house at 913 Emerson Street in Palo Alto. Lee de Forest and two fellow researchers for the Federal Telegraph Company, an early electronics firm, leaned over a table watching a housefly walk across a sheet of paper. They heard the fly's footsteps amplified 120 times, so that each step sounded like marching boots. This event was the first time that a vacuum tube had amplified a signal; it marked the birth of electronics and opened the door for the development of radio, television, radar, tape recorders, and computers. De Forest's former home on Emerson Street is now a vacant lot full of weeds and junk, but alongside the sidewalk is a historical marker, placed there by the city of Palo Alto. It says that on that spot Lee de Forest of the Federal Telegraph Company invented the amplifying quality of the vacuum tube.

Like many of the other electronics pioneers in the Palo Alto area Lee de Forest had a Stanford University connection; his work was partly financed by Stanford officials and faculty. Many of the early Palo Alto engineers were Stanford graduates and even though they might work for competing firms they remained close friends. They also shared a feeling of inferiority to the big East Coast electronics firms. Compared to RCA, the California firms were miniscule. And compared to the Eastern universities, Stanford was a young upstart.

The role of Stanford University, and specifically that of its visionary vice-president, Frederick Terman, was critical to the beginning of Silicon Valley. In 1920 Stanford was just a minor league, country-club school. By 1960 it had risen to the front ranks of academic excellence. The rise of Stanford implemented the take-off of the Silicon Valley microelectronics industry. And Silicon Valley helped put Stanford University where it is today.

Stanford University opened in 1891, a gift from Senator and Mrs. Leland Stanford as a memorial to their son, who died just before college age (hence the official name of the university, Leland Stanford Junior University). Senator Stanford, the Central Pacific Railroad magnate who drove the golden spike into the track near Ogden, Utah, linking the West with the East, endowed the new university with an estimated $20 million, at the time one of the largest philanthropic gifts ever made. The Stanfords donated their Palo Alto Stock Farm of 8,800 acres as the campus. Today the campus is still called "the Farm," and the university museum contains the golden spike.

Fred Terman knew Stanford well, having grown up on campus where his father, Louis Terman, was a noted psychology professor, creator of the Stanford-Binet IQ test, and known for his study of gifted children.

Terman was a sickly child and became intrigued with ham radio, an interest that was to shape the direction of his life. After Palo Alto High School he enrolled at Stanford, earning his B.S. in electrical engineering in 1920. Then he entered the doctoral program at MIT where his mentor was Vannevar Bush, an electrical engineering professor who became dean of engineering and later vice-president of MIT. Bush played a leading role as a scientific advisor to the U.S. government during World War II. He believed in close contact between engineering professors and high-technology firms; indeed Bush was one of the four founders of Raytheon prior to the war. Bush influenced Terman to think of a university as an applied R&D center rather than an ivory tower.

Following the completion of his Ph.D. under Bush's guidance, Terman accepted a faculty position at MIT. However, before taking up his professorial duties in 1924, Terman returned to Stanford to visit his family. While in Palo Alto he came down with tuberculosis and spent the next year in bed with sandbags on his chest. Upon recuperating, Terman stayed in Palo Alto to become a professor of "radio engineering," as electrical engineering was then called, at Stanford. He chose Stanford over MIT because of the California climate.

Thus but for the fickle fact of being struck with a serious illness in Palo Alto, Fred Terman probably would have become the godfather of Boston's Route 128, instead of its counterpart in Santa Clara County. And, without Fred Terman, Silicon Valley might never have happened.

The Hewlett-Packard Story

One of Fred Terman's most direct influences on the rise of Silicon Valley was his role in launching Hewlett-Packard, one of the area's largest, most unusual, and most admired electronics firms. In 1931 two Stanford University sophomores, David Packard and William R. Hewlett, became friends as bench-warmers on the varsity football team. Bill Hewlett was the son of the dean of the Stanford Medical School, while Dave Packard had come to Stanford from Pueblo, Colorado, where he had grown up with a ham radio set glued to his ear.

Hewlett and Packard were better students than athletes. Their interest in ham radio broadcasting took them to Fred Terman's electrical engineering classes. Terman learned that Hewlett and Packard planned to start their own electronics business after graduation and encouraged their entrepreneurial spirit. The professor was impressed with Bill Hewlett's ability and curiosity with electro-mechanical gadgets; he was always in Terman's student laboratory at Stanford, where tools and parts were available to anyone who wished to fabricate some gadget. Hewlett constructed a portable radio transmitter and receiver that he took skiing. As Terman put it: "He got a great deal of zest out of making it. . . . He found that this was a new world that was a lot of fun."[4] A few years later, when Hewlett-Packard began, its founders' shop skills were very important because Hewlett and Packard were the workforce as well as the owners of the new firm.

In 1934, after graduation, Packard was hired by General Electric in Schenectady, New York, and Hewlett went to MIT for graduate work. Four years later, Terman arranged fellowships for Hewlett and Packard so they could return to Stanford in order to earn electrical engineering degrees which required a fifth year of study. The two friends rented apartments at 367 Addison Avenue in Palo Alto, and set up a small shop in the garage behind their boarding house. During their hours free from graduate study, the two partners devised a variety of electronic gadgets and did odd-job work that Professor Terman helped them find.

Professor Terman was much taken by the concept of negative feedback, then a new idea in the field of electrical engineering. He discussed it at length in his 1938 graduate seminar, in which Bill Hewlett was enrolled. Out of this course came Hewlett's master's thesis project: to build and evaluate a variable frequency oscillator. Hewlett's machine operated over a wider range of conditions than other products then available and it cost a fraction of the existing price ($55 instead of $500). It appeared the oscillator might have commercial possibilities and Terman encouraged Hewlett to join his old schoolmate Dave Packard in a partnership to exploit it. Terman loaned them $538 to start producing the oscillator and helped arrange a $1,000 loan from a Palo Alto bank.[5] For the first year business was spotty, but Terman helped steer work their way. "You could always tell when they had any orders . . . because Packard would park his car in the driveway while they were in there working. If the car was in the garage and the doors were closed . . . you'd know there wasn't any work going on."[6]

The first big sale of eight audio oscillators was to Walt Disney Studios for the production of the soundtrack for "Fantasia." One of the original oscillators is still operating efficiently in a Hollywood sound studio. By 1940, the new firm expanded into half of a cabinet shop on El Camino Real in Palo Alto (this building still stands as Polly and Jake's Antiques); after that quarters moved into a nearby redwood building. By 1942, the H-P workforce reached about a hundred and annual sales were around $1 million. Due to the World War II demand for electronics products, Hewlett-Packard got off to a promising early start. But thereafter Hewlett-Packard grew more slowly. In 1950, twelve years after its founding, the firm had only 200 employees (although it sold 70 different products and had total sales of about $2 million). This modest initial growth indicates the slow rate of change in Silicon Valley during the 1940s, before a full head of entrepreneurial steam had built up.

Terman said of his former students: "Any place in which you put them in a new environment, they somehow learned what they needed to know very quickly . . . at really a superior level. So when they got into business they didn't need a teacher; they somehow learned as they went along. They always learned faster than the problems built up."[7] Perhaps their special talent as quick learners enabled Hewlett and Packard to shift their company's product line from electronic instruments to include computers in the 1970s, to move past their technical training in engineering to manage a huge corporation, and to avoid managerial "adolescent transition" problems. Certainly the management style of H-P, which features stock options, extensive employee benefits, and personal relationships with employees, has infected every other firm in Silicon Valley.[8] Hewlett-Packard pioneered in the formation of the distinctive Silicon Valley management style, which in essence consists of showing employees that management cares, treating them as family members.[9] Newer firms in the Valley, like Apple and Tandem Computer, are outspoken in their admiration for H-P's management style and in acknowledging their attempts to mimic it.

Today Hewlett-Packard has 68,000 employees, manufactures some 5,000 products, and has $4.4 billion in annual sales. Like many other high-technology firms, H-P invests about 10 percent of its sales revenues in R&D. The company has grown at about 20 percent per year. It is ranked 110th in the *Fortune* 500 in sales, and 62nd in profits. A recent survey of 6,000 business leaders by *Fortune* ranked H-P as one of the two most admired U.S. companies.[10]

A recent tabulation by *Fortune* magazine estimates Hewlett's holdings in H-P with 9.1 percent of the stock at $1.045 billion; Dave Packard, with 18.5 percent of the stock, is worth $2.115 billion. They ranked first and second in wealth on a national list of heads of entrepreneurial companies.[11] By this accounting Hewlett and Packard are the two most successful entrepreneurs in America.

In 1954 after the Stanford Research Park opened, Hewlett-Packard built their company headquarters on one of the choicest pieces of land on the campus. Recently H-P inaugurated their new world headquarters complex on one of the last remaining large plots in the Stanford Research Park. Their new building is located only three blocks from Polly and Jake's Antiques.

The Stanford Research Park

The chief problem facing Stanford administrators in the late 1940s was how to convert the use of the university land into money, so that the money could be converted into academic prestige by hiring star professors. The original Stanford family land gift forbade the sale of any of its 8,800 acres. Fred Terman, then vice-president of Stanford, and Wallace Sterling, its president, together hit upon the idea of a high-technology industrial park. The Stanford Industrial Park, created in 1951, was the first of its kind.[12] Terman called it "Stanford's secret weapon." Through land leasing "the purpose was simply to earn money for the University."[13] Only later did the Stanford Research Park become a means of transferring technology from the university's research labs to firms in the park.

"This idea of an industrial park near a university was completely foreign," Terman said,[14] both to Stanford University and to the firms that would become lessees. The first was Varian Associates, a Stanford spin-off for which Terman served as a board member. Varian, which was then some twenty-five miles from Stanford in rented buildings in San Carlos, signed the first lease in 1951 for four acres fronting El Camino Real and Page Mill Road. They prepaid $4,000 an acre for a 99-year lease. As there was no inflation clause in the agreement today this site is worth several hundred thousand dollars and Varian Associates has one of the sweetest land deals in Silicon Valley.

When Hewlett-Packard took a lease in the Stanford Research Park in 1954, it became the nucleus for Silicon Valley. Terman then sold leases to other high-technology firms on the basis of the advantages of being close to a university.[15] When company officials came to explore leasing a site in the park, Terman would send them "to talk to Packard or Hewlett about the advantages of being close to the University."[16] By 1955 seven companies were located in the Park, 32 by 1960, and 70 by 1970. Today, all 655 park acres are leased. The 90 tenant firms, employing about 25,000 workers, are all engaged in high technology work. Stanford Research Park has served as a model for scores of other high-technology parks in the United States and around the world.

The park contributed financially to the growth of Stanford University through the earnings from the long-term leases. These prepaid leases amount to over $18 million, a figure approximately equivalent to Senator Leland Stanford's original endowment in 1885 of $20 million. By 1981, the annual income from renting Stanford lands was about $6 million per year.[17] The clever thing about the income from the Stanford Research Park is that it is unrestricted; thus it can be put to any good use by Stanford's administrators. The earnings from the Stanford Research Park and the university's other land-rental arrangements fueled Terman's faculty recruitment.[18] This funding convinced renowned professors to move to Palo Alto from Eastern universities. Thanks to the Park, during the 1960s Stanford University began its rise to its present position as one of the nation's great research universities.

Terman used the tidy incomes from the Stanford Research Park to create a "Fighting Fund," designed to retain and recruit star faculty. At the heart of Terman's plan for Stanford's ascent was his strategy for "steeples of excellence": "Academic prestige depends upon high but narrow steeples of academic excellence, rather than upon coverage of more modest height extending solidly over a broad discipline." Exactly what is a steeple? "A small faculty group of experts in a narrow area of knowledge, and what counts is that the steeples be high for all to see and that they relate to something important."[19]

William Shockley and the Beginnings
of the Semiconductor Industry

Bell Labs is virtually a national resource with the largest basic research program in electronics in the world. Based in Murray Hill, New Jersey, Bell Labs is the R&D arm of the American Telephone and Telegraph Company. For over fifty years Bell Labs has ceaselessly spawned technological innovations; currently it holds 10,000 patents and produces about one per day. Their most significant discovery was the transistor. Some call it "the major invention of the century."[20] Arno A. Penzias, vice-president for research at Bell, says, "Without Bell Labs, there would be no Silicon Valley." He's right. Nor would there be a Silicon Valley without Dr. William Shockley, co-inventor of the transistor with John Bardeen and Walter Brattain at Bell Labs in 1947.[21] It happened that Palo Alto was Shockley's hometown; it also happened he wanted to make a million dollars.[22]

The transistor (short for "transfer resistance") was important because it allowed the magnification of electronic messages, as did vacuum tubes, but required much less current, did not generate as much heat, and was much smaller. At the time of its invention it was obvious that many useful applications of the transistor would be made. But it proved difficult to manufacture reliable transistors and the first commercial use did not occur until 1952, five years later, when transistors were adapted for use in hearing aids. Gradually transistor technology advanced and by the time co-inventor Shockley received the Nobel Prize in 1956 (soon after he arrived in Palo Alto), twenty companies were manufacturing transistors.[23] One of these was Shockley Semiconductor Laboratory.

Shockley knew what was getting underway in Silicon Valley through his many contacts in the electronics industry. His former chemistry professor at California Institute of Technology (Cal Tech), Arnold O. Beckman, had located the Spinco Division of Beckman Instruments, a manufacturer of scientific measurement equipment, in the Stanford Research Park. Beckman provided the financial backing for Shockley's new firm. Since his mother lived there, for Shockley there were both personal and entrepreneurial reasons for locating his semiconductor plant in Silicon Valley. Shockley astutely recruited eight bright young men from East Coast labs who became the founding cadre for the West Coast semiconductor industry. The eight were attracted to Shockley's firm by his scientific reputation.[24]

The beginning of the semiconductor industry in Silicon Valley is illustrated by a famous 1956 photograph of a dozen men toasting Shockley on the occasion of his winning the Nobel Prize. The photo was taken at Dinah's Shack in Palo Alto and the champagne toast was made at seven o'clock in the morning, soon after Shockley had received a telephone call from Stockholm. Robert

Noyce, one of Shockley's bright recruits, looks like a college sophomore, though he was 31, and soon to become chief of Fairchild
Semiconductor, the company he began with other members of the
"Shockley Eight." The photo also includes Gordon Moore, who
left Shockley Semiconductor Laboratory with Noyce to join Fairchild in 1957, then accompanied him to found Intel in 1968. Next
to Moore is Shelton Roberts, who left Fairchild in 1961 with Eugene Kleiner, Jay Last, and Jean Hoerni (all members of the
Shockley Eight) to found Anelco, another semiconductor company. Hoerni later left Anelco to found Union Carbide Electronics
in 1964, and Intersil in 1967. (See photo, centerfold.)

None of these firms, nor their founders, would have been in
California had it not been for Shockley. In a paradoxical sense,
Shockley deserves credit for starting the entrepreneurial
chain-reaction that launched the semiconductor industry in Silicon Valley. As Fred Terman described Shockley, "He was very
attractive to bright young people, but hard as hell to work with."[25]
When his protégés found him difficult they quit and started their
own firms.[26]

During the first year at Shockley Semiconductor Laboratory,
the boss determinedly pursued R&D on four-layer diodes, while
his research staff urged him to switch to work on silicon transistors whose circuitry could be placed on a transistor by diffusion
through openings in silicon oxide. Because Shockley refused the
suggestions of his eight engineers they obtained backing from in-
dustrialist Sherman Fairchild[27] in 1957 to launch Fairchild Semiconductor, the first company set up to work exclusively in silicon.[28] In 1960 one of the Shockley Eight, Jean Hoerni, invented
the planar process at Fairchild, in which impurities (particles that
facilitate the semiconduction of electricity) were diffused down
into the base of the silicon chip. The planar process was a great
boon to volume production of silicon transistors enabling Fairchild to get off to a fast start.

Shockley Semiconductor never recovered from the blow of
the Fairchild spin-off and finally was shut down. Shockley never
found the riches he came west to pursue.[29] In 1963 Shockley was
appointed to an endowed professorship in electrical engineering
at Stanford. During the 1970s Shockley publicized his beliefs that
not all races are genetically equal, nor are they evolving on an

equal basis. He acknowledges that he contributed to the so-called "Nobel Sperm Bank" (The Repository for Germinal Choice in Escondido, California). These controversial activities, widely reported in the media, unfortunately cause the public to overlook Shockley's scientific achievements and contributions to the growth of entrepreneurism in Silicon Valley. Along with Fred Terman, William Shockley should be considered a co-founder of Silicon Valley.

Military funding also played a role in the early days of Silicon Valley. Lockheed's move to Northern California in 1956 was crucial and U.S. Department of Defense purchases of semiconductors represented about 40 percent of total production. (Although today it is about the same dollar volume, military purchases represent only about 8 percent of total semiconductor sales.)

Pleasant climate and availability of space were other factors in attracting individuals and firms to Silicon Valley, and holding them there once they arrived. A 1963 survey of 53 companies in the area disclosed that "climate and living accommodations" were highly ranked by 70 percent of the firms. Also ranked high were "availability of brain power in the form of engineers and scientists" and "nearness to universities."[30]

Silicon Valley, once it got underway, represented an information-exchange system for technical know-how, a strong attraction for new entrants to the microelectronics industry. It also represented fresh entrepreneurial spirit, attracting those individuals who wanted to start their own firms. Silicon Valley fever, once risen, began to infect great numbers.

Crucial among the early factors in Silicon Valley growth were Stanford University, military purchases of semiconductors, and sunshine. After the mid-1960s, Stanford and the military decreased in relative importance, and the critical mass of companies and the information-exchange factors rose in significance.

Could Silicon Valley happen again in another place at another time? Perhaps so, but we doubt it. A "Silicon Valley" requires a technological innovation (like semiconductors) whose time has come. So just plain luck was also involved in the rise of Silicon Valley.

PART II

THE CULTURE

OF

HIGH TECHNOLOGY

WHILE THE CULTURE of high technology is distinctive, it is a way of life that is difficult to understand, even by those in Silicon Valley who are immersed in it. Here we present glimpses of the new high-tech culture that is emerging in the U.S. by looking inside Silicon Valley at the venture capitalists and networks that make things happen, the nature of working and living, the material rewards of success, and the social problems that are also part of high technology. We begin with the most pronounced characteristic of Silicon Valley: its free-wheeling, high-energy entrepreneurial drive.

3

Catching the
Silicon Valley Fever

"This is much more than just turning sand into gold. In a sense more and more, these days we're turning sand into intelligence. And that," he said softly, "is true transmutation."

President of a high-tech firm
in *Silicon Valley: A Novel*
by Michael Rogers

SILICON VALLEY FEVER is like a January rain in Northern California. Clouds come in off the Pacific, and pretty soon a light rain begins to fall. At first it soaks into the ground, but soon one drop runs down a leaf into another drop and ever so gradually the drops gather other drops and form rivulets which meet other rivulets and form streams. Before long the creeks are running full on their way to becoming small rivers, then large rivers. Entrepreneurial fever in Silicon Valley is now running at flood stage. And it all began with semiconductors.

While Shockley set the note for entrepreneurship in the early days of Silicon Valley, it was Fairchild Semiconductor that increased the tempo of the spinning off of new firms to fever pitch. About half of the approximately seventy semiconductor firms are direct or indirect descendants of Fairchild Semiconductor[1] (Figure 3.1). Employment with Fairchild was the gateway into the semiconductor industry elsewhere in Silicon Val-

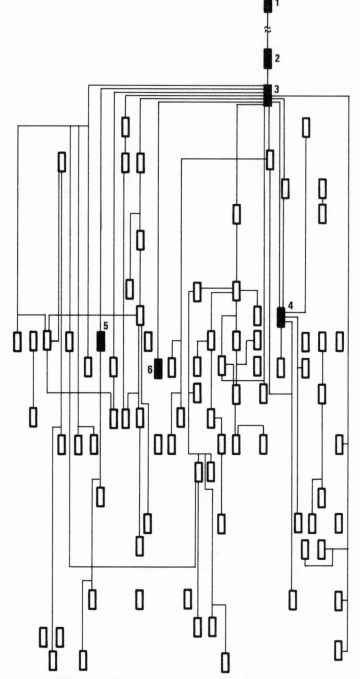

Figure 3.1. The genealogy of semiconductor firms in Silicon Valley. In this chart Firm 1 is Bell Labs; 2 is Shockley Semiconductor; 3 is Fairchild Semiconductor; 4 is National Semiconductor; 5 is Intel; and 6 is Advanced Micro Devices.

Source: Semiconductor Equipment and Materials Institute, Mountain View, California.

ley. At a 1969 conference of semiconductor engineers held in Sunnyvale, less than two dozen of the 400 present had never worked for Fairchild.

Fairchild, a huge company, could absorb the loss of top people without serious consequences to its overall technical capabilities. Further, Fairchild got the reputation for being a good springboard into the semiconductor industry of Silicon Valley and thus attracted promising young electrical engineers.

When we talked with Dr. Les Hogan, former president of Fairchild, we asked him how so many spin-offs evolved from his firm: "Well, take the case of Lee Boysel, who founded Four-Phase Systems. Lee came to my office one day, and told me 'Les, I think I want to leave to start my own company.' I said, 'Lee, I wish I had a good argument for you to stay here at Fairchild, but I don't. I think you'll become a multimillionaire; you're a brilliant engineer. But you'll need good management help and you must find marketing expertise.' He was smart enough to know what he didn't know. I said, 'You're a typical engineer, a little introverted. Now I can give you a hell of a raise, and 1,000 or so shares in the company. But you should go.' And you know, Lee Boysel made it. He made it big."[2]

Not that Fairchild enjoyed losing its talent. Company officials instituted a variety of policies designed to discourage defection from Fairchild, but none of these deterrents to job mobility effectively slowed the outflow of engineering talent. The firm has one of the toughest no-return policies in Silicon Valley—Fairchild refuses to hire back anyone who leaves. A decade ago, then-president Wilf Corrigan became so concerned by the number of Fairchild R&D employees who left to spin off new semiconductor firms that he abolished the R&D division.[3] However that failed to slow the outflow, and when Fairchild began to lose its place in the industry, R&D had to be reinstituted.

In 1979 Fairchild Semiconductor was purchased by Schlumberger, a French multinational corporation, primarily because Fairchild badly needed a major infusion of capital.[4] The sale of Fairchild to a foreign firm caused considerable muttering in Silicon Valley. It was as if the family farm back in Iowa had been sold to a housing developer from New York.

The Life and Times of a Semiconductor Engineer

The rise and fall of firms in the Silicon Valley semiconductor industry is reflected in the career of Howard Z. Bogert, who has gone through ten jobs in the past 23 years. This works out to a job mobility rate of around 30 percent, which is characteristic of Silicon Valley engineers.

1. After earning his B.S. in electrical engineering (BSEE) at Stanford in 1957, Bogert served in the U.S. Navy as a computer maintenance specialist. While in the service he wrote to Dr. William Shockley and was offered a job in his company in 1960 (two years after the Shockley Eight had made their exit to Fairchild). After a taste of Shockley's management style, Bogert resigned.

2. Bogert was hired by Fairchild at a $10 per month salary increase, where he worked under Bob Norman on the first integrated circuit.

3. In 1963 Norman and several other Fairchild engineers spun-off General Micro-Electronics (GME). Norman took Bogert with him. They designed the first large-scale integrated circuit of metal oxide-on-silicon (MOS). However military buyers banned existing MOS technology, so in 1966 several GME people spun-off a new firm, American Microsystems (AMI), in order to produce more reliable MOS semiconductors for military consumers.

4. In 1967 Bogert switched to AMI, a struggling semiconductor house then on the edge of bankruptcy and selling stock to its employees to raise needed cash. Burroughs and General Electric became customers for AMI's MOS semiconductors after attempts to sell to military buyers had failed. Sales shot up from $500,000 in 1967 to $8 million in 1968.

5. In 1970 Bogert left AMI to launch his own firm, International Computer Modules (ICM). Several partners put in $10,000 each. A recession knocked out ICM's financing. Then Bogert's former employer, AMI, sued ICM for stealing company secrets. Unable to handle the stress of the start-up period, ICM was dissolved.

6. In 1971 Siliconix offered to buy out the former partners in AMI in Siliconix stock. Bogert stayed with Siliconix for one year.

7. Bogert joined Unicom, a former AMI subsidiary that manufactured pocket calculators. However prices for pocket calculators dropped from $200 to $20 in four years and smaller firms could not ride out the profit decline. In 1976 Rockwell purchased Unicom.

8. Bogert became an independent consultant, working part time for Memorex and Dataquest. Later he joined Dataquest full time as Director of Technology, Semiconductor Division. (Dataquest is a subsidiary of A.C. Nielson of TV ratings fame.) Bogert's work entailed monitoring innovations in the semiconductor industry, a position for which his history of job mobility aptly prepared him.

9. Four years later, in 1982, Howard Bogert announced that he was resigning to go into semiconductor consulting.

10. After a year of being his own boss, Bogert accepted a job back at Dataquest, as director of the Semiconductor Industry Service.[5]

The Adolescent Transition

One of the special problems of rapidly growing high-technology firms is the adolescent transition, the phase during which size outgrows managerial ability. When a firm increases from one to 100, to 500, to 1,000 employees, transition problems occur at around 500 workers. At this size a firm must have personnel, advertising, and accounting departments, as well as a training division. The growing company can no longer operate effectively as an informal and dedicated group clustered around a charismatic entrepreneur-engineer. An engineer may have started the firm in order to escape the bureaucracy of an old-line company. Suddenly success demands that the new rapidly growing firm must return to the bureaucratic style from which its founder fled. This paradox is frustrating to the entrepreneur who enjoys success, but dislikes being unable to call all 500 employees by their first names. The entrepreneur also wants the firm to continue to outgrow the competition, but is reluctant to give up a piece of equity in the company to venture capitalists (in order to keep growing at a skyrocketing rate). Puzzled, the entrepreneur asks, "Why isn't it as much fun around here as it used to be?"

Most entrepreneurs are engineers, poorly trained in business management, financial, and legal matters. Passing through the adolescent transition ultimately means that the chief executive has to learn to delegate responsibility to employees. Letting go of details is not easy for the can-do individuals who captain new start-ups. Harry Garland, president of Cromemco, liked to review all advertising for his firm, which had 500 employees. His company officers couldn't convince him that his time was too valuable for that task. Until August 1982 Cromemco's ads were appropriate for a computer-buying audience of engineers and scientists. But when Cromemco launched a home computer aimed at the general public, Garland wisely brought in an experienced marketing man to plan effective nontechnical consumer ads.

In a 20-year study conducted by Dr. Albert Bruno, a professor of marketing at the University of Santa Clara, 95 percent of the new Silicon Valley companies survive their first four years of life. This rate is much higher than that of the average U.S. manufacturing firm; only 75 percent survive the first two years. Why are the California start-ups more successful? Bruno says it is due to the "Silicon Valley maternity ward," the infrastructure of venture capital, consultants, peer information networks, and support industries.[6] All the "pieces" for a start-up's birth and nurturing are plentiful in Silicon Valley.

But Bruno cautions that the new microelectronics firms face a particular threat posed by the adolescent transition. Approximately 25 percent collapse in the second four years as they fail to pass from entrepreneurial to established management. In addition there is a high rate of acquisition by other firms in the second four years. Of 250 firms founded in the 1960s, 32 percent had been acquired or merged by 1980, 31 percent were surviving and independent, and 37 percent were bankrupt.[7] The companies that survived were an average age of fourteen in 1980, had average annual sales of $9 million, and employed an average of 135 people.

How a Chip Goes from Rising Star to Cash Cow to Dog

Just as a new company goes through stages as it develops, so does a new product. The story of how a new semiconductor chip goes through the usual sequence from being "a fast-rising star" to being a "cash cow," to being a "dog" was related by David Drennan in the Corporate Planning Department at Advanced Micro Devices. "AMD started as a 100 percent second source company and for the first three or four years after our start-up in 1969 we just sold 'me-too' products created by Fairchild or Texas Instruments or some other firm. The first important device that we designed ourselves [in late 1975] was the 2901 microprocessor using bi-polar technology. The 2901 is flexible because it is a universal device like a crescent wrench that can be programmed to many different needs. It is used in computers, telecommunications and instruments. Most of our competitors were producing MOS microprocessors, each geared to a specific application. Our bi-polar device was faster and used less electrical power, important advantages in the computer field. So the 2901 looked promising to us.

"Well, back in 1975, our salesmen began to discuss the idea of a bi-polar microprocessor with our customers. AMD has the reputation of being close to our customers, by helping them design their systems around our chips. We decided that the high development costs for the 2901 were justified by the broad base of demand. This product was a big risk for us; we put our life-blood on the line, along with our image, a fine group of engineers that we did not want to lose, and a lot of emotional commitment. We began design work, and then about a year later we got to 'first silicon'—meaning the test wafers with the mask applications. [A wafer is a flat disc of silicon on which semiconductor chips are formed and the masks are the templates for the chips]. During this period we were still talking with customers, and then redesigning the 2901. For instance, we began using 3-inch wafers, so as not to be changing our production process as well as the architecture of our chip. Later we switched to 4-inch wafers.

"Finally we began sampling the product to certain customers. Concurrently we geared up to make the 2901 in large volume, hoping that large orders would come. Sales started slowly. We had to find a second source for the 2901 because no one wants to design their computer around your device if you are the only supplier; they want a safety valve. So we licensed Raytheon and Motorola as second sources. One of our competitors, Signetics, soon produced a rival to the 2901. We did not patent our product because we did not want other companies to see our design in the patent pages. Anyway, it takes too long to get a patent.

"About four years from our decision to create the new chip [in 1979], we sold our millionth 2901! This product is now our 'cash cow'; it gave a big boost to AMD sales. We sold nothing in 1969, the year of our start-up in May, $1 million in 1970, $4 million in 1971, $11 million in 1972, $26 million in 1973, $25 million in 1974—a bad year, $34 million in 1975, $62 million in 1976, $92 in 1977, $148 million in 1978, and we had sales of $220 million in 1979."[8] But like all semiconductor chips, AMD's 2901 would soon become an out-dated "dog," and sales would dribble on for only a few more years.

The life of a semiconductor product is very short. Jerry Sanders, president of AMD, says that 80 percent of the semiconductor chips that his company produces are based on designs less than five years old. In this sense generations of chips turn over like a geneticist's fruit flies.

An Intel sales manager, Mark Larsen, seconds this notion: "If you stop for a week in this industry, I swear you would lose your technological state of the art knowledge. There is nothing about a two-year-old product that I couldn't divulge to my competitors. A one-year-old product, you might not be able to tell everything, but a two-year-old is old."[9]

Jerry Sanders: Impresario of Silicon Valley

A colorful character in Silicon Valley is Walter J. (Jerry) Sanders, III, president and CEO (Chief Executive Officer) of Advanced Micro Devices. He positions himself, his company, and his chips in the public eye as shrewdly as a Hollywood promoter. "I'm an engineer by education, a marketing man by background, and an entrepreneur by circumstance...."[10] Sanders is first and foremost a marketer and AMD's success shows that aggressive marketing in microelectronics can pay off.

Sanders began life in a poor Irish family in Chicago, and his humble beginnings may explain his new-rich lifestyle today—his Savile Row suits and Paris neckties, his movie star stable of expensive autos, and his lavish homes. He studied electrical engineering at the University of Illinois and came west to work for Douglas Aircraft in Santa Monica. In 1959 Sanders joined Motorola as an applications engineer and sales trainee in their Chicago office. Fairchild, then the industry leader, began to notice they were consistently losing sales to Motorola in Sanders's territory; his wining-and-dining strategy was winning customers. The Sanders charm was stronger than Fairchild's outstanding products. So Fairchild hired Sanders and assigned him to their Los Angeles sales territory (thus Sanders began his Hollywood connection, which he maintains today with a Malibu residence). A few years later, Sanders was moved to the home office in Mountain View and named director of marketing at Fairchild. He was 31 years old.

Shortly thereafter Fairchild officials balked at Sanders's demand for a higher salary and he quit, retreating to his Malibu home.[11] After some months of meditation, Sanders joined seven other refugees from Fairchild to form AMD in 1969. They had $50,000 of their own funds, and, with much effort, raised a pile of venture capital. As Sanders recalled: "Arthur Rock used to say it took him five minutes to raise $5 million for Intel's start-up. I like to say it took me five million minutes to raise five dollars, because we had a hell of a time putting together the $1.5 million on which our company was started. Today $1.5 million seems to be a cough in a telephone call."[12]

Sanders said that AMD was able to live through its early years because "doors kept slamming just behind us, but never just ahead of us." One very close call for AMD occurred on July 22, 1969, when the new company was trying to raise capital. They were still short of their minimum by $5,000 at 4:55 P.M., five minutes before the final deadline. Then the phone rang and an investor notified AMD that he wanted to put $25,000 of his capital into the firm. That saved the day.[13]

As David Drennan said, initially AMD sold chips as a second source for other companies. Customers usually demand a second source for any semiconductor chip, otherwise they feel too dependent upon the primary seller who could charge them an arbitrary price, and who might not always be able to deliver a shipment of chips on time. A semiconductor firm like AMD which served mainly as a second source and seldom came out with new products did not earn much prestige in the eyes of other semiconductor companies. But Jerry Sanders raised second-sourcing to a high level of expertise, boasting about the excellence of his firm at second-sourcing. A few years ago Sanders claimed that AMD's 8080 microprocessor was the "leading follower" of the Intel 8080.[14]

AMD's rate of growth in the past 12 years outdistanced any other semiconductor firm in Silicon Valley. Many of the special marketing strategies used by AMD came from the creative mind of Jerry Sanders. "It was Jerry that thought of producing all of our semiconductors to Mil Spec 883 [military specifications for semiconductor quality, set by the U.S. Department of Defense] so that our customers knew we were up to a high quality standard, even though we sold very little to Defense," said Sanders's former co-worker Tom Skornia. He also credits Sanders with creating a variety of price incentives for customers. For instance, AMD was the first firm to offer price breaks on the purchase of a mixture of 100 semiconductor chips.[15] Sanders realized the crucial importance of public image in marketing, and he worked hard to shape the AMD image as an aggressive outfit.

In *Business Week*'s 1982 executive compensation survey, Sanders was one of the highest paid CEOs in the industry with a $622,000 annual salary in 1981 (which included a $147,000 reimbursement for interest on loans to exercise his stock options).[16] In other terms, Sanders's salary amounted to $278 per hour (assuming an eight-hour day). For comparison, John S. Young, the president and CEO at Hewlett-Packard, earned $493,000; and Charles E. Spork, number one at National Semiconductor, was paid $216,000 in 1981. Sanders's earnings approach the $692,000 paid to the president of IBM, J.R. Opel.

PHOTO: ADVANCED MICRO DEVICES

Catch the Wave with Jerry Sanders

Perhaps some of the "go-go" ideology of Jerry Sanders is expressed by one of AMD's 1979 employee recruitment ads:

Ten years ago, Advanced Micro Devices had no products, zero sales, and eight of the best people in the business.

Today, Advanced Micro Devices has more than 600 products, $200 million in sales, and 8,000 of the best people in the business.

We want more. We want *you.*

You'll work for the nation's fastest-growing integrated circuit company. And you'll work with people who really like to win, people who are as good at what they do as you are.

Every place has its time. Ours is now.

Join Advanced Micro Devices.

CATCH THE WAVE.

Gene Amdahl: Recycled Entrepreneur

Some entrepreneurs successfully build a new company from scratch, find their success unsatisfactory, then leave their firm to launch another start-up. A case in point is Gene M. Amdahl, a storied personage of Silicon Valley regarded as a true computer genius who had the audacity to take on IBM, the giant of mainframe computers. Amdahl began his career in the 1960s as a computer designer at the IBM R&D center in Menlo Park, California. He was the principal architect of the family of IBM 360s, the most successful mainframe computers in history. But when Amdahl had an idea for another new computer, IBM, for reasons of price, decided to stick with its established products. So in 1970 Gene Amdahl picked up his marbles and spun-off his own firm, Amdahl Corporation, to manufacture IBM plug-compatible equipment. "Plug-compatible" means that Amdahl's machines would plug in to other IBM equipment. Essentially Amdahl was beating IBM at its own game and one might expect IBM to wage total war on Amdahl. They did, but Amdahl succeeded because he had a superior product. He shipped his first computer in 1975. In four years Amdahl had sales of $300 million and had helped launch the "pcm" (plug-compatible manufacturing) industry.

What Amdahl lacked was sufficient capital to support his superior technology. Amdahl Corporation staggered from one cash-flow problem to another. A former employee relates how meeting each monthly payroll was a major crisis. On one occasion Amdahl flew a company accountant to Tokyo to bring back payroll funds, an exchange for the sale of a piece of the company's equity to Fujitsu, a Japanese electronics firm. Bit by bit Gene Amdahl sold off ownership until he had only a couple of percentage points left for himself. He also experienced the usual difficulties of an entrepreneur-inventor in passing his company's adolescent transition. For example, instead of delegating the task to an employee, Amdahl insisted on personally meeting with the officials of each company that purchased one of his mainframe computers. That soon became quite a chore, but Amdahl insisted on the ceremony.

Amdahl's main problem, however, was with IBM. Amdahl

had one or two percent of total sales in mainframe computing equipment; IBM had 80 or 85 percent. Its dominance of the industry allowed IBM to wage war on the pcm's in a variety of ways. They could drop prices and dare pcm's like Amdahl to compete. The powerful aura of IBM made it extremely difficult for Gene Amdahl to obtain venture capital from American sources.[17]

With those kinds of problems, 1979 was a disastrous year for Amdahl Corporation. A stockholder vote brought in Eugene R. White as the new president and Gene Amdahl resigned. He felt it was intrinsically unfair that he was no longer chief of a company carrying his own name. He then spun-off yet another start-up, Trilogy Systems, whose name derived from its three-way ownership by Gene Amdahl, his son Carlton, and a trusted friend, Clifford Madden. An entrepreneur's second venture profits from lessons learned from the first and Gene Amdahl wasn't letting go of his ownership control of Trilogy. He lined up $160 million so that the co-founders owned 99 percent of the Trilogy stock.[18]

Even after his involvement with Trilogy, Amdahl's entrepreneurial fever wasn't satisfied. In 1982 Amdahl invested in yet another computer venture, GRiD Systems Corporation, a firm that produced an expensive portable computer. GRiD's Compass computer sells for $8,000 to executives who want an attaché-size unit they can carry with them on the road and connect by telephone with their home office.

Gene Amdahl is now 61 years old and his hair is white. Some of his friends in Silicon Valley, however, say they expect him to start up at least a couple more computer firms before he quits.

John Linvill: Professor-Entrepreneur

At Stanford University even some of the professors are Silicon Valley entrepreneurs, and a few are millionaires. In the School of Engineering most professors are somehow involved in entrepreneurial activities either as partners, founders, board members, consultants, stockholders, or all of the above.

Dr. John G. Linvill is Professor of Electrical Engineering at Stanford. Over the years he has taught semiconductor electronics to thousands of students who now work in Silicon Valley. Like many of his colleagues in the School of Engineering, Linvill has a variety of close relationships with the nearby microelectronics firms; he serves on the board of Spectra-Physics (a laser firm) and several other local companies.

Linvill's claim to entrepreneurial fame is co-founding Telesensory Systems, Inc., in 1971, a company located in the Stanford Research Park that manufactures the Optacon (Optical-to-Tactile-Converter). The Optacon costs $4,295 and is a four-pound black aluminum box about the size of a book. Its phototransistors scan printed text and transmit these images as electronic impulses to 144 vibrating rods, which reproduce the messages on a blind person's fingertips. The Optacon allows the blind to read at an information flow rate approaching normal speaking speed (about 50-90 words per minute). In essence the Optacon bypasses Braille reading via the magic of microelectronics.

As a result of John Linvill's invention over 9,000 blind people now read electronically. One of them is Candace Linvill Berg, the professor's daughter, who has been blind since age three. With the help of her Optacon she went through Stanford and earned her Ph.D. in psychology.

When his daughter was younger, Dr. Linvill watched his wife spend three or four hours a day translating books into Braille for Candy's schooling. To replace this laborious process, Dr. Linvill began to experiment with using a miniature camera over a line of type, then converting this information into electronic impulses which drove tiny vibrating pins.

The basic work and testing of the Optacon were carried out by Linvill's electrical engineering students in their campus laboratory. When a working instrument evolved, Linvill discovered that electronics companies were not interested in producing the Optacon commercially. So Telesensory Systems, Inc., was established. It was financed by Linvill and three colleagues; by a $250,000 order for 50 Optacons from the U.S. Office of Education; and by an $85,000 investment, including $25,000 from Stanford University. Telesensory Systems had annual sales of $8 million and employed 160 persons in 1982.

Jimmy T. of Tandem

How many times have you been at an airline desk to make a reservation and been told that "the computer is down"? Thanks to James Treybig of Tandem Computer it is less often these days than in the past. The market niche for Tandem was created by the vulnerability of most computer systems, which often break down at the worst possible time. Treybig and his co-founders devised a means of hooking two computers in double-harmony—both can work independently, but if one goes down its partner immediately steps in and takes over both tasks.

Nine years ago Tandem Computer was just an idea on a sheet of yellow paper. Since then the firm has had a spectacular rate of growth, increasing at 100 percent a year to sales of $208 million in 1981. With 3,800 employees, Tandem appears not to have been troubled by the adolescent transition. The reason may be the unorthodox management style that Treybig instituted in the company. A Texan with a BSEE from Rice University and an MBA from Stanford, Treybig is known as "Jimmy T." by his employees. His people-oriented management style is familial, the company motto "Success through team effort." Tandem offers trendy Silicon Valley emoluments: Friday afternoon beer blasts, a swimming pool, stock options for every employee, and a generous package of incentives.

Tandem also has the sayings of Jimmy T., a blend of human relations wisdom and shrewd observation: "You can no longer optimize profits and screw people. Tandem's a socialist company."[19] There is indeed a great deal of equality at Tandem; the firm's strategy is to treat its employees like human beings, recognizing that brain power is the most important resource in a high-technology company. Tandem's computer engineers embrace Jimmy T.'s leadership with considerable enthusiasm. Tandem reports a turnover rate of seven percent, far less than the 30 percent that is par for Silicon Valley firms.[20]

Jimmy T. learned the basics of people-oriented management at Hewlett-Packard, where he was marketing manager for six years. His customers' nightmares centered around computer failures, which could shut down an airline reservation system, a bank, or some other vital service. Existing fail-safe computer systems at that time required a second, redundant computer that lay idle except in times when its partner failed. Tandem's first hot product was the Nonstop 16, in which up to 16 computers were hooked up in a network with each one devoting a small fraction of its capacity to monitoring the other computers in order to watch for a breakdown.

Jimmy T. not only had technical ability and management skills, but he also knew how to obtain venture capital. He gained this capacity by working for Kleiner and Perkins, a San Francisco venture capital firm. In 1974 they put up the initial funding in response to Jimmy T.'s business plan, which is still regarded as something of a marvel. At the end of 1979 Tandem came within $1 million in sales of its 1974 projection. Jimmy T. plans on Tandem becoming a $1 billion firm in 1985, an ambitious goal. Tandem presently has fourteen vice-presidents, more than the company currently requires—they are on hand for the anticipated growth of the firm.

Jimmy T. credits his company's success to forward planning, a unique management style, and to Silicon Valley. He's said: "There is nowhere else in the world we could have started this company. Silicon Valley is an attitude. We found risk capital, we found suppliers and vendors who wanted us to succeed, and we found people with an attitude that made us succeed."[21]

Entrepreneurship According to Nolan Bushnell

Nolan Bushnell, founder of Atari, Pizza Time Theatres, and Catalyst Technologies, explained entrepreneurship: "A guy wakes up in the morning and says, 'I'm going to be an entrepreneur.' So he goes in to work and he walks up to the best technologist in the company where he's working, and he whispers: 'Would you like to join my company? 10 o'clock, Saturday, my place. And bring some donuts.' Then he goes to the best finance guy he knows, and says, 'Bring some coffee.' Then you get a marketing guy. And if you are the right entrepreneur, you have three or four of the best minds in the business. Ten o'clock Saturday rolls around. They say, 'Hey, what is our company going to do?' You say, 'Build left-handed widgets.' Another hour and you've got a business plan roughed out. The finance guy says he knows where he can get some money. So what have you done? You've not provided the coffee. You've not provided the donuts. You've not provided the ideas. You've been the entrepreneur. You made it all happen."[22]

Proliferation of Cottage Industry

Dr. Richard Schmieder, a geographer who works as a local head-hunter, recently published *Rich's Complete Guide to Santa Clara County's Silicon Valley*. This excellent little atlas identifies 2,736 electronics manufacturing firms,[23] an astounding number, far greater than any previous estimates that have been made for Silicon Valley. And in addition to these 2,736, Silicon Valley also includes many non-manufacturing electronics-related firms engaged in marketing, advertising, public relations, selling, consulting, headhunting, supplying, R&D, training, management, market research, design, venture capital, legal, and numerous other support services that are important ingredients of the microelectronics industry and other high-tech industries in Santa Clara County. There are at least as many non-manufacturing companies as manufacturing, so the total number of firms in the electronics industry in Silicon Valley is approximately 6,000. Further, we estimate that non-electronics firms number at least another 2,000. So the total number of high-technology firms in Silicon Valley hovers around 8,000.

In addition to this surprising number of firms in Silicon Valley, our analysis of Schmieder's data on electronics manufacturing firms discloses another striking characteristic: their small size! Figure 3.2 shows the distribution of the companies by size (measured in number of employees). Over two-thirds (70 percent) have from one to ten workers, and 85 percent have fewer than 50 employees.

TLC Moves Out of the Garage

Not long ago a CBS News team arrived to do a documentary on Silicon Valley. They interviewed Bob Noyce at Intel, Regis McKenna of a public relations firm that specializes in high-tech cli-

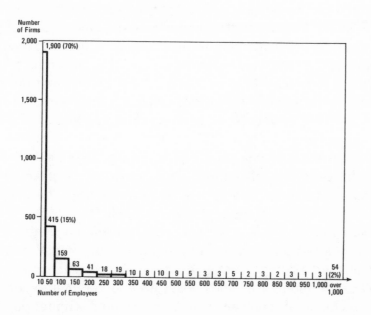

Figure 3.2.   More than two-thirds of the electronics manufacturing firms in Silicon Valley employ fewer than ten workers.

ents and various other industry leaders. During their discussions with us, the CBS team asked to visit a garage-type company with less than a dozen employees. We arranged for them to meet Dr. Ann Piestrup, chairperson and founder of The Learning Company (TLC), a rather special kind of Silicon Valley firm in that it develops and markets children's learning games, which are both fun and educational. *InfoWorld* magazine has said: "Every so often a company appears that challenges the accepted notions of an industry. The Learning Company of Portola Valley, California, is such a firm."[24]

TLC began in 1979 when Ann Piestrup was home with her small daughter Sarah and began to realize how inadequate existing computer games were. Video games held children's attention, but chiefly taught violence. Like John Linvill when he was faced with a personal problem, Piestrup decided to do something about hers. She was 36, had a Ph.D. in educational psychology, and several years of experience working for private R&D firms.

With a grant from Apple, Piestrup began studying how nursery school children reacted to computer color graphics, music, and voice. The kids loved the computer and showed none of the fear that many adults display in their first computer experience. Piestrup hired a computer programmer and they began to design educational programs for very small children. One program, called "Juggle's Rainbow," helps kids learn such concepts as left, right, upper, and lower. If the child strokes any key on the left half of the keyboard, a beautiful colored butterfly appears on the computer screen. Touching any key on the right-hand side brings out a different set of colors. This program is geared for three-year-olds; the ability to read is unnecessary. The Juggle's Rainbow program won an award from Apple.[25]

TLC's goal is to avoid violent programs and concentrate on teaching children complex concepts in an exciting way. While the first games were being developed and pretested with small children TLC fell upon hard times. Piestrup and her small staff (including a couple of refugees from Atari) worked without pay. At one point the struggling firm almost lost its furniture, until an employee loaned TLC some emergency funds.[26]

The big break for TLC came in November 1981, when Melchor Venture Management invested $300,000. All TLC programs run on Apple computers and Tom Whitney, an Apple official, was impressed with the market niche being carved out by TLC. When Whitney left Apple for the Melchor venture capital firm, one of his first acts was to interest President Jack Melchor in TLC. Melchor is a strong family man with children and TLC's ambitious, altruistic goals appealed to him. Melchor's backing was accompanied by the conditions that Tom Whitney be placed on the TLC board and that Jack Smythe, an MBA with business experience, become president of TLC.[27]

TLC now has eleven employees, five games are offered for sale, and others are in the works. The Learning Company expects sales of $5 million by 1984.[28] Leslie Grimm, the eleven-year-old daughter of a TLC employee, earns royalties from a TLC program that uses her graphics.

It may appear that most Silicon Valley entrepreneurs are electrical engineers. Many of the successful start-ups indeed are headed by electrical engineers, physicists, or computer scientists:

Bob Noyce, Jerry Sanders, Gene Amdahl, John Linvill, and others. After all, the semiconductor and computer industries are applications of electrical engineering know-how. However the reverse is also possible—a non-engineer can be the entrepreneur and assemble a team of technical people to assist him, or her, as with Ann Piestrup and TLC or software entrepreneur Bill Gates of Microsoft, a former Harvard student who is not an engineer.

As Silicon Valley fever spreads, it becomes clear that entrepreneurship is not a specialty of any particular field or occupation. Anybody, even an eleven-year-old, can be an entrepreneur.

4

Venture Capital

"Cash is more important than your mother. That's Al's Law."

Al Shugart, Founder, Shugart Associates and Seagate Technology, 1982

"We venture capitalists plant seeds, water them, and hope there will be a harvest."

Pitch Johnson, President, Asset Management Co., 1981

SILICON VALLEY is the prime center of venture capital activity in the United States. Over one-third of the nation's largest venture capital companies have an office located in or near Silicon Valley. Many of the remaining venture firms, although based elsewhere, are heavily involved in Silicon Valley. Venture capital goes hand-in-hand with entrepreneurship and one cannot understand a high-tech system like Silicon Valley without understanding how venture capitalists operate.

Venture capitalists are powerful gatekeepers, deciding whether or not a new start-up will go. But venture capitalists do much more, providing management assistance and technical advice throughout the early stages of a company's growth. In some cases, they may even fire the company president and take over the firm until a new leader can be found. Yet they tend to shun publicity and remain a shadowy and often misunderstood entity to the public. Many Americans do not even know that venture capitalists exist, and few recognize their power in directing technological innovation.

Venture capital is money placed in new or young high-technology companies with a high potential for growth. A venture capital firm serves as an intermediary between investors looking for high returns and entrepreneurs in need of capital. Venture capital firms often invest money solely on the basis of an entrepreneur's promising idea, a form of collateral that conventional bankers consider worthless. Entrepreneurs trade a percentage of the ownership of their company (often 50 percent) in exchange for venture capital. Understandably, entrepreneurs have little love for venture capitalists, sometimes referring to them as "vulture capitalists." But venture capitalists are as essential for the entrepreneur as a bank account.

Venture capitalists obtain the money they invest from four major sources: wealthy individuals; pension funds; universities and similar institutions; and the special investment arms of banks, insurance companies, and other large corporations. These investors choose the high-risk investment of venture capital because it offers tax advantages and the opportunity to make much higher returns. Some of the most successful venture capital funds have yielded more than a 50 percent annual return in recent years, and earnings of 35 percent are fairly typical. As a result the amount of financial resources committed to venture capital has surged.

Only a decade or so ago the venture capital industry was in decline. In 1969 the U.S. Congress increased the maximum tax on long-term capital gains from 28 to 49 percent. This decision had a devastating effect on the amount of financial resources available for venture capital, and the incentive to invest in new companies was greatly diminished. In 1969, $171 million of new private capital was committed to venture capital firms; by 1975, after the new tax law took effect, this figure dropped to $10 million, a mere 6 percent of the capital available six years previously[1] (Figure 4.1).

In 1978, after intensive lobbying by Silicon Valley and high-tech firms elsewhere, Congress reversed its earlier decision and rolled the maximum capital gains tax back to 28 percent. The tide began to turn as venture capital investments again became attractive. Later a decision by the U.S. Department of Labor allowed pension funds to be invested as venture capital. In 1981 Congress further decreased the maximum capital gains tax to 20

3000 Sand Hill Road

A recent directory lists 59 venture capital firms in or around Silicon Valley. Within the Valley, 15 venture capitalists are located under one roof, at 3000 Sand Hill Road in Menlo Park, just off the Stanford University campus.[4] It is a beautifully designed complex in a lovely setting with a hilltop view across the San Andreas Fault to the coastal range beyond. The trees, shrubs, flowers, and lawns at 3000 Sand Hill Road are exquisitely kept, and the parking lot is filled with Mercedes, Jaguars, and BMWs. The scene conveys an image of pastoral establishment, of well-appointed, gracious living.

This concentration of high-technology financiers is functional for the venture capitalists as well as the entrepreneurs. A venture banker can have lunch with a friendly competitor and pick up useful information about a particular entrepreneur whose business plan he is considering. Such handy networks can work against a potential entrepreneur—if rejected by one venture capitalist, the whole community knows immediately. Such "pack investing" works against the ideal of free market forces. There is much subjectivity in investment decisions; one capitalist's instinct may be wrong, and thus may influence others.

If you are an entrepreneur with a start-up in mind and looking for backing, drive over to 3000 Sand Hill Road. There's $80 to $100 million in annual venture capital investment waiting for you.[5]

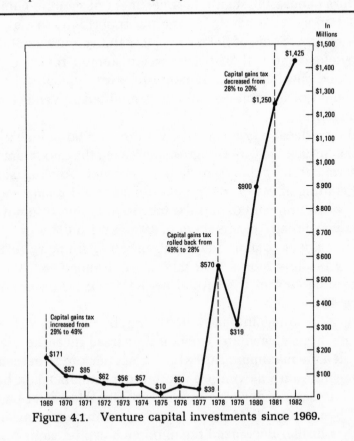

Figure 4.1.   Venture capital investments since 1969.

percent. The net result was that by the end of 1982, the amount of new private capital committed to venture capital firms had risen to over $1.4 billion, eight times the amount of 12 years before.[2] That's enough money to start 2,800 small high-tech companies or 350 good-sized ones.[3] Some keen observers of the Silicon Valley scene are now worried that perhaps there is too much venture capital. Their concern is that it is becoming so easy to obtain funding, that too many start-ups are being launched; if many fail in a few years, venture capitalists will be left with a black eye.

Steps in the Birth of a High-Tech Start-up

In order to better understand the role venture capital plays in start-up businesses, let us examine the process through which a typical Silicon Valley company is born.

1. INSPIRATION

A start-up firm begins with inspiration, the creation of a new product or service that serves an unmet need. Nolan Bushnell foresaw the potential of video games as the result of his work in a Coney Island amusement park coupled with playing a computer video game at the University of Utah. So he launched Atari. Steve Jobs and Steve Wozniak wanted a microcomputer, but couldn't afford to buy one. So they started Apple.

2. PURSUIT

A decision to form a new business around an innovative idea often involves acceptance of risk and a departure from a secure lifestyle. Sometimes pursuit is the only option available. Bill

Hewlett and David Packard began their firm in 1938 as a means of providing themselves with jobs after graduation from Stanford. Silicon Valley entrepreneurs have widely different backgrounds, business orientations, educations, and personal characteristics, but they often have the following in common: they leave well-paying jobs with mature companies in a similar field for their start-ups; they desire a greater sense of control over their future; they have a very high level of energy, motivated in part by dissatisfaction with their present position; and they know role models who are successful entrepreneurs. They all have the determination to pursue the promise of their "hot idea" for a new product by forming their own company.

3.   FORMATION OF A TEAM

A balanced and talented team includes a president with management and technical experience; and specialists in finance, marketing, engineering, and other fields like software development perhaps, or product design. To create a team of dedicated individuals the entrepreneur must convince the others of the potential rewards. When Activision, the video game company, started in 1979 its chief entrepreneur was Jim Levy, who came from the record industry. He quickly assembled four other founding members, refugee video game designers from Atari. Activision obtained $700,000 in venture capital, created a couple of video games that became big hits, and shot up to sales of $60 million in 1981. Without the four co-founders on the team, Levy says he couldn't have secured the venture capital to get Activision started.[6]

4.   FOCUSING THE VENTURE

A team begins development of a new product by pursuing available information on customer needs and possible markets. Typically they work in someone's home or garage ten to fourteen hours a day, six or seven days a week. They likely will have pooled their financial resources, working without pay, living on their savings. Bursts of energy and excitement occur at this early stage. A venture capital company rarely will finance this initial development stage (with "seed" financing); in most cases, venture capitalists wait until the new business has reached further development.

5. FORMATION OF THE BUSINESS PLAN

A business plan is both a game plan for starting a new firm and the principal means by which a start-up is evaluated by venture capitalists. A business plan encourages an entrepreneur to recognize potential obstacles and to formulate strategies for overcoming these barriers. The business plans of certain companies are legendary in Silicon Valley. For example, Tandem's business plan, written in 1974, still came close to predicting the firm's sales in 1982 of over $200 million. And Bob Noyce's business plan for Intel was written on just a single sheet of paper.

6. MAKING THE DEAL

Most entrepreneurial teams do not possess enough capital for creating a new business and must search for outside capital. They often begin with friends and relatives, then approach business associates, banks, and other lending institutions. Given the high risks and lack of collateral associated with most new high-technology ventures, conventional lending institutions will not provide capital until a new company shows signs of success in terms of sales or orders. Therefore the entrepreneurial team's next stop is often a venture capitalist.

Through a friend or associate, the entrepreneur sends a business plan to one or more venture capital firms. An active venture capital firm receives hundreds of similar business plans each year and will only invest in a handful. If the business plan looks promising, a venture capital firm will set up a meeting with the entrepreneurial team. The venture capital firm meanwhile pumps their informal networks to obtain information about the entrepreneur and the innovation.

An initial presentation by the entrepreneurial team to the venture capital firm usually takes place in the venture capitalist's office. With millions of dollars resting on the outcome, this meeting is serious drama. The entrepreneur presents the business concept while the venture capitalist interrupts with questions of clarification. One issue might be whether several venture capital firms would invest together in the start-up. An advantage is that the entrepreneur receives the benefits of wider experience, more contacts, and greater financial strength, while the venture capital firms can spread their risks. Venture capitalists commonly invest in groups of two to five ("pack investing"). There is a great deal of cronyism among venture capital firms and one venture capitalist would be considered greedy to hog an especially attractive investment. The venture capital community in Silicon Valley is like a country club. Everyone knows everyone else, news and gossip travel quickly within the group, and the activities of the club members remain hidden to most of the public.

7.   LAUNCHING A START-UP

Let's assume that the entrepreneur's business plan (usually after some modification) is finally "bought" by the venture capitalist. The deal is struck, usually after several months of negotiation. The entrepreneur and the capital backers break out the bubbly. The next morning it's back to work for both partners. The new firm expands from its garage into larger facilities, and gears up toward beginning production. The venture capitalist not only is on the new company's board of directors, but also provides regular management advice, perhaps even on a daily basis, which is why it is convenient to be located near a start-up. Pitch Johnson, president of Asset Management in Palo Alto, states: "The venture capitalist's role is that of chaplain, a kind of psychological masseur for the entrepreneur."[7] The chemistry must be right, for the entrepreneur and backers must work hand-in-hand for the next several years.

As the new company grows in size and sales, the entrepreneur often comes back to the venture capitalist for further financing in order to fuel expansion in the race to outgrow the competition.[8] As time goes on risk decreases and establishment funders (like bankers) may buy in to the high-technology firm. At this point, the venture capitalist begins to think about withdrawing; his role is about over.

8. GOING PUBLIC

Five or six years after its launching, if the start-up has been successful, the venture capitalist helps the new company "go public" by offering its stock for general sale. This event involves great excitement and is the real moment of pay-off on the venture capitalist's investment. On this day the value of the young firm is established and its entrepreneurs may become instant millionaires.

This is the point at which the venture capitalist often picks up his moneybags and goes home, to invest in yet another risky start-up.[9] Most venture capitalists hope to earn ten times their initial investment within five years. But of course these hopes are not always realized; they may get a return of zero and take a loss if the new firm fails. About 20 or 30 percent of new firms die an early death. Another 60 or 70 percent are modest successes. Only 5 percent are the Apples, Rolms, and Tandems that make it big.[10] Venture capitalists say there are few opportunities outside of microelectronics and other high-tech fields that can meet their expectations for a high pay-off. So if you have a business plan to manufacture a better mousetrap, don't bother approaching venture capitalists. Unless it's an electronic mousetrap.

A venture capitalist offers the entrepreneur consulting, recommendations about personnel, technical advice, and business and financial management. Bill Hambrecht, a San Francisco venture capitalist, is a member of 37 boards of directors for firms in which he's an investor. Unlike bankers and stock investors, venture capitalists become very involved with their start-up companies. As Pitch Johnson put it: "We don't just roll the dice. We blow on them, a hell of a lot."[11]

Venture capitalists look for certain traits in the entrepreneurs they back: honesty; the ability to admit mistakes and be flexible in different situations; absolute dedication; a hunger to succeed; and a sound managerial and technical background. As one venture capitalist put it: "In real estate, it is location, location,

location. In venture capital, it is people, people, people." Pitch Johnson looks for intensity and determination as indicators of the successful entrepreneur: "I want to see him leave heel marks all the way to the edge of the cliff." A similar notion is expressed by Don Valentine of Capital Management Services in Menlo Park: "Just bring me your 140-IQ egomaniacs, your driven guys who are hard to deal with, and I'll take them all."[12] Valentine should know; he's invested over $70 million launching forty firms in the past decade, including Apple, Atari, and Altos Computer.

Venture capitalists portray themselves as urbane, sophisticated businessmen, though they are basically seen by entrepreneurs as shrewd and rich. The popular Valley nickname for them—"vulture capitalist"—depicts the venture capitalist as a greedy, obnoxious scavenger, living off the entrepreneurial spirit and hard work of Silicon Valley's engineers. The vulture capitalist's objective is to gain control of as much of someone else's company as possible. If the founders have to be dumped in the process, so be it. Since the vulture's goal is to make money when the company goes public or is acquired, the long-range viability of the firm is unimportant. Therefore capitalist and entrepreneur may have very different objectives, and at least a certain degree of conflict.

The amount of capital finally committed to a start-up is specified in shares of company stock at a set value per share. Once this agreement is made, it is only the beginning of dealings between founders and venture capitalists. The first deal is known as first round financing; usually there is a second round when the fledgling company asks for still more capital, negotiating more shares of stock at a different price (usually higher). There may be third and fourth rounds of financing. Subsequent rounds may then involve only the venture capitalists from the first round, or other venture capitalists may come into the game. Since the venture capitalists possess the capital, new firms feel powerless in dealing with them. One can understand why a firm's founders can have mixed feelings toward their financiers.

Going It Without Venture Capital: Cromemco[13]

Cromemco is a computer firm headed by two Stanford Ph.Ds in electrical engineering who began operations in a garage in 1975 and now inhabit a luxurious 200,000-square foot plant in Mountain View. The company had moved five times in five years as annual sales had gone from $50,000 in 1975, $600,000 in 1976, $4 million in 1977, $11 million in 1978, $20 million in 1979, $30 million in 1980, $50 million in 1981, and about $100 million in 1982. In its first five years, the firm's sales soared over 8,000 percent, a dizzying compound rate of 216 percent per year.

Cromemco's may sound like the familiar Silicon Valley success story except for one crucial difference: Cromemco *never borrowed a dime.*

If Cromemco has a model, it's Hewlett-Packard. But there's one big difference—Bill Hewlett and Dave Packard started their firm in 1938, before the concept of venture capital even existed. Also H-P only grew to a few hundred employees in its first 20 years while Cromemco increased to 500 employees in its first seven years. In contrast, the negative model for Cromemco founders Harry Garland and Roger Melen is Gene Amdahl, who built Amdahl Corporation from scratch, but in the process lost all but a few percent of ownership in the company that today still bears his name. Garland and Melen own 100 percent of Cromemco (aside from some stock they contribute to a profit-sharing plan for their employees). How they pulled off this coup is fascinating.

Cromemco's history began when Garland and Melen were undergraduates at Stanford living in Crothers Memorial Hall and dreaming of owning their own high-technology firm. In the mid-1970s they authored a few articles in *Popular Electronics* describing electronic gadgets (not computers) they had created. Readers could order the components for these gadgets from "Cromemco," a "firm" that Garland and Melen dreamed up named after their dormitory. On a 1975 trip to New York to meet the magazine's editor, Melen was introduced to Ed Roberts, founder of MITS-Altair, the pioneering microcomputer firm (Altair was named after a fictitious planet by that name in a "Star Trek" television episode). Melen and Roberts hit it off immediately, and, on an impulse, Melen flew back to Albuquerque with the Altair founder. After an all-night bull session, Melen designed some gadgets to hook-up the Altair home computer with a home television screen, thus enhancing its practical utility. Then Melen went home to Palo Alto to tell his friend Garland that they were in business with their "Dazzler" hookup system, peripheral equipment for the Altair. The two electronics wizards moved out of their Stanford dormitory when they completed their doctorates and became junior faculty members. Their professorial salaries provided the "venture capital" to begin manufacturing the Dazzler.

The two entrepreneurs used their savings of $2,500 to formally found Cromemco. Neither drew a salary at first (in fact, Garland and Melen today are 16th and 17th on the company's payroll).[14] From the start, they made a fetish of avoiding "Amdahlization." They received valuable fiscal advice from Keith Argabright, a CPA with Main Hurdman's office in San Francisco (the firm that does Cromemco's accounting work), who insisted they open a credit line of $250,000 with the Bank of America. Today Cromemco has upped their credit line to over $5 million, but it is largely unused. They view it as a lifesaver for their company if there were a disastrous recession in the industry.

Liquidity of assets is a key to Cromemco's success. The company rents its office and manufacturing facilities in Mountain View; they could afford to buy, but prefer not to. Their game plan is to operate with as little profit as possible, plowing back most of their gains into the purchases of equipment and into hiring more employees. Because they are not a publicly traded firm, Garland and Melen do not have to answer to a board of directors. Nor do they have to produce a profit for stockholders. No annual reports, no executive committees, and complete fiscal secrecy about Cromemco's operations can be very advantageous in a highly competitive industry.

Garland and Melen's unitary command of Cromemco enables them to make rapid decisions and pursue company policies that are strictly their own. Cromemco produces a family of computers that are top-of-the-line; they charge a higher price than most competitors and they deliver top quality. Their products have sold themselves, with little promotion.

Two key factors in going it without venture capital are technological competence in a product line, and filling a felt need for those products. Cromemco primarily sells its computers to engineers; they don't need high brand-awareness via media advertising to persuade them to buy.[15] Such technology minded customers look first at product performance. Without doubt, Cromemco has excelled at selling to technically competent buyers who want the best and are willing to pay for quality. Cromemco's Systems 3 computer has been "wildly successful," admitted Roger Melen.

Cromemco's motto, printed on employees' business cards, is "Tomorrow's Computers Today." It might be appropriate to add another slogan: "And We Never Borrowed a Dime."

Meet Some Venture Capitalists

Frank Chambers

On the 26th floor of San Francisco's Bank of America building is the office of one of venture capital's old pros, Frank G. Chambers.[16] He can look out over San Francisco Bay, Golden Gate Bridge, and Marin County beyond, and reflect on twenty years in the venture capital business and investments in over fifty start-ups. Chambers helped pioneer such phenomenal success stories as Dataproducts, American Microsystems, and Rolm. He has also experienced frustration, failure, and disappointment, like the time he turned down two kids in the mid-1970s who wanted funding for a start-up called Apple Computer.

In 1947 Chambers and his brother Robert founded Magna Power Tool Corporation in San Francisco. Their product was a new type of multipurpose power tool named the Shopsmith, which combined the functions of individual shop tools like a lathe and drill press. The partnership was a tremendous success with $3 million in sales during the first year of operation. They accomplished this with only $30,000, keeping expenses at a minimum and financing their production through a clever sales strategy. They had one large buyer, Montgomery Ward, which paid for shipments within 20 days. The Chambers brothers farmed out production to a San Francisco machine shop which agreed to payment in 30 days. Shopsmith began on a shoestring, and prospered.

After several years the Chambers brothers sold their company, but Frank Chambers did not forget the frustration he had experienced while trying to meet cash flow problems. A few years later, in 1959, he and a close friend, Fred Cox, formed one of the first venture capital companies in Northern California, Continental Capital Corporation. Since then, Continental Capital has given way to two limited partnerships. Chambers's venture capital schemes are not the largest in this field; his strategy is to pursue market niches where the smallest amount of money invested will produce the highest multiples of return.

Now in his sixties, Chambers enjoys gracious living. He belongs to the esteemed Bohemian Club and San Francisco's Bankers Club. After a day of reviewing business plans, he returns home to a 240-acre ranch in Marin County which he shares with five other families. But Frank Chambers hasn't yet learned to slow down; in the past two years Continental Capital has invested in sixteen new start-ups ("Too many," says Chambers). In ten years, Chambers insists he'll still be in venture capital. The reward, he says, is the excitement of shaping technological change. The power of venture capitalists is great and it is highly concentrated. Chambers says that 100 main decision-makers control the venture capital in the United States. He ought to know.

Arthur Rock

Bookish-looking Arthur Rock came to San Francisco from the East Coast in the mid-1960s. Since then he has been involved in creating about fifty entrepreneurial start-ups, including Intel and Apple. Yet there is no name on the door of Rock's office in San Francisco's financial district. Despite his fame for such accomplishments as raising $5 million for Intel in 1968, Rock favors a low profile.

Rock doesn't claim to know much about electronics, a lack he considers an advantage. "Although it slows me down a bit, it helps me understand the character of a person who is seeking venture capital. I see how he explains his proposal." What does Rock look for in the entrepreneurs he backs? They must really want to be rich. "Few people are willing to do what's necessary to be rich—to put that above everything else, to have the drive, the energy focused on making a success. Being tough with themselves."[17] Rock is very selective about the new ventures he finances. He culls only one or two proposals from the hundreds of business plans he reviews each year.

Despite the crucial importance of venture capital in Silicon Valley, it is a murky topic that is little studied in a scientific way and seldom taught in university courses. However, past inattention to venture capital is beginning to change. Pitch Johnson is now a part-time professor at the Stanford Business School where he teaches courses on entrepreneurship. His MBA students are required to write a business plan for a new firm and form an entrepreneurial team. Other business and engineering schools are also starting to teach their students about venture capital. Arthur Rock recently endowed a professorial chair for entrepreneurial studies at the Harvard Business School.

Pitch Johnson

The typical venture capitalist in Silicon Valley usually majors in engineering as an undergraduate and follows this training with an MBA. After several years' work experience in a high-technology company, the typical West Coast venture capitalist trains with an experienced venture capitalist, learning what to look for in entrepreneurs and their business plans. Finally, around middle age, the venture capitalist organizes a fund and strikes out on his own.

Pitch Johnson of Asset Management in Palo Alto has led a

life that closely parallels this typical career path. Johnson grew up in Palo Alto; his father was a coach at Stanford University. Johnson became a track star at Stanford, where he majored in engineering. After getting his Harvard MBA, Johnson worked for eight years in the steel industry in the Chicago area. In 1962 he went back to Palo Alto to launch a venture capital company, one of the first in Silicon Valley, in partnership with his friend Bill Draper. A few years later Johnson went out on his own. Looking back on his twenty plus years in venture capital, Johnson takes satisfaction from the start-ups he has helped launch. "Of course," he says with a small grin, "It's nice to make a little money too."[18]

There is one atypical characteristic of Pitch Johnson. His office is not at 3000 Sand Hill Road. In fact, it's in Palo Alto, in a converted residence right next to Johnson's own home. He says that he has one of the shortest commutes in Silicon Valley, about 35 feet.

Jack Melchor

Almost all venture capital companies are pretty much one-man operations. There may be an assistant or two, a secretary, and perhaps some part-time consultants, but the main decision-maker is usually just one man.[19] He weighs evidence about an entrepreneurial venture, considers his hunches, and then comes to a decision. A group of partners do not seem to work running a venture capital firm. One test of this proposition is provided by Melchor Venture Management in Los Altos, headed by Jack Melchor. A former Hewlett-Packard executive, Melchor is an unusually successful venture capitalist. He has assisted seventy companies in getting off the ground in Silicon Valley (among them Rolm, Osborne Computer, and TLC) and said: "I suspect I've helped 100 to 150 people within 15 miles of where we are sitting to make their first million."[20]

In recent years Melchor had expanded his venture capital firm by adding partners and his staff grew to ten. But in late 1982, Melchor concluded that big was bad. With the increased size Melchor found he was spending too much time teaching junior partners the skills of venture capital and was no longer devoting enough time to evaluating promising business plans. Nor was he having enough contact with the entrepreneurs he had financed. So he returned to being a one-man show.

Melchor looks at venture capital in statistical terms: "You can only lose 100 percent of what you commit, but you can make more than 100 percent. So even if you make half of them, you come out ahead." Melchor admits to losing about 20 percent of his investments in start-ups. In addition, every venture capitalist is plagued with what are called "zombies" or the "living dead," firms that seem to hang on but that do not create much return. A typical scorecard on ten investments by a well-managed venture capital firm would include two failures, two zombies, two fairly good investments (nothing spectacular, but returning a nice profit), two or three "winners" (providing capital gains of seven to fifteen times the venture capital firm's initial funding), and, with luck, perhaps one legend-making "super-winner," returning 100 or more times the initial investment.

Burt McMurtry of Technology Venture Investors (at 3000 Sand Hill Road) looked back at eleven start-ups in which he invested from 1969 to 1973.[21] His scorecard looked like this:

- Five failed or became stagnant.
- Five were good investments or winners.
- The eleventh firm took his investment of $250,000 to $75 million, a growth of 230 percent.

Jack Melchor was the initial venture capitalist to back Rolm Corporation. It had been turned down by a variety of venture capital firms, for understandable reasons. All three founders of Rolm were younger than thirty and had little previous experience in electronics. Though the key figures at Rolm were Jewish, Melchor's venture funds came from Saudi Arabia (a nation that at the time would not even provide visas for American Jews to work in their country). Despite the circumstances Melchor Venture Capital Management invested in Rolm and today Melchor is glad he did.

One of the several venture capitalists who rejected Rolm was Tommy Davis of the Mayfield Fund. Davis has also turned down Apple and several other Silicon Valley successes. The American

Electronics Association invited Davis to serve on a panel to discuss entrepreneurial firms at a 1982 banquet. The other speakers were all executives in successful electronics firms to whom Davis had refused venture capital. Davis was introduced by the master of ceremonies as the man who had said "no" to his fellow panel members. During the laughter from the audience that followed, Davis stood up and placed his dinner napkin over his head.

5

Networks

> "There's a magic here in Silicon Valley that we don't under-
> stand. This critical mass took some years to build up; it had
> its roots in the 1950s, but it began to really blossom in the
> 1980s. And Silicon Valley has been a really special kind of
> information environment ever since. An intellectual pot is
> boiling here."
>
> Les Hogan, former president of Fairchild
> Semiconductor, 1982

INFORMATION-EXCHANGE is a dominant, distinguishing characteristic of Silicon Valley. Because innovation entails coping
with a high degree of uncertainty, such innovation is particularly
dependent on information.

While most microelectronics firms have company secrecy
policies, individuals and firms utilize various information strategies to circumvent such mandated secrecy. Job mobility of R&D
workers among semiconductor firms is one means of technological information-exchange, and, in some cases, information-exchange may be one reason for job mobility. The close location of the firms facilitates freewheeling information-exchange in
Silicon Valley. "The easy information-exchange here is like the
scientists who feel that their technology *belongs to the world, to
humanity.* It's just too important to keep this technical information to oneself or one's firm," said Fairchild's Les Hogan.[1]

One ought to think of Silicon Valley not as just a geographical place, nor simply as the main center of the microelectronics

industry, nor even as several thousand high-tech firms, but as a *network*. An experienced semiconductor engineer said: "I know someone, and they know someone. But I don't know who they know. The power of this network is that the participants all know it exists. We all know that we all know lots of other people in the Valley. This is mainly due to the high rate of job mobility. The rate of rumor-passing in Silicon Valley is simply phenomenal. Reputations, successes, people leaving a firm, new products. The mill grinds out these rumors at a prodigious rate. Part of this rumoring comes about because all of these firms are so close together. You can look out your office window and see the other company."[2]

Bill Grubb, president of Imagic, an Atari spin-off video game company, said of the network: "Before we sold our first product, our vice-president and I already knew 90 percent of the potential buyers. We immediately signed up such customer firms as Sears, J.C. Penney, and Toys-R-Us. And since then we just kept on going. Up."[3]

The close networks that characterize Silicon Valley give the region an advantage over other areas. Nolan Bushnell illustrated this point: "There's a tremendous amount of networking here in Silicon Valley, unmatched anywhere else. I recently visited a group of engineers in London who were working on a new product in competition with a group here in Silicon Valley. Both started at the same time, but the Silicon Valley team got the jump by six months. Our group included an engineer that had a friend working at Intel. He smuggled out a couple of prototypes of a new chip that was just what they needed. The chip was soon to be on the market, but it wasn't yet in the catalog. Intel was very happy because there were some immediate buyers. Just that six months shows that we have tremendous advantage here. That's why Silicon Valley is always ahead."[4] Indeed, a Federal Trade Commission report said that the unique strength of the U.S. semiconductor industry derives from its firms' rapid copying of each others' innovative chips.[5]

As 3000 Sand Hill Road is the center for venture capital, the Palo Alto Square building on El Camino Real at Page Mill Road is the center for high-tech law. At last count, Palo Alto had 865 lawyers, twice the number of ten years ago and six times that of twenty years ago.[6]

The high-tech legal business is booming. Gordon Davidson, a lawyer at the firm of Fenwick, Stone, Davis and West, often has a new start-up case each day of the week.[7] Davidson plays a key networking role for start-ups, helping entrepreneurs complete their business plans and search for venture capital. He has ideal educational qualifications for this matchmaking, a BSEE and a Master's in computer science, plus his law degree. This training helps him judge an important issue for microelectronics spin-offs: whether the entrepreneur is taking trade secrets from his former employers.

The largest Palo Alto high-tech law firm is Wilson, Sonsini, Goodrich and Rosati with 50 lawyers. John Wilson said that on one day in mid-1982 his firm closed $20 million in deals involving high-tech start-ups.[8]

The fact that Palo Alto Square has become the center of high-tech legal operations also shows the importance of networks. In addition to knowing their legal statutes, the Palo Alto Square lawyers' main stock in trade is who they know. They can match an entrepreneur who has a hot idea with a venture capitalist who has dollars to invest. Business luncheons, after-work drinks, cocktail parties, and other social occasions are the stuff of which a high-tech lawyer's career is built. Their Roladex card-files are as indispensible as their law books.

Information must be given in order for it to be obtained. The nature of the technical information-exchange process in the microelectronics industry demands a high degree of reciprocity among the participants. An illustration of such person-to-person trade-offs is provided by a young Ph.D. at Hewlett-Packard's Central Labs who told of a professional meeting of semiconductor engineers at which he was describing his R&D project. Some of his H-P colleagues became concerned that he was telling "secret" information. But the Ph.D. knew exactly how far he could go. "I was fully aware of where the line was drawn. I went dangerously close to it. And in the public discussion of my results, some of our competitors asked questions that indicated to me how much they already knew. This was valuable information to our company."

How Networks Helped Us Write This Book

Rather early in writing *Silicon Valley Fever* we realized that a personal interview with Dr. Marcian E. "Ted" Hoff, inventor of the microprocessor at Intel in 1971, would be essential. Ted Hoff is a rather shy man and we knew that he generally avoided talking about his important invention. Author Judith Larsen had several network connections at Intel, but none of her contacts knew Ted Hoff. During most of 1981 and the first half of 1982 we waited patiently for an opportunity to approach Hoff.

In February 1982, author Rogers invited Vicky McConnell, a free-lance consultant on organizational communication, to lecture to his Stanford class. After class several of Rogers's students talked with McConnell. One was Anthea Stratigos, a communication major. Later, when McConnell was consulting at Intel headquarters in Santa Clara, Scott Pfotenhauer of Intel's corporate personnel unit asked her to recommend someone for a summer internship. Vicky McConnell remembered being particularly impressed by Anthea Stratigos and told Scott about her. He called her and an interview followed.

The job didn't work out for Anthea, but Scott phoned her again and they became social friends. Anthea told Scott about her professor, Ev Rogers, who was writing a book on Silicon Valley. Scott agreed to have lunch with Ev and Anthea, at which he offered to arrange an appointment for Ev to interview Ted Hoff about the invention of the microprocessor. A few days later Ev met with Ted Hoff at the Intel R&D building in Santa Clara.

Scott Pfotenhauer also arranged for us to visit Intel's Fab 3, the wafer fabrication facility at Livermore, California, that is the star of the company's semiconductor production process. Few outsiders are allowed to tour a wafer fab facility due to Silicon Valley security practices.

The results of the interview and visit are described in Chapter 6.

Key figures in the technical information network of Silicon Valley learn to manage the knowledge they possess. Karl Harrington, an engineer with a semiconductor company, told us: "Nobody comes forward with everything they know. It's like playing cards. If you keep something back, it provides some job security. Nobody tells you all the little tricks and nuances. You hold back a little so you can trade it later on. I could give information about equipment, for instance, to a company that I might go to work for someday. But I won't give information that would hurt the company that I'm with now."[9]

In Silicon Valley an engineer may disclose technical information to a former colleague who now works for a competing firm.

Information-exchange due to friendship was described by Floyd Kvamme, a former executive at National Semiconductor now with Apple Computer. "We all know each other. It's an industry where everybody knows everybody because at one time or another everyone worked together."[10]

Dataquest, the market research hub of the microelectronics industry, holds an annual conference for semiconductor firms each fall. It is usually held at a posh resort like the Camelback Inn in Phoenix, or the Double Tree Inn in Monterey. Participants are company CEOs and presidents. Dataquest utilizes a computer program to arrange the seating at dinners and seminars so that individuals will get to know each other and so that unfortunate combinations do not occur.[11] For example a customer would be placed next to a vendor; two Japanese would not be seated next to each other, as they would want to meet Americans; but individuals from directly competing firms would not be seated together.

Hans Reiner, chief of the Technology Center at Standard

Hey, Our Neighbor Owns a Computer Company[13]

Interpersonal ties can also be important in starting a new firm. A recent example occurred in Los Altos Hills, a nest of newly rich Silicon Valley technologists. Al Horley had no intention of talking business with his next-door neighbor. But one day Horley's wife Jeanette went over to ask the curly-headed Texan for some of his horse's dung for her garden. Turns out that the Texan owned a computer company. Jeanette Horley returned home to urge her husband to go over to meet their neighbor. Horley now recalls: "That day was an act of fate. It was unquestionably the event that led to my company."

The neighbor was James Treybig, founder of Tandem Computer. He and Al Horley talked over a few beers that Saturday afternoon, and then Horley invited Treybig to his garage to see a prototype satellite receiver that Horley had made out of some sheet metal. Within a few days, Jimmy T. brought over a team of his executives to determine if Tandem could use the satellite to link their computers around the world. Treybig also introduced Horley to his venture capitalists, Kleiner, Perkins, Caulfield & Byers. Soon Horley had raised $24 million in backing.

Two years later, Al Horley's Vitalink Communications Corporation sold satellite systems at $5 million a year. His first customer was Jimmy Treybig's Tandem. You could say that Vitalink got its start over a pile of horse manure.

Electrik Lorenz (SEL), a German electronics firm, told of his surprise when he first encountered the information-exchange network in Silicon Valley: "I was sent by my company to visit our representative in Sunnyvale, in order to get help with a particular technical problem that they were having. Our guy had part of the answer, and he knew where to find the rest of the information. After work, he took me to a bar in Silicon Valley. Then he called over engineers from adjoining tables, who were acquaintances of his. They really enjoyed telling us what to do. By 9 P.M., I had the solution to our company's problem. The next morning I flew back to Stuttgart. I was really amazed at how freely people cooperate in California."[12]

A Guide to Where the Networks Are

Bars and restaurants in Silicon Valley are more than just places to eat and drink; they are favorite places to talk shop. The oldest and most famous of these gathering places is Walker's Wagon Wheel Bar and Restaurant located in Mountain View at Whisman Avenue and Middlefield Road, practically in the shadow of Fairchild Semiconductor. A number of the "Fairchildren" spin-offs were planned here. However the center of the microelectronics industry has moved south down the peninsula and a new set of luncheon places and after-work bars have become centers of information-exchange: the Cow Girl Bar in the Sunnyvale Hilton Inn; the Peppermill just off Highway 101 on Bowers Avenue (near Intel's headquarters); and The Lion and Compass owned by Nolan Bushnell, who opened it when he couldn't find a good place to eat lunch near Atari. Its bar has an electronic ticker tape flashing on the wall, featuring stock listings for top Silicon Valley firms.

The bars and restaurants provide a neutral meeting ground for old friends who may have worked together but now are employed by competing firms. They chat over a glass of California chablis not about their families, sports, or hobbies, but about EEPROMs, flip-flops, and gate-arrays—Computerese.

Breakfasts at the Peppermill are now a Silicon Valley tradition, especially for semiconductor marketing people. A sales manager at Intel said: "I can go to The Peppermill at eight in the morning and always meet somebody I know. After all, this is Silicon Valley. All of my customers and all of my competitors—and that's about five hundred people—eat breakfast there regularly. In fact, I have to be careful about who is sitting in the next booth; you can gain a lot of information by overhearing conversations. All the distributors are there and these are the guys that I work with. A customer may be sitting there with one of my competitors, but I walk around and shake hands. Then I say, 'Oh, by the way, why don't we meet for breakfast tomorrow?' You make appointments. The Peppermill is just a giant meeting place."

An engineer in Intel's Sales Division feels that sales people are more careful in managing their information networks than other types of employees: "People in design or production have to be careful, but they aren't. They just don't think much about the importance of being careful. Anyway they don't spend so much time in restaurants. If somebody invited a design engineer at Intel to meet for lunch, he probably wouldn't even think to keep his mouth shut. And he wouldn't know who the people are around him anyway."

Fairchild, Atari, and Home Brew

For each of the different microelectronics industries in Silicon Valley, a particular organization played a central role in forming the informal networks among the individuals and firms in that sub-industry. Almost all of the pioneering figures in the semiconductor industry at one time worked together at Fairchild, providing a kind of fraternal bond among the now-competing firms in the same industry. Most game designers worked together in the Nolan Bushnell days at Atari in the last half of the 1970s and are all on a first-name basis today. The equivalent to the Fairchild-Atari old-boy network in the microcomputer industry is the Home Brew Computer Club. This unique organization had its first meeting in March 1975 in the garage of microcomputer enthusiast Gordon French in Menlo Park. Twenty-two microcomputer companies have since been launched by club members, and twenty of them are still in operation. Many are, or were, leading companies in the microcomputer industry: Apple, Cromemco, and North Star, just to name a few.[14] Some of the Computer Kids in Home Brew pioneered in computer software, others like Paul Terrell and Boyd Wilson launched computer retail stores, while other members like Jim Warren founded computer trade shows.

When Home Brew was founded it had a regular membership of 500 or so computerphiles, mostly young and male. The purpose of Home Brew (so named because the original members who had computers had assembled them from kits) was to facilitate information-exchange among microcomputer lovers. There were no dues, initiation rites, or bylaws.

The typical meeting began with a "mapping period"— individuals with something to announce, trade, sell, or give away would stand up and identify themselves. Then a "random access period" allowed like-minded individuals, such as devotees of the Intel 8080 microprocessor, to break up into small groups for a free-flowing discussion. People exchanged computer programs and circuit designs, information that would in a few years be company secrets. In the mid-1970s Steve Wozniak handed out Xerox copies of his circuit designs for the Apple computer. In return he got peer reinforcement and suggestions for improvement. No one at Home Brew then thought that microcomputers would become a competitive industry.

Home Brew was started by Fred Moore, who with his friends posted notices around Silicon Valley which said: "Exchange information, swap ideas, talk shop, help work on a project, whatever." To their surprise, hundreds came to the first meetings and they soon had to move out of Gordon French's garage into an auditorium at Stanford. Moore hoped that the Home Brew Club would provide an alternative to the commercialization of microcomputers and would help give computing power to the people. Moore was a political activist who had spent two years in prison as a draft protestor during the Vietnam War; he favored useful applications of microcomputers over profits. "I was hoping that those of us who were renegades, mavericks, anarchists, in the Home Brew Club would go beyond just [forming commercial companies]. But basically the idea of company and industry is what caught on."[15]

When several of the Home Brew members started microcomputer companies the free information-exchange at club meetings began to cease. Wozniak says, "For many people I know, their days at Home Brew were the best times of their lives. But it's all over now."[16] Fred Moore is nostalgic and somewhat bitter about what happened to Home Brew. He feels that capitalistic urges replaced his original altruistic ideals in the computer club. Today Moore devotes himself to editing a newsletter, *Resistance News,* for draft-resisters. He writes it on a microcomputer.[17]

Some of the original Computer Kids still come to Home Brew meetings today. Gordon French, who now heads a microcomputer consulting firm called Square 1, thinks that Home Brew is still the center of the informal network of microcomputer experts. Whether it is or not, Home Brew established that network.

Job Mobility

"All a guy has to do here if he wants to change jobs is drive down the same street in the morning and turn into a different driveway," Jerry Sanders of AMD once said.[18] One of the most striking characteristics of Silicon Valley is an amazingly high rate of job mobility. Some estimate that job-changing may be 50 percent each year. This turnover rate is highest among line-operators, board-stuffers, and assemblers; and somewhat lower among engineers and managers, who may turn over "only" about 30 percent per year.[19]

Paul Hess, a Silicon Valley company manager, said: "I do lots of hiring and recruiting, so I've read a million resumes in the last 15 years. One guy worked for 15 companies in 24 months. That was a little too much. But I'm not turned off by someone who has a history of two years with a company and then on to the next one."[20]

High job mobility is a boon or a disaster, depending on one's perspective. For employees, the assurance of being able to leave one company and move to another with an increase in salary provides a form of security. Each shift means a raise of 10 or 15 percent and perhaps a move up the management ladder. Companies have a quite different view of job-hopping; the loss of experienced employees is a major problem. A constant staff turnover creates difficulties in establishing consistency in internal operations. When an engineer who is key to a design project leaves, much of the thinking behind the project leaves with him.

The high rate of job change is perhaps encouraged by the companies as they urge employees to aspire to better positions. A Silicon Valley executive stated: "If we were to hire five secretaries at the same time, within a couple of years there would be a wide range in what they were doing and what they were getting paid."[21] Stan Thomas, an executive vice-president of finance, said that when individuals interview for a specific job, they look at what their next step up might be: "Say your firm has 400 employees today; three years from now you expect 3,000 employees. What's the organization going to look like? Where will the new employee fit in? When a company is growing so fast, a new employee can write his own job."[22]

The most common incentive for job-hopping is money; a move to a new job usually represents a raise of 15 percent. The shortage of technical people means that paying more is sometimes the only way to attract needed personnel. Design engineers are especially scarce in the semiconductor industry. "There are more individuals involved in playing basketball and baseball professionally than ever designed an integrated circuit," says Albert Bel Sale of Wang Laboratories.

Job-hopping is also a way of advancing a career through a series of moves up the corporate ladder. Unlike elsewhere, in Silicon Valley job-hopping provides greater opportunity for advancement than staying with the same company. By job-hopping the employee can move to a more responsible position with more pay.

Headhunting

Beneficiaries of job-hopping are the headhunters, whose going rate for engineers is 25 percent of the new hire's first year's salary, usually about $6,000 to $8,000. "All you need is a bag of nickels and a phonebook and you're a headhunter," says Sid Wilkins, a headhunter in Mountain View. Estimates are that there are 400 to 600 headhunters operating in Silicon Valley. Wilkins says: "A good percentage of them are working off the kitchen table. Most do not stay in the business for more than a year. By then they have run out of their old friends and other contacts, and they begin the tough part of the business."[23]

Not all Silicon Valley job placements are handled by local headhunters. Premier jobs are referred to executive search firms with worldwide operations and Silicon Valley offices. These firms work on a retainer fee and are paid regardless of their success in filling a specific position.

There are also employment agencies who receive fees contingent on the placement of a new employee. These are established firms with a staff of recruiters paid on a commission basis. The classic Silicon Valley headhunter operates independently, without a formal administrative structure.

Headhunters, employment agencies, and executive search firms agree that their greatest problem is recruiting prospective employees from outside Silicon Valley. Sid Wilkens says: "A few years ago you could go down to Phoenix with a flat-bed truck, load it up with engineers, and come back to the Bay Area and place them all. No more. Housing is the key. I have failed to close more deals because of housing problems than any other issue."[24]

Lynn Dwigans, head of Executive Search Services for Peat, Marwick, Mitchell in San Jose, also feels that nationwide recruiting for Silicon Valley jobs has ended. "Our fee for recruiting a $70,000-a-year executive could run about $20,000 plus $5,000 in expenses. Add to that relocation costs of about $50,000. That means the company has $75,000 invested before the executive is on the job. Our client companies say it's not worth it. They want to fill the position from the talent pool available in the Valley."[25]

Although the executive search firms and employment agencies stress their credibility and integrity, reality does not always bear this out. Within an hour after Exxon Office Systems announced the closing of its Summit Research Center in 1982, calls from headhunters flooded the switchboard. When the laid-off workers walked out to their cars in the parking lot, each found a card from a local headhunter on the windshield.[26]

The high rate of job mobility among professionals in Silicon Valley is encouraged by the shortage of qualified, experienced personnel. Accordingly business management style must be generally oriented to short-term employment; high job mobility demands a primary concern with the short-range future.

Another reason for high job mobility in Silicon Valley is the desire to obtain technical information from the competition. An engineer who leaves Company A for another firm probably signed a nondisclosure agreement not to take secret information from his firm if he ever left. While an employee cannot give specific product information to new co-workers in Firm B, this nondisclosure agreement with Firm A does not prevent transferring the valuable information that *surrounds* the new product. For instance, perhaps there are twenty different ways to approach the technological solution to an important microelectronics design problem. Firm A tried ten of them and found them to be unsuccessful. This information about paths not to take can be extremely valuable to Firm B. In a competitive industry, purchasing such knowledge in the form of a professional R&D worker offers one strategy for circumventing company secrecy policy, and it's completely legal.

But there are counter-strategies available to Firm A. Leaving a firm does not preclude a later return—after six months or a year with a competing firm, a key engineer may be even more valuable to the previous employer. The individual may be rehired by the original firm, in part to gain information from the competition. Indeed, his original firm may have *allowed* the professional to go in order to rehire him at a later time. So job-hopping in Silicon Valley can be a game of byzantine strategies and counter-strategies, with the exchange of technical information one of its main purposes.

A knowledgeable industry observer stated: "It has been industry policy for years that the minute someone resigns, that person is out. They call a company guard, who escorts him to the door. They then mail your personal stuff to your home. The company may make a counter offer to try to re-recruit you, but once they decide you are going, you go right now. Firing can be pretty gross too. I know of a high-level official in one firm who returned from lunch to find that the lock on his office door had been changed. That's how he got the bad news."[27]

The transfer of key employees from firm to firm helps create a cross-fertilization in Silicon Valley. There is no legal way to erase what is in someone's head. If an employee is really valuable, his former employer may sue, but that's mostly a holding action, intended to slow down the other (hiring) firm. Such legal action can put a year's lag in a new company's start-up. If the firm is undercapitalized, it may go under. A few years ago a semiconductor company, International Computer Modules (ICM), was started up by Howard Bogert with Japanese money as a spin-off from American Microsystems, Inc. (AMI). American Micro sued. The Japanese backed out, and ICM was finished.[28]

In such legal suits the employee and the new employer are usually both defendants. The charge is theft of trade secrets and often the former employer can't prove his case. "But sometimes a person will do a dumb thing like take along a process manual. That occurred in the Rheem case a few years ago. The employee walked off with a manual. Mailed it back to Fairchild in a plain brown envelope about six months later. Fairchild got a small judgment. But the energies of key people at Rheem were diverted by the lawsuit from getting their new company going. Ultimately Rheem gave up on manufacturing semiconductors and sold those operations to Raytheon."[29]

The only instance that criminal charges can be brought for stealing trade secrets is when someone physically copies or steals an item that incorporates a trade secret. An artful company can easily skirt around such illegal activities. One way is for a firm to advertise for a nonexistent job and then pick an applicant's brains during an interview to learn his company's secrets. Another technique, entirely legal, is to ask a trusted employee to go undercover and accept a key position in a competing firm. Such rogue engineers earn two salaries, each in the $50,000 range;

when a company discovers the "mole" they usually just fire the individual rather than prosecute.

Anything a company can do to limit the rate at which key employees leave is a means of diminishing the rate at which company secrets get out. There are major differences in turnover rates from company to company: about 6 percent of engineers at Hewlett-Packard, only 4 percent at IBM, but 30 percent or more for many other Silicon Valley firms.

Regarding firms with a low turnover rate, Don Hoefler says that "Hewlett-Packard people are very loyal. It's difficult to recruit out of H-P. But it takes a certain kind of individual to like H-P, as it's a pretty structured kind of existence. If you're free-swinging and have entrepreneurial spirit, you would be unhappy at H-P. Most people that I know at H-P are in for life with no intention of leaving."[30] Naturally, there is a cost to achieving such low job mobility at H-P; the generous emoluments paid to employees amount to a sizeable share of company profits. Early on H-P's officials decided they did not want to be one of the typical Silicon Valley hire-and-fire operations.[31] An important pay-off from this lifetime employment policy is that very few of H-P's company secrets walk out the door.

The importance of long-term employment as a means of preventing information-exchange in a high-technology industry is shown in Japanese firms. Microelectronics employees in Japan have the security of lifetime employment. Nondisclosure agreements are unknown in Japan, as there is not enough job mobility for such employer-employee agreements to serve a purpose.

Another means of limiting job mobility and the concomitant loss of technical information is to isolate key R&D engineers in the boondocks. This may mean any location outside of Silicon Valley. In order to maintain secrecy around the development of the 432 "microframe," Intel moved the design team to a suburb of Portland, Oregon.[32] This isolation effectively prevented the 432's secrets from spreading prematurely through the grapevine of Silicon Valley. Sending their design engineers up to rainy Oregon was a strategy for keeping their know-how inside Intel. Unfortunately for the company, its isolation strategy later backfired. In early 1983, eighteen Intel employees at the Portland plant resigned to form a new company. This rupture was serious for Intel;

three of the key defectors had been running operations that represented about 20 percent of Intel's sales and 20 percent of the company's R&D budget.[33]

Patents, Trade Secrets, and Potting

A patent theoretically guarantees a monopoly over a technological innovation, but in Silicon Valley this is not exactly the case. A patent is a grant issued by the federal government giving an inventor the right to exclude all others from making or selling an invention within the U.S. for seventeen years. Two to five years are usually required for the U.S. Patent Office to review a patent application in order to determine whether the invention is new and useful.

Most innovations in Silicon Valley are not patented because the inventor must disclose the invention to his competitors at the time of the patent's issue. That's why Thomas Edison denounced patents as a "license to steal." Silicon Valley executives fear patent disclosure would encourage competitors to copy their invention, perhaps in a modified form making legal recourse difficult or impossible. Patent infringement suits are expensive and lengthy. A competitor may also "invent around" a patent; there are often various means by which an effective equivalent can be achieved.[34] In a high-technology industry in which change occurs rapidly patents are negligible as a legal means of ensuring ownership of technological information.

However some Silicon Valley firms do own patents. One reason is for public relations purposes, to create an image of the firm as a technological leader. This function of patents is unlikely to impress industry insiders but it may sound good to investors with less technical knowledge. Framed patents make attractive decorations on the wall of a firm's visitors' lobby. Ted Hoff of Atari, who holds fourteen patents himself, says: "Patents are of little real use in the semiconductor industry. There are so many innovations taking place that you are bound to infringe on somebody else's patent. If everybody in the industry decided to defend their patents, the only guys who would make any money are lawyers. So instead it's more customary to grant an agreement that I won't bother you if you won't bother me. When the agreement is set up, if I have more patents in my file than you do, maybe you should pay me a small fee."[35]

An alternative to patenting is the *trade secret* strategy in which the innovation is kept under wraps after development and before commercial exploitation is underway.[36] Essentially a trade secret is whatever a company says it is. The innovative firm's competitors can try to learn the trade secret through the common practice of *reverse engineering*—purchasing the new product and taking it apart to learn how it was produced.

A counter-strategy to protect a trade secret from reverse engineering is called *potting*, in which the innovation is packaged in a way that makes it very difficult to remove the packaging without destroying the innovation inside. Some Silicon Valley semiconductor firms pot their own new products but use reverse engineering on their competitors' new chips. Neither technique is very successful in the long range, but a semiconductor firm can gain a short-term advantage of a few weeks or months. In a highly competitive industry with continuous innovation a short time can be very important and may be worth the cost of reverse engineering.

In mid-1982, two giant Japanese computer firms, Hitachi and Mitsubishi, and 18 of their employees were charged with conspiring to steal IBM secrets which included the design workbook (called "Adirondack") for IBM's newest and most powerful computer, the IBM 3081K. The FBI had set up a "sting" operation in Santa Clara, establishing a phony consulting firm called Glenmar Associates which offered the IBM secrets to Hitachi and Mitsubishi. In June 1982 the FBI swooped down on officials of the Japanese firms who came to Glenmar to pick up confidential IBM information and computer tapes. Hitachi had paid $622,000 for the information, and Mitsubishi paid $26,000 (and was preparing to pay $1 million). The Japanese and the two companies initially denied the charges, and Hitachi's top management claimed they had no knowledge of their employees' actions. When the case against

Hitachi came to trial, a plea bargain agreement was made in which Hitachi pleaded guilty and was fined $10,000. The U.S. agreed not to file additional charges against the firm.

Spokespersons for the Japanese computer industry pointed out that Hitachi and Mitsubishi were only doing what most Silicon Valley firms regularly do: seeking to tap into networks of technical information. Why were the two Japanese firms singled out by the FBI? It could only be that the U.S. government and IBM wanted to create a major embarrassment for the Japanese microelectronics industry.

Further, the Japanese were hurt and puzzled by the events leading up to the sting. Hitachi relied for certain technical information on Maxwell Paley, president of Payne Associates, a Silicon Valley consulting firm, and a former IBM employee. While under contract to Hitachi, Paley tipped off the FBI that he believed Hitachi had confidential IBM documents in its possession. That led to the sting operation. Hitachi claims that Paley introduced Hitachi employees to Glenmar Associates, the FBI's undercover operation. By Japanese standards, Paley committed an unforgivable act of disloyalty. A noted Japanese journalist stated: "Japanese feel that when they are hitting someone they are in a fight, and when they are shaking hands they are friends. . . . Hitachi's losing out to Maxwell Paley, a consultant on contract, is a clear example of the drawbacks of Japanese-type one-handed boxing. . . ."[37]

However one may view the IBM sting operation, it illustrates the thin line between legal and illegal industrial intelligence operations in Silicon Valley. The Japanese are correct in their claim that "everybody's doing it." IBM spends more than $50 million annually to guard company secrets.[38] One doesn't spend that much for defense against industrial espionage unless there is a very real threat.

6

Winning at the Game: Intel

"Intel is working on the edge of disaster. We are absolutely trying to do those things which nobody else could do from a technical point of view."
Robert N. Noyce, Intel Corporation, 1980

IT IS ONE THING to be innovative, quite another to get rich from innovation. Fortunately for Intel, technological innovation equals profit in the semiconductor industry, thanks to what is called the "learning curve." In the semiconductor industry the learning curve means that the price of a chip typically declines 20 to 30 percent for each doubling of its total production during the years of its life cycle. This downward sloping trend is called a learning curve because the lower price is made possible as a firm gradually *learns* how to produce a chip with higher and higher degrees of quality, thus lowering the rejection rate of defective chips(Figure 6.1). Because more saleable chips are produced for the same amount of manufacturing effort, the firm can afford to charge a lower and lower price for each chip.

Because of the learning curve, unless a firm gets an early start in producing a chip, it is difficult to compete. The sooner a company gets on the learning curve, the greater its advantage over competitors. It is this law that rewards technological innovation and punishes laggardliness in Silicon Valley. The only sure route to survival in the Valley is via continuous innovation, and the model for this strategy is Intel. Indeed the learning curve behavior in the semiconductor industry was most clearly ennunciated in 1964 by Dr. Gordon Moore, Intel's co-founder, who formulated Moore's Law, the principle of the learning curve.

An example of the learning curve in action is the cost of pocket calculators. When they first became available around 1972, a four-function (add, subtract, multiply, and divide) calculator averaged $250. There was a tremendous demand for this product and a large number of firms began producing them. The vital component in each calculator was a semiconductor chip. Due to the learning curve, the cost per chip began to decrease precipitously and the cost of pocket calculators also began to drop—from $250, to $100, to $50, to $20, and, around 1977, to $10 or less. Meanwhile, as price competition sharpened, the smaller firms, who had not benefitted from the learning curve, dropped out of the race, and soon only Texas Instruments, Hewlett-Packard, Casio, et cetera, were left. Such an industry shake-out occurs because of the learning curve.

A consequence of the learning curve for semiconductor chips is a long-range decrease in the cost of computing. The more years that a chip, say the 4K RAM, is produced, the cheaper it becomes. And as the electronics industry moved from the 4K to the 8K to

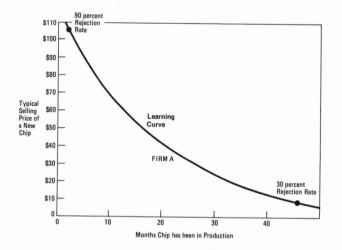

Figure 6.1. The selling price for a new semiconductor chip decreases rapidly after its introduction as the firms producing it learn how to fabricate the chips with fewer rejects, and thus at lower cost per chip. A competitor introducing a chip a few months later is at a considerable disadvantage, due to lost time on the learning curve.

the 16K and on to the 64K RAM, the cost per thousand bits of computer memory dropped very sharply. Cost per bit has been decreasing by about 28 percent per year since 1973. In order to put increasing amounts of electronic circuitry on a smaller and smaller chip, extremely fine patterns must be etched on the silicon wafers. The present width of an electrical connection is only 4 to 6 microns (a micron is 1/25,000 of an inch). In contrast, a human hair is 100 microns in diameter. Objects smaller than 25 microns cannot be seen by the naked eye.

In the mid-1960s, the complexity of a chip was comparable to the network of streets in a small town. Today's chip is comparable to the streets of greater Los Angeles. And an ultimate complexity like that of the quarter-micron chip is similar to a street map covering the entire North American continent.[1]

As chips become cheaper and smaller in size, they are utilized as components in more and more new and redesigned products for the consumer. A major advantage is that the number of moving parts in a consumer product can be greatly reduced by using microelectronic components. For instance, a new model sewing machine can use a single microprocessor to control the stitching pattern in place of 350 gears, cams, and other mechanical parts. The microprocessor not only simplifies the sewing machine and lowers its selling price, but the electronic model will be more reliable.

Intel is successful because it turns this growing demand for new semiconductor chips into sales. Technological innovation has provided the boost for the company's success. Growing at about 25 percent per year, Intel now has over 20,000 employees in locations around the world. After its founding in 1968, Intel grew rapidly.

How Intel Does It

Intel got off to a *very fast start.* Soon after its founding, Ted Hoff, a young Intel engineer, invented the microprocessor (a computer on a chip). Since then the inventions have kept on coming, creating a confidence that Intel could out-invent competitors. As Hoff stated: "Intel has its image, its policy of maintaining its position as a leading-edge firm. So we invest heavily in R&D. We have lots of new products and we try to pick carefully which innovations to produce, and which to drop, on the basis of what is interesting and leads to a sound future."[2]

Early successes in technological innovation provided Intel with *the resources and the reputation* to stay ahead. Intel has one of the highest ratios of R&D to sales of any semiconductor firm.

Intel has faith in the *quality of its personnel,* and is reluctant to let any of them go, even in times of economic downswing. Intel's second-priority goal is to recruit the best people in the microelectronics industry (its number one goal is to lead the industry in innovation; profit-making is well down the list of official corporate goals). A continuous stream of high-caliber young engineers flows into Intel's R&D labs, most of them directly out of university engineering schools. College recruiting gets lots of attention at Intel and personnel recruiters say they don't only go for the 4.0 student. Instead they would rather hire the individual with 3.0 grades and a strong goal orientation toward innovation, someone who has completed a really creative student project.

Intel brings it all together with a *management style* that is highly structured and thorough. CEO Andy Grove is an intense individual, intimidating to most Intel employees. He feels it is better to bring up failures and discuss what's gone wrong, rather than to compound a problem by allowing it to continue. A lot of executives' time—at least 70 percent of working hours—are spent in meetings. About 100 standing councils at Intel meet regularly to make monthly reviews of such topics as marketing, customer service, facilities, human resources, and so forth. The structure of these review committees provides a close monitoring of the innovation process at Intel. The stream of new products emanating from Intel is carefully managed.

The top managers at Intel are Bob Noyce, Gordon Moore, and Andy Grove. Each has a say in key decisions, which are made by consensus. Noyce is the outside man who deals with government and the rest of the industry; Moore, the thinker, focuses on planning; and Grove is the man of action. All three are technical men who hold Ph.Ds. As Bob Noyce pointed out: "Our three top officers have grown up in technical positions. Not as lawyers, not as accountants, not as paper-pushers, but as doers. That signals that the way to get ahead at Intel is to make a technological contribution."[3]

Long-range planning at Intel is integral to its success. Over a decade ago, the firm's leaders realized that the housing costs in Silicon Valley would force them to locate new plants elsewhere. They found locations in the U.S. with conditions similar to Silicon Valley and then purchased future plant sites in Phoenix, Portland, Sacramento, Livermore (California), Texas, and Florida. In addition, Intel has off-shore production facilities in Penang (Malaysia), Manila, Barbados, Puerto Rico, and Israel. Thus, the company became an international empire.

Intel chooses to avoid certain areas. Noyce said: "We *build on strength* and try to stay out of competition where we're weak." A few years back, the company learned a lesson the hard way about digital watches. It looked simple to put an Intel chip in a watch and sell the chip along with the watch. But that involved marketing to consumers, rather than to other electronics firms. "We thought it was a technology game, and it turned out to be a merchandising game. That's not our game," said Noyce.[4]

The challenge for Intel today is to stay on top of the microelectronics industry. That's a pretty tough act, as recent events show. Some cracks in Intel's vaunted reputation appeared during 1981, when profits dropped to $27 million, down 72 percent from the year before. Because of the continuing recession in 1982, Intel's profits stayed down. Company executives expected the recession to lift during 1982 and hired 3,000 new employees, anticipating higher production in the face of economic recovery. Their strategy backfired when the recession did not end. As 1982 drew to a close Intel found itself short of cash; it cut salaries by up to 10 percent and froze them for 1983. Then in December 1982 Intel sold 12 percent of its stock to IBM for $250 million and in 1983 IBM bought additional shares, bringing its total ownership to 15 percent; IBM got one seat on Intel's board of directors. Things became worse for Intel in January 1983 when the Intel employees at the Portland plant defected to launch a new start-up. Problems were compounded the following month when Ted Hoff, Intel's star inventor, resigned to go to Atari. But thanks to an upturn in the economy later in the year, Intel's star brightened.

If a single individual personifies Silicon Valley fever, it is undoubtedly Bob Noyce. Any understanding of microelectronics entrepreneurship would have to include the career of this talented man.[5]

Dr. Robert N. Noyce was born in 1926, the son of a small-town Iowa minister. He attended nearby Grinnell College, an institution which he later endowed with Intel stock estimated to be worth $10 million today. Noyce's physics professor at Grinnell interested him in transistors and when Noyce went on for his Ph.D. in physics at MIT he studied transistor technology. After three years at Philco Corporation in Philadelphia Noyce arrived in Palo Alto in 1956 to work at Shockley Semiconductor Laboratory as one of the original Shockley Eight. He left the firm a year later as the leader of the "Traitorous Eight," as Shockley dubbed them, to found Fairchild Semiconductor.

By his own description, Bob Noyce was a somewhat reluctant participant in the Shockley walkout; the other seven Shockley dissidents had already lined up their connection with the Fairchild Camera and Instrument Company. However they needed a leader and approached Noyce, who was still in the good graces of Shockley. As Noyce tells it, "Suddenly it became apparent to people like myself, who had always assumed they would be working for a salary for the rest of their lives, that they could get some equity in a start-up company. That was a great revelation, and a great motivation too."[6] Indeed, seven years later when the parent, Fairchild Camera and Instrument, bought out its Semiconductor Division, Noyce and the other seven members of the Shockley Eight each were paid about one-quarter of a million dollars.[7]

While director of R&D at Fairchild, Noyce developed the integrated circuit. The same concept had been invented by Jack Kilby at Texas Instruments (TI) a few months before. In July 1959 Noyce filed a patent for his conception of the integrated circuit. Jack Kilby's employer, TI, filed a lawsuit for patent interference against Noyce and Fairchild, and the case dragged on for some years. Today Noyce and Kilby are generally regarded as co-inventors of the integrated circuit, although Kilby alone was inducted into the Inventors' Hall of Fame as the inventor.[8] Noyce is credited with improving the integrated circuit for industrial purposes.

Relationships deteriorated between Fairchild management on the East Coast and their Semiconductor Division in California. Noyce stayed on as Fairchild's talent dribbled away to start competing firms. Gordon Moore began to agitate for a spin-off. Finally, in June 1968, Noyce resigned from Fairchild to launch Intel with Moore. The price of Fairchild stock dropped sharply on the day Noyce's resignation was announced.

In order to replace Noyce, Sherman Fairchild pulled off one of the most sensational recruiting deals in the history of Silicon Valley when he snared Les Hogan from Motorola. Hogan was an ex-physics professor at Harvard, who had been heading Motorola's semiconductor work. Fairchild gave him a starting salary of $120,000, a 33 percent increase over his Motorola wages and part of a three-year contract totaling $1 million. Hogan also got 10,000 stock shares at the cut-rate price of $10 each; the market price was $60. Thrown in was an interest-free loan of $5.4 million to exercise an option on 90,000 shares of Fairchild stock. Hogan also insisted that the corporate headquarters for Fairchild Semiconductor be moved to Mountain View, in order to avoid the conflicts with the East Coast that had bedeviled Noyce.[9] The Hogan package was so sweet that it serves as the ultimate measure for other job offers in Silicon Valley, as in: "I was offered half a Hogan." When Hogan's move was announced, Fairchild stock shot up seven points, and Motorola's dropped eight points on the same day.

The millions Noyce needed to found Intel came mainly via venture capitalist Arthur Rock. Rock had been impressed by Noyce since the 1950s, when Rock helped arrange the financing for Fairchild Semiconductor. Noyce: "It was a very natural thing to go to Art and say, 'Incidentally, Art, do you have an extra $2.5 million you would like to put on the crap table?' "[10] Noyce and Moore indicated their willingness to invest about $250,000 each of their own money, amassed from their original investments of $500 in Fairchild. Rock got on the phone, and in thirty minutes he had lined up the $2.5 million (and became a legend in the process).

In 1982 Noyce's net worth in Intel, with 3.4 percent of the company's stock, was estimated at $36.6 million.[11] Like many others in Silicon Valley Noyce invests his earnings in other start-ups, thus continuing to convert his inside knowledge of Silicon Valley goings-on into yet more money. Noyce presently serves on the board of directors of about seven firms and spends only part of his time at Intel.[12] In 1975 Noyce stepped down from chairman to vice-chairman of the board at Intel in order to pursue his many outside activities.

From the outset Intel concentrated on memory chips, and it was almost accidental that it got a big boost from microprocessors, invented at Intel in 1971. Just as invention of the planar process and the integrated circuit had made Fairchild a commercial success for Noyce, the microprocessor boosted Intel into the big time.

How Ted Hoff Invented the Microprocessor

Other than the invention of the transistor at Bell Labs, and the integrated circuit by Bob Noyce and Jack Kilby, the most significant innovation in the microelectronics industry was the 1971 invention of the microprocessor by Ted Hoff. Given that fact, it's surprising that Dr. Marcian E. (Ted) Hoff, Jr., has not received much public recognition for his invention.

When we met Ted Hoff, we sensed that this middle-aged engineer prefers to keep a low profile, as his out-of-the-public-eye status allows him to keep on inventing new products. Hoff relates the details of inventing the microprocessor in a matter-of-fact way, rather like a boy telling his teacher what he did last summer. Hoff's modest attitude, however, doesn't mask the fact that inventing the microprocessor was a heck of a lot of fun.[13]

Hoff grew up in a rural area outside Rochester, New York, where his father worked as an electrical engineer. Hoff's uncle, a chemical engineer, gave young Ted a chemistry set, a subscription to *Popular Science,* and introduced him to hobbyist catalogs like *Allied.* "I got interested in science at an early age," says Hoff.

He majored in electrical engineering at nearby Rensselaer Poly-technic Institute (RPI), writing his undergraduate honors thesis on switching behavior in transistors. By 1958 Hoff already held two patents. The first patent, when Hoff was a sophomore, was for an electronic train detector based on the audio frequencies transmitted through the railroad tracks; the second was for a lightning protector he invented while in his junior year.

Hoff had never been west of Niagara Falls, so when he ap-plied for a National Science Foundation fellowship for graduate study, he specified Stanford University. He had heard of Fred Terman, and Hoff's professors thought highly of Stanford. When he arrived on the Palo Alto campus, Hoff enrolled in a course on the theory of transistors, a topic that made a big impression on him. He soon became involved in semiconductor research and, after earning his Ph.D. Hoff stayed on at Stanford as a research associate. But after a decade in academe, Hoff was bitten by the entrepreneurial bug: "I wanted to work on an idea that had an economic potential. The greatest flattery is when someone is will-ing to pay for your idea."

In 1968 Intel had just been founded and was looking for R&D workers. Hoff was highly recommended by the Stanford faculty, but Intel first offered the R&D job to someone at IBM, who chose to remain in New York. Next the job was offered to a Fairchild engineer, who rejected the offer. Hoff finally got a call from Bob Noyce; Hoff was Intel's third choice for the R&D job and became Intel's twelfth employee. He worked in a small lab in one of Intel's original offices in Mountain View, sharing the space with other staff and with boxes of supplies from Union Carbide, which rented the other half of the building.

Intel's main emphasis was on semiconductor memory chips at this point, but it welcomed customers like Busicom, a now-defunct Japanese manufacturer who wanted Intel to design special chips for its proposed family of desk-top calculators. On June 20, 1969, a team of Busicom engineers arrived from Tokyo to meet with Hoff; that night he left for a long-planned vacation in Tahiti. When he returned, the Japanese engineers were still waiting. They presented their design for a set of six highly com-plex chips to drive their new calculators. Hoff told them their de-sign was too complicated for Intel to handle.

Near Hoff's desk was a PDP-8 minicomputer which he used in his research. He had thought about the possibility of designing something like a microcomputer. The idea of a computer-on-a-chip was still on Hoff's mind: "I looked at the PDP-8, I looked at the Busicom plans, and I wondered why the calculator should be so much more complex." Hoff worked out the design for a microprocessor. A microprocessor is a semiconductor chip that serves as the central processing unit (CPU) controlling a computer. In other words, a microprocessor is the computer's brains. In designing the world's first microprocessor, Hoff had the inspiration to pack all the CPU functions on a single chip. He attached two memory chips to his microprocessor—one to hold the data and the other chip to contain the program to drive the CPU. "Hoff now had in hand a rudimentary general-purpose computer that not only could run a complex calculator (like Busicom's), but also could control an elevator or a set of traffic lights, and perform many other tasks, depending on its program."[14]

Oddly, the Busicom engineering team weren't impressed by Hoff's microprocessor design. Instead, the Japanese set to work redesigning their chip-set. However Hoff continued to work on his design for a microprocessor, even if Intel's Japanese customers weren't interested.

Bob Noyce was a firm supporter of Hoff's project. He had anticipated the possibilities of the microprocessor several years before. At a conference in the late 1960s, when Noyce predicted the coming of a computer-on-a-chip, one of his critics in the audience remarked, "Gee, I certainly wouldn't want to lose my whole computer through a crack in the floor." Noyce responded: "You have it all wrong, because you'll have 100 more sitting on your desk, so it won't matter if you lose one."[15]

At this time most computer designers were not interested in working on small computers; they felt the real action was in the larger mainframes. But Hoff was able to convince Stan Mazor, an Intel employee recently hired from Fairchild, to join him in the microprocessor work. In October 1969 the manager of Busicom and his engineers presented their revised design for the calculator chip-set at Intel's headquarters. Then Hoff made his argument for the microprocessor, claiming that it would have more general applications. Busicom's top manager was convinced, essentially telling Hoff, "I hope it's as good as you say." An Intel-Busicom contract was signed, granting exclusive rights to Busicom for the Intel microprocessor.

Hoff and Mazor now set to work in earnest to design the microprocessor. In March 1970 Federico Faggin came to Intel from Fairchild; he did the chip layout and circuit drawings. Faggin came up with a "nice clean design," in Hoff's opinion. Meanwhile Busicom was going ahead with the calculator in which the Intel microprocessor would be a key component. Less than a year later, in January 1971, Hoff and his colleagues had a working microprocessor.

Intel labeled this first microprocessor chip the "4004" ("four thousand four"). The four thousand number meant that it was a custom product, designed for Busicom. The final number four designated the 4004 as the fourth custom chip made by Intel.

Gordon Moore, president of Intel, described the power of Hoff's microprocessor: "Now we can make a single microprocessor chip and sell it for several thousand different applications."[16] That was the beauty of the microprocessor—it could serve as a component in any electronic product where one wanted miniaturized computing power. This flexibility of application had tremendous commercial implications. Ted Hoff had invented a means for Intel to get rich quick.

Meanwhile, in October 1969, Victor Poor of Computer Terminals Corporation had approached Intel with a need for a custom chip for a terminal he was building. Hoff and Mazor designed a microprocessor for Poor that had a larger capacity than the 4004; they called it the Intel 8008. When Mazor showed it to Poor, he was flabbergasted, not believing that a computer could be put on a chip. The 8008 came out in 1972. Poor wanted a second source for the chip, as customers often do, and took the "target spec" (essentially a blueprint) to Texas Instruments in Dallas. Shortly thereafter, Hoff and Mazor added some "bells and whistles" to the 8008, and began its production. Not surprisingly, TI's version of the Intel 8008, which became available in June 1972, looked a great deal like Intel's specs, but it lacked the bells and whistles that had been added at the last minute. Soon Intel's competitors were beginning to climb on the microprocessor bandwagon. But Intel continued to lead with superior design.

The Intel agreement with Poor's Computer Terminals Corporation for the 8008 was not as exclusive as the Busicom contract for the 4004; it allowed Intel to sell the 8008 to other buyers. Fortunately for Intel they were approached by Busicom in January 1971 about renegotiating a lower price for the 4004, which the Japanese felt they must have in order to cope with competing calculator firms. When Hoff heard about this turn of events, he told Intel's marketing division: "For God's sake, get the rights from Busicom to sell the 4004 to other people." In exchange for a lower price, Busicom gave up its exclusive rights to the 4004, except that Intel was precluded from selling it to other calculator firms.

The Intel marketing division wasn't convinced that microprocessors were a viable product worth the cost and effort to manufacture. Even though Intel had been selling the 4004 to Busicom since January 1971, this microprocessor had still not been announced publicly by Intel so there was no demand for it. As 1971 passed, Hoff and Mazor and their little team of microprocessor enthusiasts would appear before Intel's marketing people and urge them to announce the 4004. Hoff says: "We pleaded with them each month, but each time they decided not to announce it yet." Finally Edward L. Gelback came on board as Intel's marketing chief; he'd been at TI and had a more positive view of the microprocessor as a product line.

There is a natural tension between technical people and the marketing department in every high-technology company.[17] It is a battle between creativity on one side and merchandisers who know customers' needs on the other. The conflict can arise when the R&D people proudly present their concept of a new product and the marketers tell them it won't sell. Or the conflict may occur over the allocation of company resources, whether funds should go to R&D or to marketing.

In November 1971 Intel finally decided to announce the 4004 by taking out an ad in *Electronic News,* an industry trade publication. Intel's ad announced not just a new product, but "a new era of integrated electronics . . ., a microprogrammable computer on a chip." Semiconductor companies had made exorbitant promises in the past, and the industry reaction to the Intel 4004 was wary. Typical was the reaction of a customer at the fall 1971 computer show in Las Vegas who, at the Intel display, exclaimed over the nerve of Intel saying they could have a computer on a chip. When Stan Mazor gave him a data-sheet on the 4004 the customer had to grudgingly admit that sure enough it was a computer.

Ted Hoff and Stan Mazor went on the road for three weeks in mid-1972, holding seminars and meeting with design engineers in various companies. The Intel enthusiasts for the microprocessor encountered a range of doubt; a frequent question was, "Well, how do you repair it?" People couldn't get the idea that a computer could be a throwaway item like a light bulb. Other customers scoffed, "How would you keep them busy?" Hoff recalls that at this early stage in the life of the microprocessor, what many customers really wanted was the power of a minicomputer at the price of a microprocessor chip. "We still could not do what a minicomputer could do in processing power. Not then."

In March 1972, four months after Intel had announced the 4004, TI advertised its eight-bit microprocessor in an electronics magazine. But the next month Intel announced its own eight-bit microprocessor, the 8008 (this was the product designed for Victor Poor). TI's eight-bit microprocessor was three times the size and higher in cost than Intel's. As Hoff explains: "The cost of a chip is a function, a strong function, of its size. The smaller a chip, the more of them you can get on a wafer, so the price is correspondingly cheaper." TI saw the main use for its microprocessors in calculators, while Intel foresaw a tremendously wide range of applications for the microprocessor.

Hoff, Mazor, and Faggin continued working on an improved microprocessor, leading to the Intel 8080 which came out in August 1973.[18] This product started out as simply a minor redesign of the 8008, but just tinkering would require a new set of masks anyway, so Hoff and Faggin decided to completely rebuild their previous microprocessor. "N-channel MOS technology was moving along by this time, and we incorporated this advance in the 8080." MOS is the abbreviation for metal-oxide-on-silicon, a type of microelectronics technology that is used in large-scale integrated (LSI) circuits.

"The 8080 is one of the most successful microprocessors of all time, in terms of sales. The numbers just took off," recalls Hoff. The original $360 price of the 8080 soon began to drop as the experience Intel was gaining in producing the microprocessor helped move down the learning curve. The Altair microcomputer kit sold in the pre-Apple days of the mid-1970s for $395. How could they have sold this kit for only $35 more than the Intel 8080 it contained as a component? For one thing, Altair paid a lower price due to volume purchase, and the steep drop in the learning curve was driving down the price of the 8080. "The 8080 sells today for about $2.50 each in large quantities," says Hoff. "I've even seen single chips listed at $2.95 in hobbyists' magazines." Hoff chuckles about Gelbach's Law, named after Ed Gelbach, the former marketing chief at Intel, now Intel's senior vice-president: "Every chip eventually sells for five dollars. Except for those chips that sell for less than five dollars."

When the Intel 8080 came out in 1973, it opened up the market for microcomputers. The 8080 was twenty times faster than the Intel 4004. The microcomputer boom had begun with the Altair and then the Apple. Microcomputers were possible due to the prior invention of the microprocessor. The boom in microcomputer sales gave a tremendous boost to the market for microprocessors. Apple co-founders Steve Jobs and Steve Wozniak recognized the need for microcomputers and in Hoff's opinion, "That was their contribution, and it was a very important one." However, he adds he is "most surprised at the use of microprocessors in personal computers; I didn't think that people would buy microprocessors just for hobby uses. With the development of video games, personal computers became another form of entertainment. If any inventor can create something for entertainment use, he has it made."

The microprocessor represented such a radical invention that the mass media did not pick up on it for almost a year after Intel's announcement of the new product in late 1971. The idea of putting a computer on a semiconductor chip amazed the public and soon many magazines had articles about it. One effect of the media attention was a reversal in attitude among computer professionals. In 1969, when Hoff began R&D work on the first microprocessor, he had difficulty attracting programmers to join his team; they were all thinking mainframe. But now, says Hoff, "Computer programmers come in our door every day, wanting to work on microprocessors."

Hoff sees the impact of microprocessors as revolutionary: "We are going to be in a revolution that will last for the next 50 to 100 years in which more and more functions that have traditionally been thought of as doable only by humans will be done by machines. Muscles have already been replaced, now its our brains. Computing will be available, thanks to miniaturization, to a much broader part of the community. Young people today are growing up without fear of computers. They will apply computers to a wider and wider range of uses. And advances in computer technology mean that the new tools will be there for them to apply."

However the tools are becoming more expensive and time-consuming to produce. There were less than a dozen people working with Hoff and Faggin on the 4004. With a small budget, in only one and a half years they went from the concept of the microprocessor to delivery. Today's microprocessors require hundreds of thousands of man-hours and millions of dollars for their development.

Hoff points out that even though microprocessors benefit society in general, it is also inevitable that they work to the disadvantage of particular occupational groups. An example is the installation of point-of-sale computers that have enabled supermarkets to employ poorly educated teenagers at minimum wage in place of skilled, usually adult check-out clerks. Meanwhile consumers benefit from somewhat lower food prices and from greater accuracy at the checkout stand.

The prestigious British magazine, The Economist, named Hoff "one of the seven most influential scientists since World War II."[19] He was also honored by being named an "Intel Fellow"—there had only been one other—which meant that he had a great degree of flexibility in the research projects on which he worked. Mainly Hoff worked on various leading-edge technological problems at Intel, an assignment he enjoyed. After microprocessors, Hoff worked on a speech recognition device that copied human speech built around the Intel 2920. Hoff and two of his co-workers were awarded a patent for the 2920. That was Hoff's fourteenth patent.

Hoff is quite modest about his contribution in inventing the microprocessor. He feels he was just at the right place at the right time: "If we had not made the 4004 in 1971, someone else would have invented the microprocessor in a year or two."

In 1983, Hoff resigned from Intel and accepted the post of vice-president of R&D at Atari. He explained that he had been working at the same place for fourteen years and needed a change. He also stated he looked forward to inventing technologies that would soon have a huge impact on consumers.

Fab 3: Producing Semiconductor Chips

Fab 3, Intel's largest wafer production facility, is located in Livermore, California, about forty miles east of Intel's headquarters in Santa Clara. Fab 3 was built in 1973 outside Silicon Valley to escape the skyrocketing housing prices of the Valley and to tap the cheaper labor force available at Livermore.

Fab 1 and Fab 2, located in Santa Clara, were built soon after Intel's founding in 1968. Intel's practice is to identify their plants on the basis of function and when they were constructed. Intel's newest wafer fabrication plant, Fab 7, has just begun production in Israel, the first Intel wafer fab facility outside the United States. Other fabrication takes place in Portland, Phoenix, and Albuquerque. Many of the wafers produced at Fab 3 in Livermore go to "A 2," assembly plant #2 in Manila, where the tiny gold leads are bonded to the semiconductor chips by young Filipino women. Because an assembly plant requires lots of labor, most operations are located where labor is relatively cheap: Puerto Rico, Barbados, Mexico, and Malaysia.

The wafer fab plant in Livermore is a one- and two-story affair that from the outside does not look large enough to produce 1,200 wafers per workday. Not counting rejects, there are about 160 or so good chips on each wafer, so Fab 3 turns out an average of 200,000 chips daily. If each chip is worth an average $10 after assembly and testing, almost $2 million of chips go out the door of Fab 3 each workday.

Fab 3 is actually a factory within a factory. The "outer factory" contains offices, receiving and shipping facilities, a training room, a cafeteria, bathrooms, and other facilities. The inner factory is the "cleanroom," a particularly antiseptic area that looks like a hospital operating room. Except that it is cleaner—a wafer fab cleanroom contains fewer than 100 dust particles of one micrometer or more in diameter per cubic foot, while the dust level in a modern hospital is about 10,000 particles per cubic foot.[20] Ordinary clean air contains about one million dust particles per cubic foot, which is actually not so clean, when looked at from the viewpoint of a semiconductor chip.

The cleanroom is used to manufacture wafers. Each wafer is a 4-inch flat circle of silicon on which from 8 to 10 layers of intricate electronic circuitry are painstakingly built up through a complex series of chemical and electrical processes. The basic idea of creating chips by laying down layer after layer of circuitry, called the "planar process," was developed by Jean Hoerni when he worked for Fairchild in 1960.

Dust specks are anathema to semiconductor production as they shortcircuit the miniaturized electronics, thus leading to rejection of the chip. Great care is taken to ensure that the cleanroom is entirely closed off from its external environment. Workers must wear "bunny suits" of lint-free cloth, all of the report forms used in the cleanroom are made of lint-free paper, and only ball-point pens are used, as pencils are great dust-generators. One enters and leaves the cleanroom through airlocks (there is a negative vacuum inside). Intel requires its employees and visitors to read and sign a 13-page manual of cleanroom procedures. A violation, such as wearing makeup if one is a woman, or not wearing a face cover if a bearded man, can result in a written warning. Fab 3 has a "yield" of about 70 percent, meaning that only 30 percent of the chips are rejected because they do not pass quality tests, which is high relative to the rest of the semiconductor industry. Bob Wigger, manufacturing manager at Fab 3, does not intend to let this standard slip; Intel's profits rest directly upon yield, and Wigger is proud of the quality standard that his 370 employees have set at Fab 3.

Each square foot of cleanroom space is extremely expensive to build and maintain; therefore the density of workers is high. An impression of Fab 3's cleanroom is that of a surrealistic world, as if it were located on the moon. The bunny suits make everyone

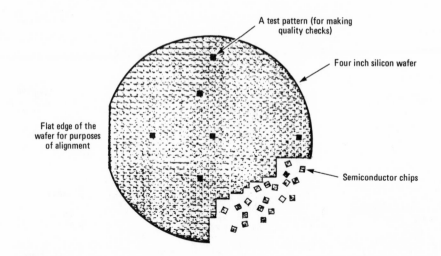

A test pattern (for making quality checks)

Four inch silicon wafer

Flat edge of the wafer for purposes of alignment

Semiconductor chips

Figure 6.2. A silicon wafer typically contains up to two hundred semiconductor chips, which are separated from each other at the assembly plant after the miniature circuitry has been built up on the wafer at the wafer fabrication plant. Note that the semiconductor chips on a wafer look very much like a sheet of tiny postage stamps.

look like bulky spacemen; indeed it is often difficult to distinguish men from women until one learns that all of the 300 or so line-operators are female; the only men in the cleanroom are 30 engineers and 40 maintenance men. The workforce is crammed into the rather constrained area of the cleanroom along with several million dollars of equipment. And the main object of everyone's attention is the silicon wafer.

An equivalent of the expression "womb to tomb" in the semiconductor industry is "beach to customer." The wafers come from plain old sand, which is purified chemically, then heated to 1,420 degrees Celsius, after which it crystallizes and is sliced into wafers, each about half a millimeter thick. The raw silicon wafers arrive at Fab 3 from Monsanto, one of several vendors who supply Intel. Each wafer costs about $10, and by the time it leaves Fab 3 two months after it arrives, it will have a thin epidermis of complicated circuitry built up through several basic processes that take place in the cleanroom: photolithography (or masking), diffusion, and thin films. About 200 different operations involving one or another of these processes will occur. If we could follow a particular wafer through this manufacturing process, it would require about four hours just to walk through the labyrinthian sequence of steps as each layer of circuitry is built up on the wafer

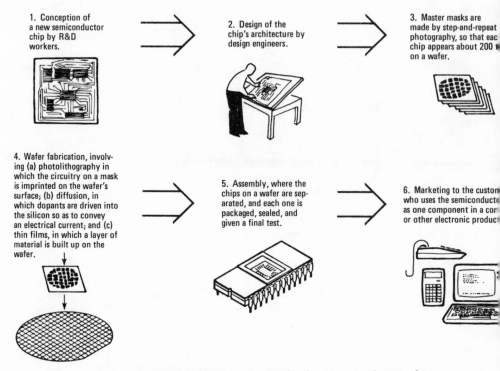

Figure 6.3.   Main steps in the birth of a semiconductor chip.

followed by another layer. To add further to the difficulty of understanding the birth of a chip, a variety of different kinds of wafers are produced. Some will be RAMs (random access memory), others ROMs (read-only memory), PROMs (programmable read-only memory), EPROMs (erasable PROMs), EEPROMs (electrically erasable PROMs), et cetera. A variety of chips are manufactured at Fab 3 at the same time by different sequences of basic operations.

The masks come to Fab 3 from a corps of design engineers at Intel 4, a large R&D building adjacent to Intel headquarters in Santa Clara. Designers are the uninhibited free spirits of the microelectronics industry who combine artistic creativity with the precision of electrical engineering. Designers are often called "witches" by others in the semiconductor industry, implying that they combine their engineering skills with a special brand of black magic. Design engineers are one of the highest paid and loftiest prestige occupations in the industry, somewhat akin to brain surgeons in a hospital. An Intel team of designers may have worked for several months or several years, depending on the complexity of the chip being designed, to produce the set of master masks that they send to Fab 3 at Livermore. Each mask is made of glass and is about 4 inches square. It is the negative, in a photographic sense, of one layer of circuitry to be placed on the silicon wafer at Fab 3. If a wafer with ten horizontal layers of circuitry is to be built up in the wafer fabrication process, then at least ten different masks are involved—in most cases, two or more masks are used to imprint one horizontal layer of the chip's architecture. Each of these ten layers is connected with tiny electrical circuits passing vertically through the three-dimensional structure of the wafer, adding to the complexity of wafer fabrication.

Back at Intel 4 in Santa Clara, design engineers have labored over a chip blown up 500 times. The tricky task here is to position and reposition thousands of component parts of the circuitry so as to maximize efficiency of production and to minimize the size of the chip, as tinier chips mean more of them can be manufactured on a wafer. Much of this design work is done with computer simulation, in which various combinations of the components are arranged and rearranged. A magnified version of the chip is then drawn on an oversized drafting board and this blueprint is then reduced by photography, assisted by a computer, to the miniaturized actual size of the semiconductor chip. Then this tiny blueprint is reproduced several hundred times through a "step and repeat" process to produce each of the ten or so masks, each a template for the identical chips that are to be soul mates on a silicon wafer. The set of ten masks are mounted in the photolithography machines at Fab 3, where they are used to clone thousands and thousands of semiconductor chips. Each of Intel's masks is guarded very carefully; employees are reminded that the world of Silicon Valley contains lots of industrial spies who would love to steal them.

Building Up the Layers of Circuitry on the Wafer

At Fab 3, an intense ultra violet light is projected through the mask onto the wafer. Chrome lines on the mask block this light from certain sections of the wafer, in order that the circuitry on the mask is conveyed to the surface of the wafer (which has previously been covered with photoresist) by a process akin to photoengraving. Each line on the wafer is less than five microns in width, much less than the width of a human hair. This is the essence of the masking process in the Fab 3 cleanroom. Following the masking operation, the wafer is washed with a solvent which removes the film wherever the mask was opaque. Hydrofluoric acid dissolves the oxide coating on the surface of the wafer except where the masked patterns were implanted. Thus the circuits are placed on the silicon wafer, layer by layer.

Diffusion is the process of introducing layer after layer of impurities into circuits upon the surface of a wafer. When the wafer is heated to 1,100° C (four times the heat at which you bake a cake) in a specially controlled environment, a thin film of silicon dioxide forms on its surfaces. This film is an excellent insulator. Then the wafer is subjected to a high temperature to drive impurities (called dopants) deeper into the silicon. These impurities are what make the wafer a "semiconductor" of electricity; it is somewhere between an electrical conductor like copper, and a nonconductor like glass or plastic. Thus it is a *semi*conductor. Later, when the chips on a wafer will be operating to provide a computing function, small electrical currents will flow through the designated circuits, channeled by the narrow lines that are diffused onto the wafer during the processes in the wafer fabrication plant. The tiny currents will open or close little gates or valves on the chip, thus expressing the "0" or "1" binary code of computers.

Ion implantation is yet another means of introducing impurities into the wafer. Dopant ions, stripped of one or more of their electrons, are accelerated by high energy until they strike the wafer, where they penetrate to various depths depending upon the masked impression, which has been put on the wafer previously. An advantage of ion implantation is that it can be done at room temperature. Also, the amount of dopant implanted on the wafer can be controlled very precisely by the operator of the ion implanter.

Another basic process in the Fab 3 cleanroom is called "thin film." A molten metal-like aluminum is transferred under vacuum

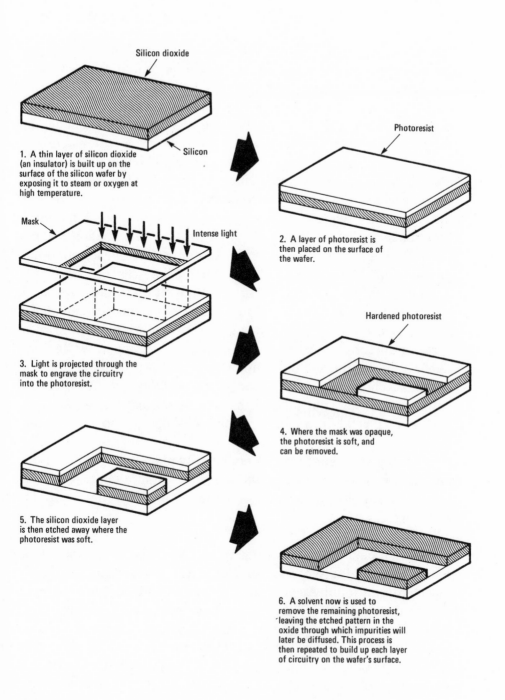

Silicon dioxide

1. A thin layer of silicon dioxide (an insulator) is built up on the surface of the silicon wafer by exposing it to steam or oxygen at high temperature.

Silicon

Photoresist

2. A layer of photoresist is then placed on the surface of the wafer.

Mask

Intense light

3. Light is projected through the mask to engrave the circuitry into the photoresist.

Hardened photoresist

4. Where the mask was opaque, the photoresist is soft, and can be removed.

5. The silicon dioxide layer is then etched away where the photoresist was soft.

6. A solvent now is used to remove the remaining photoresist, leaving the etched pattern in the oxide through which impurities will later be diffused. This process is then repeated to build up each layer of circuitry on the wafer's surface.

Figure 6.4.   A simplified diagram of how each layer of circuitry is built up on a wafer's surface through the process of photolithography.

conditions as a thin film about one micrometer thick onto the wafer's surface. This metallic layer is thus coated on the wafer.

Each wafer moves through its complicated process in the cleanroom with a batch of 48 peers, loaded together in a quartz or plastic carrier. Each of the 49 wafers is stacked on its edge in the carrier, with a space between each wafer. A wafer is never touched with the bare fingers; instead it is picked up with a small clamp on a vacuum wand so that its tiny circuits are not damaged. Despite the tender care with which a wafer is treated throughout its two-month lifetime in the cleanroom, some, and perhaps many, of the hundreds of chips it contains become damaged. Perhaps a dust particle inadvertently becomes embedded in the chip. Perhaps one of the ten masks was not perfectly aligned with the previous layers of circuitry that had been laid down (in this case all 200 chips on the wafer must be rejected). In the case of one reject wafer given to us during our tour of a semiconductor cleanroom, a line-operator hiccupped while conducting one of the 200 operations involved in producing it. Each of the 200 chips on the wafer was marked with a red-ink dot, indicating that it had not passed the final electrical test at the end of the wafer fab production process. That hiccup cost about $2,000.

Finally, a layer of glass is chemically placed atop the wafer's surface, in order to protect the wafer from scratches. Now the wafer's life in the cleanroom is completed and it graduates to the outer world.

Twice each day, at 10:30 A.M. and 3:30 P.M., a van carries a load of completed wafers from Fab 3 at Livermore to San Francisco International Airport, where they are air-freighted to A 2 in Manila, or to one of Intel's other assembly plants. The workers will scribe each wafer between the chips, then break the wafer along the scribe lines. The good chips that passed the final test at Fab 3 are then bonded into plastic packages with electrodes leading out of the package on fine wires. Each chip, now encased in its protective package, looks somewhat like a caterpillar with many legs. The packaged chip is subjected to an exhaustive set of electrical, heat, moisture, and vibration tests to ensure that it functions perfectly and will do so reliably for years of future use.

After marking the survivors of this testing with the Intel insignia, the finished chips are loaded back on a 747, and shipped to customers around the world, who will utilize the chips as components in computers, small appliances, autos, and other products. That's the end of the beach-to-customer process in manufacturing semiconductor chips.

The real heroes of Fab 3, and, more generally, of the entire semiconductor industry, are the line-operators. Most are women, representing a wide cross-section of age and ethnicity. Many are young, fresh out of high school with perhaps a few months' experience working at McDonald's or Burger King. Others are middle-aged mothers, whose children have grown up. Almost all live within a few miles of the wafer fab plant at Livermore, which means that in this part of California, the majority are Caucasians. They are attracted by a starting salary of $4.10 per hour, low compared to skilled manual jobs in other U.S. industries, but better than alternatives in the Livermore area. The base salary is little more than the legal minimum. On the basis of good work performance, a line-operator at Fab 3 can climb to as much as $9.00 per hour after about five years. All of the line-operators we talked to at Fab 3 complain about the endless monotony of their work, performing routine operations hour after hour. They cannot dawdle under the watchful eyes of their supervisors, but the women talk almost constantly with nearby peers (although Intel policy discourages such conversation).

Most line-operators are women. When we asked a Fab 3 worker why, she replied: "Because our fingers are faster than men's. And we can better cope with the monotony of this work." Further, men won't work for such low wages. Females, because they're glad to have a job, may also be less likely to join a labor union, the nemesis of Silicon Valley executives.

When looking through a microscope at a wafer during a plant tour of Fab 3, one of the authors exclaimed to the female operator at this station: "What beautiful circuitry." She replied, "Not if you look at it hour after hour, day after day, week after week." How do the line-operators cope with such monotony? Some don't, they simply quit after a few months or a year. In 1982, Fab 3 expanded its workforce by 150 additional workers—2,000 women applied in response to a local newspaper ad. Six months later, 17 of the new employees had already quit. But most operators stay on the job, or at least in the industry. Within months they develop a skill that is in demand and are assured of having a job when other industries are laying off workers.

Most line-operators cannot realistically look forward to becoming a trainer or a supervisor, as there are few job openings. But there are exceptions. One woman was hired as a line-operator at Fab 3 when it opened in 1973 and set an outstanding performance record in the cleanroom. By 1976 she was promoted to supervisor of a group of 15 line-operators. Her unusual ability then led to a further promotion to acting production manager at Fab 3, an "exempt" position. Last year the once line-operator was promoted to production manager of Fab 2 at Santa Clara. She was not yet thirty.

Line-operators can earn up to $75 per month bonus if Fab 3 has superior production, although this bonus usually is only about $30–$40 (about 5 percent of the workers' base salary). Nevertheless the bonus plus other incentives like stock-purchase options appear to motivate the line-operators to high quality production.

Most line-operators do not simply push buttons. Some of the machines, like the ion-implanters, require considerable skill to operate properly; fine gradations of judgment are required. Intel has a careful training program. An experienced operator provides extensive one-on-one instruction to the novice in learning to use a new machine and a 200-page manual is provided by Intel. This training typically continues for two or three weeks until the trainee demonstrates a high level of proficiency in performing an operation. The success of the training period, however, rests on the trainer, a peer who has had several years' experience on the machine. Even then there are failures. At Fab 3 one day an ion-implanter was not working and the production of several thousand wafers was backed up. The huge machine carried a plaintive, hand-lettered sign: "Sorry, down for repair." Earlier that day, a trainee with only one week's on-the-job training had panicked and hit the "stop" button, crashing the machine. The trainer said, "Well, she still has a ways to go in learning how to operate the ion-implanter."

About 30 engineers are assigned to Fab 3's cleanroom (another 70 work in an Intel R&D unit also located in Fab 3). Almost all are male, many just out of engineering college. Their main responsibility is to monitor various wafer fab operations. They also solve unexpected problems when they occur, as happened during our visit to Fab 3. At about 10:30 in the morning, a sudden spurt in the rejection rate was noticed at one of the wafer test stations in the cleanroom. A team of engineers galvanized into action. X-rays disclosed that minute cracks were occurring inside the latticed architecture of the wafer. After following several likely leads the engineers traced the problem to warping of the wafer. When we left Fab 3 at 5:30, the young engineers were still seeking to determine why the warping occurred. Later we learned that the problem was solved, only after an all-night session.

7

Losing: Companies That Don't Make It

"If failed business ventures leave ghosts behind them, the air in Silicon Valley must be thick with the phantoms of departed start-ups."
Business Week, February 28, 1983

"I ran a company that didn't make it. There was no stigma attached to that. I could start another company at the drop of a hat and people have approached me about doing so. But I won't; trying again would be just too painful."
Name withheld by request

Acquisitions and Take-Overs

LIKE SUCCESS, failure has its own style in Silicon Valley. In established industries, most failing corporations file for bankruptcy. In Silicon Valley, some failing high-tech firms do go bankrupt, of course, but many once-active companies are acquired or merged.

A company take-over can be good news or bad news. Some start-ups are in fact developed to the point where they demonstrate enough success so that another company will step in and take them over, paying handsome amounts for the stock. For the founders, a take-over can bring the riches of their dreams. But in other cases, a take-over may not be welcome, either by management or by the employees of the company being absorbed.

When a take-over occurs, changes soon follow. In about half

of the cases, top management of the acquired company stays in place, at least for a while.[1] Other executives leave because they have become millionaires from their stock sale. Others may find their jobs are duplicated in the parent company, especially if they work in customer relations, finance, sales, or marketing, and are laid off. When Schlumberger acquired Fairchild in 1979 the first act by the new CEO (from Schlumberger) was to cut the number of employees from 32,000 to 23,000, the number of vice-presidents from 52 to 5, and the corporate staff from 600 to fewer than 100.[2]

One of the biggest take-overs in recent years was when Gould, Inc., a $2 billion conglomerate based in Illinois, acquired American Microsystems, Inc., (AMI), a Silicon Valley custom chip maker.[3] Negotiations lasted over two years with advance and retreat strategies that at times resembled the courtship of whooping cranes more than a business deal.

In 1979 Gould lost out to United Technologies in a bid to buy Mostek, a semiconductor manufacturer in Texas, then lost to Schlumberger in a bid for Fairchild Semiconductor. In October 1979 an Illinois banker breakfasted with Glenn Penisten, president and CEO of AMI, at Hugo's Restaurant in Palo Alto, and extended feelers on behalf of Gould. Penisten was not interested. Four months later the banker called again and persuaded Penisten to meet William Ylvisaker, CEO of Gould. Later that month the two got together at the Marriott Hotel in Santa Clara for a talk, but nothing further happened.

In October 1981 the Illinois banker phoned again, and convinced Penisten to meet Ylvisaker for more discussions. They met three times during the next few weeks, twice in San Francisco and once in Illinois. These negotiations proceeded in earnest and when Ylvisaker went to London on business he kept in phone contact with Penisten. The deal was consummated on November 24, 1981, in a private suite at the Fairmont Hotel in San Francisco. The two CEOs talked about employees, working conditions, trade secrets, business philosophies, customers—and money. Then they signed a letter of intent to merge the two corporations.

The next morning, four of AMI's eight directors met in the Palo Alto office of the company's lawyer. A teleconference was set up with the other four directors in Germany, Palm Springs, New York, and Los Angeles. They approved the merger. So for

$217 million in stock, the once independent chip maker known as American Microsystems, Inc., became a wholly owned subsidiary of Gould, Inc.[4]

Size is no guarantee of success. TRW, a multinational corporation with 1982 sales of $5.1 billion, recently decided to abandon its joint venture with Fujitsu, the giant Japanese computer company. The announcement, phrased discreetly, stated that Fujitsu would take control of TRW-Fujitsu "to link market requirements to product developments more directly, to simplify communications, and to improve responsiveness to customers." TRW-Fujitsu had jointly manufactured minicomputers and electronic cash registers. The joint venture had not been profitable for TRW, and a Fujitsu American spokesman said there had been "some communication problems."[5]

Silicon Valley companies that are acquired by a large corporation usually become a subsidiary or division of the parent. When the acquiring corporation has headquarters outside Silicon Valley, problems often occur. The Silicon Valley microelectronics industry does not operate like other industries; distant corporate offices that take away local control and hamper decision-making may bring on failure. Absentee owners may not be sensitive to the special problems and benefits of Silicon Valley. For example, the need for special policies to compensate for high housing prices may not be appreciated by an East Coast board of directors. They also may fail to realize the amount of job-hopping that occurs, and the need for perquisites to counteract it. An example of problems with absentee landlords occurred in the late 1960s, when the East Coast headquarters of Fairchild could not understand why its semiconductor division in Mountain View needed to offer stock options to its star engineers: So Bob Noyce defected from Fairchild to start Intel.[6]

The Adolescent Transition

Of all the reasons Silicon Valley companies don't make it, perhaps the adolescent transition is the most common. A brilliant

THE MAGAZINE FOR
GROWING COMPANIES

OCTOBER 1981
$2.00

Inc.

HIS MAN
AS CHANGED
USINESS
OREVER

t personal computers
o for you

J AND YOUR
RETARY

T BUCHWALD VS.
E ATTORNEY
NERAL

W THE TAX CUT
ECTS YOU

Apple
Computer
Chairman
Steve Jobs

ven P. Jobs, one of the Computer Kids who
nched the microcomputer revolution, now
airman of the board of Apple Computer Inc.
urtesy *Inc.*

e godfather of Silicon Valley, Dr. Frederick E.
man, former Vice-President and Provost of
nford University. Courtesy *Stanford Univer-*

In 1938 Bill Hewlett and Dave Packard launched their company in this garage, which still stands behind their old rooming house at 367 Addison Street in Palo Alto. *Hewlett-Packard Company*

A toast to Dr. William Shockley on the day he won the Nobel Prize in 1956 for his invention of the transistor. Standing center, with glass, is Robert Noyce, who later launched Fairchild Semiconductor. Others of the "Shockley Eight" shown here were to comprise the founding cadre of the semiconductor industry, spinning off new firms from Shockley's and from Fairchild. Courtesy *Robert Noyce*

A South American fire ant examines a 64K RAM, a Random Access Memory chip that stores and provides access to more than 64,000 bits of data instantaneously. *Western Electric Company*

Semiconductor chip designers lay out the architecture of a new product with the assistance of a computer. When completed, these chip designs will be greatly reduced in size and placed on masks. *National Semiconductor Corporation*

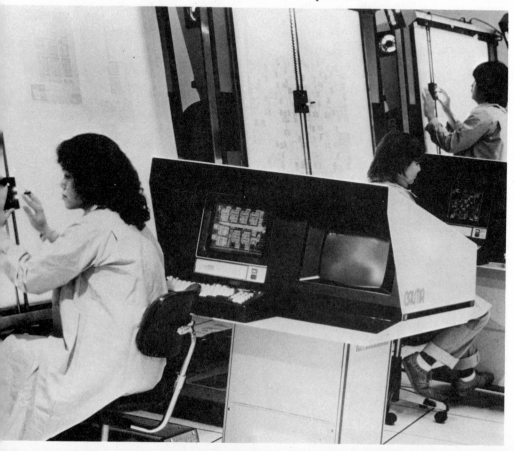

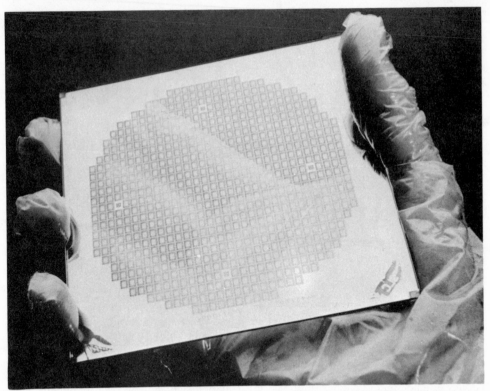

This mask contains 712 identical designs for a semiconductor chip that will be reproduced by photolithography on a silicon wafer. Five or more similar masks are utilized to layer miniature circuitry on the surface of the wafer, then the chips will be broken off, tested, packaged, and used to build computers or other microelectronics products. *National Semiconductor Corporation*

The greatly magnified surface of a partially completed silicon wafer. The raised lines are the circuits, each about one micron in width. *GCA Corporation*

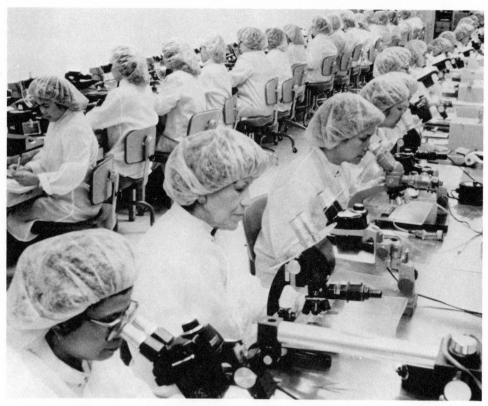

A crowded wafer fabrication lab in Silicon Valley, where silicon wafers are checked by microscope for possible defects. Protective clothing is worn in order to maintain a dust-free environment inside these "cleanrooms." *National Semiconductor Corporation*

The Intel 4004, the first microprocessor, invented by Dr. Marcian E. "Ted" Hoff in 1971. Microprocessors contain the control functions for a computer, and made possible the development of the microcomputer. *Intel Corporation*

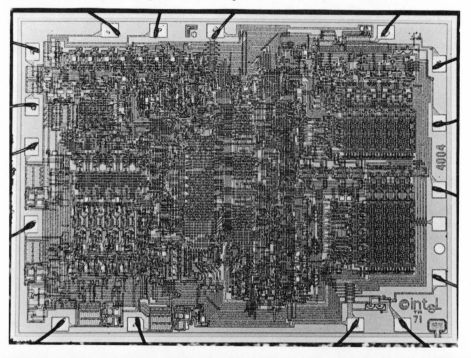

An aerial view of the heart of Silicon Valley: semiconductor plants and other microelectronics facilities in Santa Clara and Sunnyvale. *Dataquest*

A latter-day Stonehenge, Silicon Valley style, these walls for a tilt-up building went up 97 tons at a time in the Marriott Business Park in Santa Clara in 1983. Each 48-foot high cement section was poured on the ground, then raised into position. *San Jose Mercury News*

Sarah, daughter of Dr. Anne Piestrup, founder of The Learning Company, using one of their software programs on a microcomputer. Photo: *Mark Tuschman*

engineer-inventor starts a company based on an innovative idea. The product catches on and the company grows. New staff are hired at a furious rate. With growth comes paperwork and complications; policies are established and formal procedures announced. The founder-inventor no longer knows everyone by first names. He begins to reminisce about the good old days when it was so much more fun at work. His company is experiencing the adolescent transition.

Not all engineer-founders are able to make the transition to successful managers. The qualities that contribute to entrepreneurial success may mitigate against corporate success. The saga of the engineer caught in the adolescent transition is so common that it seems almost inevitable. The companies that avoid it are few.

Verbatim's is a classic example of the adolescent transition.[7] Reid Anderson, an electrical engineer, founded Verbatim after working in electronics R&D for 24 years, mostly at Bell Labs. His research convinced him that magnetic tape would replace paper tape in storing computer data. In 1969 he borrowed money from friends and relatives and took out a loan to start his company. Tape casettes were giving way to faster floppy disks. The 8" floppy disk was introduced in 1973 by IBM as a sideline to their main product, mainframe computers. So when Anderson asked IBM if he could license the floppy disks, IBM agreed. From 1974 to 1979 Verbatim's sales grew from $4.3 million to $36 million and earnings rose from $260,000 to $2.3 million. By 1979 Anderson was worth $14.7 million on paper.

Then came the adolescent transition. It began with a minor problem that quickly escalated. Verbatim changed the liner paper on the jackets enclosing the floppy disks without first properly testing them. The new liner caused the disks to dry out, making the disks wear out faster. To make matters worse, Verbatim had also changed the chemical coating on the disk, which reduced wear. In 1980 the company issued a recall of its 8" floppies.

What went wrong? The company had been so concerned with expansion that they did not take time to install adequate monitoring procedures. New processes were rushed into production without sufficient testing. In addition Anderson's skill as an inventor had persuaded him to steer the company into research on an expensive rigid disk that stored more information. However this time Verbatim was not alone in the market. Computer manufacturers decided to make the rigid disk, as did the Japanese. In 1980 earnings dropped 43 percent, and the board of directors decided to bring in an experienced manager. Malcolm Northrup was named CEO in 1981 and soon things turned around. In 1982 Verbatim had sales of $85 million, up from $54 million in 1981.

Former CEO Anderson is now spending most of his time as a venture capitalist, investing in new start-ups. Presumably he gives entrepreneurs advice about the adolescent transition.

Management Problems

"I don't think I know of any really well-managed electronics companies that went belly-up," commented the former president of a failed high-tech firm. "I didn't run my own company with strong enough control."[8] Richard Lee, co-founder, chairman, CEO, and chief financial officer of Siliconix, agrees: "I subscribe to the theory that there's no such thing as bad business—just bad management."[9]

Silicon Valley's management philosophy frequently is a holdover from earlier days when a start-up's founders favored an atmosphere that promoted technical research above financial savvy. Many high-tech firms are founded by engineers with little background in managing corporations and as the start-up begins to grow large, management problems frequently occur.

"ABC" (a fictional name) is a Silicon Valley company that didn't make it, largely due to management problems. Almost anyone who has been in the Valley for any length of time has worked for a company that didn't make it. Most prefer not to talk about it on the record. "Herb" (a pseudonym) joined ABC in summer 1979 as engineering manager. By March 1980 the company was in serious trouble.

ABC's founder and president was extremely charming, spoke capably, had impressive educational credentials, was intelligent, and painted an image of entrepreneurial success. His previous experience was in sales and he excelled at selling the idea of the company. His company easily got started and during its first year, ABC achieved its objectives and things looked good.

However in the company's second year its new product was supposed to be in volume production, but the yield was zero. The president lacked technical or manufacturing experience. He had hired technically competent people, but he had not delegated responsibilities to them. As the manufacturing problems continued, the president made a fatal mistake: He personally assumed responsibility for making technical decisions.[10]

The first chink in ABC's armor appeared in November 1979, when the company's venture capitalists came for a routine review of progress. The president presented ABC's ambitious plans for getting into pilot production and initial marketing projections. The venture capitalists thought the product needed more testing. The president stated that the product had been tested and that it should be announced and brought to market. The venture capitalists reluctantly agreed.

A few months later in June 1980, when the yield was still zero and there was no product in the marketplace, the venture capitalists became furious and scheduled a special meeting. Each of ABC's five top managers gave a presentation. The president had not reviewed the speeches prior to the meeting and did not know what information would be presented. Yield was still zero. The market had not developed as rapidly as expected and orders were not coming in. The president tried to "sweet-talk" the venture capitalists. This time it didn't work; they "cut him off at the knees." The venture capitalists had considered the president as competent, but now they no longer thought so. They regretted their earlier decision to support the new product announcement. It was obvious that the meeting was a disaster and, to make matters worse, the board of directors was scheduled to have dinner together that evening. Everyone knew that ABC was in dire trouble. Top staff started dusting off their resumes. In September 1980 the president was fired. The venture money dried up and the company died shortly thereafter.

ABC's failure could have been avoided. There was adequate capitalization, the product was technically feasible, timing was good, the price was right, and the quality of the staff was excellent. The problem was poor management.

ABC was funded by East Coast venture capitalists. ABC's president had graduated from an Ivy League university and came from an upper-class background. Herb: "You never experience that stuff being important in Silicon Valley. People come from some dinky school in the Midwest but they are real competent. Often a company hires an engineer who has a degree in one area but they assign him to work in another. Venture capitalists here in the Valley know everybody, so when they are considering financing someone they will call around until they find people who once worked with the guy and ask about him. If you don't give the straight story, watch out. Once you lose credibility with the venture capitalists, you are dead." It's a common opinion in Silicon Valley that East Coast venture capitalists are more difficult to deal with than are those on the West Coast; the former often don't understand the fast pace at which the California entrepreneur moves.

Under-Capitalization

Business problems resulting from under-capitalization are not unique to Silicon Valley; no cash means trouble in any industry. But when the company is a start-up, and when venture capital is involved, lack of money has its own set of problems—and solutions. High-tech start-ups usually rely on venture capitalists for initial financing. The new company and the venture capitalists both know when they agree on the initial deal that it may be only the first step in a protracted financial relationship.

Usually a new company is not yet producing or selling a product so the marketplace cannot pass judgment on the company's activities or products. But corporate officials and venture capitalists agree on milestones—specific targets that the company must reach by a certain date. Achieving a milestone is as important for a start-up as reporting quarterly profits is for a publicly held corporation. If a milestone is reached the company proves itself to the venture capitalists, and manages to stay alive awhile longer. Even meeting milestones, there are often ensuing rounds of financing before the initial product comes out.

Both the company and the venture capitalists hope that the product makes a splash in the marketplace and that sizeable profits will be realized. Sometimes this happens, but more often the hope remains only a hope. The company may run into problems and an important milestone not be achieved. The venture capitalists may decide that the company's product is not likely to pay off in the near future and that their money can earn a better return with another new company. If they pull out at these early stages, the company will go under.

New companies that are producing a product and need more capital have other options, such as going public or issuing new stock. In the near future the need for more capital may force privately held firms to go public and encourage established companies to raise capital by selling more stock. Rumors of a firm going public or of a new stock offering are hot gossip in Silicon Valley, with fortune-hunters following closely in their wake.

Scale-Up Problems

There is a dramatic difference between making two or three of something and producing a product in volume. In manufacturing microelectronics products like semiconductors which require thin-film processes, the problem generally involves yield. Ideally a company develops the processes, writes process specifications, and trains operators to perform the tasks. While this sounds straightforward, in reality it can be convoluted. Most high-tech manufacturing consists of many steps using different machines involving exact mixtures of gases and chemicals performed in cleanrooms.

Scale-up problems are an area of high-tech industry where the Japanese show great achievement. The Japanese excel at methodically organizing the hundreds of steps in a process, of testing one change at a time and noting its results, and of systematically considering every alternative. Silicon Valley entrepreneurs, by contrast, have a penchant for "winging it." The dominant attitude in time-pressured companies is to turn out the product—first 10, then 100, then 1,000, and write it all down later.

Mike Nary, an industrial engineer in semiconductors with twenty years' experience, concluded about basic American-Japanese differences: "Planning is a worthy approach. You lay out a thirty-day scenario but after four days you're so far off that you forget the plan. It's better to get some smart people in there and pound on the part until it works. You've got to have some planning, but brute force is probably more effective."[11]

Correct market definition is essential to Silicon Valley success. When corporate giants march into a marketplace they intend to take the middle and leave the edges to the little guys. These corners are the special domain of the start-ups. As Nolan Bushnell put it: "Think of the marketplace as being a large field of wheat. As a company gets bigger and bigger, the size of the combine blade gets bigger. But when they get to the end of the row, they have to turn around. The big company says those little corners are too small for us. But the new little company says, 'Hey, let's harvest those.' Small companies can fill that market need."[12]

The small market niche that the new company defines may soon become a huge market segment. But if the niche is too small, the company will not grow. GRiD Systems is a case in point. GRiD was founded in 1979 with $20 million from some of the biggest venture capitalists in Silicon Valley. The company got off to a flying start with its first product, the Compass, a powerful portable computer in a trim case (the computer is just two inches high and weighs 9.5 pounds). GRiD's Compass was a big hit at the 1982 San Francisco Computer Faire; everyone was talking about this sleek product. But despite its rave reviews, the Compass, priced at $8,000, sold only about 200 units in two years. The market niche that GRiD went after was the top executive who needed a powerful, portable computer. Evidently there just weren't that many executives who depend on a microcomputer they can slip into their attaché case.

Besides its problem with market definition, GRiD was also coping with the problem of adolescent transition. GRiD's founder, John Ellenby, is a systems designer. In early 1983 he turned over the titles of president and CEO to David Hanna, a GRiD vice-president with business experience. As Ellenby put it, "I'm an inventor and a developer and I've been looking for some time for a business partner to focus on the operating problems of the company, particularly on marketing and sales." GRiD is now in the process of modifying its market definition and making product revisions.[13]

The Economy

When the 1982 recession resulted in massive layoffs of factory workers in the East and Midwest, workers in high-tech companies seemed sheltered from job insecurity. Yet even Silicon Valley is affected by the economy. The recessions of 1971 and 1975 had far-reaching ramifications; semiconductor firms have never recovered from the gains made by the Japanese following the 1975 recession. The depression of the early 1980s also took its toll, and small start-ups were the first victims.

Kleis Bahmann, who was a top manager at a semiconductor equipment company that went under during the 1975 recession, recalled those times.[14] His company's 125 employees enjoyed using the company swimming pool, sauna, and volleyball court. They were a close group with justified pride in their reputation for producing fine products. But the company was small and got caught in the recession. First the billing rate dropped; in three months the order rate dropped 90 percent. Since there were so few orders, management decided to build up the inventory and be ready to get rich when good times returned. But they didn't come back soon enough. As a semiconductor supplier, the company was dependent on big manufacturers like National Semiconductor and Intel. As long as these giants weren't buying their equipment, suppliers were in trouble. The company simply could not sustain its cash flow and it folded. The employees were laid off and the equipment and facilities were sold to a larger supplier that incorporated the acquisition into its on-going operations.

In March 1983 Atari decided to lay off 1,700 employees in Silicon Valley, most of them line-operators, and move manufacturing operations to Taiwan and Hong Kong.[15] In 1981 video games were a hot consumer item and Atari produced the best-selling game, Pac-Man. Orders exceeded supply and Atari went on a hiring spree, adding 1,000 people in a four-month period during 1982. Atari announced plans to add 10,000 new jobs.[16] But things didn't work out that way. Other companies realized there was big money to be made in video games and the competition steadily cut away at Atari's profits. Atari's market share fell from nearly 90 percent in 1977 to only 41 percent by the end of 1982.[17]

The rapid increase in its number of employees, the fierce competition, and the depressed economy all combined to hurt Atari. In an attempt to cut costs and make money, Atari decided to move its assembly operations off-shore. Workers in Hong Kong make about $1.20 an hour, compared to about $9.00 an hour for American workers.[18] Atari is not the only high-tech company to move its operations to Asia. About half of the 500,000 jobs in the semiconductor industry are located there. However, Atari's decision to lay off American workers while hiring Asian workers was a first in Silicon Valley.[19]

Atari was unusual in being able to afford the luxury of manufacturing in Silicon Valley. When its business was booming and profits were generous, Atari could absorb the Valley's high manufacturing costs. But the competition adopted a calculated strategy; they manufactured off-shore from the beginning and beat Atari by lowering prices on their video games. Atari had to re-learn the lesson of digital watches and electronic calculators in the 1970s: A company can afford to be inefficient until the marketplace matures the product, produces it in quantity, then competes with your prices.

Atari claimed that its move off-shore was necessary for the company to remain viable and to maintain its other Silicon Valley jobs. The implications for the future are clear: Microelectronics jobs in America will increasingly focus on design and development, not on manufacturing and production. High-tech is not an industry to provide many jobs for production workers laid off from old-line industries. Microelectronics is not the answer to America's unemployment problems.

Osborne Computer blended elements of big success—a confident leader, technical expertise, a defined market niche, problems of the adolescent transition, rumors of undercapitalization, scale-up problems, and really tough competition. And in 1983, Osborne was in trouble.

Osborne Computer had just one product: the Osborne 1, a 24-pound portable computer that folds into a case that can fit under an airplane seat. It included a video display, keyboard, internal memory, disk drives, and software—and sold for about $1,8000. The Osborne had been described as a "cheap brute."[20]

Adam Osborne, the company founder, originally established himself as a computer industry author and gadfly. After earning his Ph.D. in chemical engineering, he worked for Shell Oil, where his entrepreneurial bent clashed with the bureaucracy. In 1970 he quit to set up a consulting company. He soon got interested in computers and began writing about them; one of his books, *Introduction to Microcomputers,* sold more than 300,000 copies.

Characteristically, Osborne formed his own company and published some forty books, twelve of which he wrote himself, before selling the company to McGraw-Hill in 1979. As a columnist for *InfoWorld,* the microcomputer magazine, he became known for his bold, muckraking style. His knowledge of the computer industry enabled him to recognize a market niche waiting for exploitation: "I saw a truck-sized hole in the industry and I plugged it."[21] In December 1980 Osborne founded Osborne Computer Corporation with the goal of producing a low-priced computer that would make computing available to everyone. Capital for the new company came from $250,000 in profits from Osborne Publishing, and from venture capital supplied by Jack Melchor and by the venture capitalist firm of Rothschild-Unterberg-Towbin.

Skeptics said that Osborne should stick to writing; an inexpensive computer was impossible. Osborne proved his critics wrong when within two months of the first shipment of the Osborne 1, the company reported a profit. Osborne's strategy was to build the Volkswagen bug of microcomputers. The Osborne 1 used standard components and relied entirely on programs written by independent software companies. If one were to buy each of the software programs that came with the Osborne 1, the cost would be more than the total price of the computer. Costs were reduced by low overhead, capitalizing on declining semiconductor prices, and by getting vendors to carry the company's inventory.

Osborne sales reached $80 million in 1982, with 10,000 computers sold per month. However, the company was growing so rapidly (with over 1,000 employees) that it desperately needed additional capital, despite denials by corporate officials.[22] It took exactly 40 screws and 68 minutes to put together an Osborne 1.[23] With this speed of production came problems. One retail store that sold 225 Osborne computers had to make 400 repairs on them and dropped the line.[24] The company admitted there were some production difficulties, blaming them on inadequate inspection of vendor sub-assemblies.

In January 1983 a sign of the adolescent transition occurred. Adam Osborne was replaced as president and CEO by Robert Jaunich, an experienced corporate executive who was known as a "results-oriented" manager. Osborne is an entrepreneur who admitted he didn't "feel qualified to run the company on a day-to-day basis. I enjoy being an entrepreneur and I don't enjoy being a manager."[25] The transition was friendly. But the greatest challenge to Osborne's success lay just ahead. Among the 250 or so microcomputer companies, several aimed at Osborne's low-end market. In 1983, Kaypro began selling a portable computer with a larger screen than the Osborne, and at a lower price. Osborne Computer announced a new machine, but was not able to start selling it. By mid-1983, Osborne sales dropped to practically zero. On September 13, 1983, Osborne Computer declared bankruptcy.[26]

Bankruptcy

The last chapter for some Silicon Valley firms is bankruptcy. Magnuson Computer Systems, a producer of mainframe computers, filed for bankruptcy in March 1983. The bankruptcy announcement wasn't unexpected; in early 1982 columnist Evelyn

Richards of the *San Jose Mercury News* stated that Magnuson had failed to meet its payroll on time.[27] The Magnuson story could have been the Apple or the Intel story or the story of any Silicon Valley start-up. Similar transitional forces were at work—the same problems and the same hopes were involved.

Magnuson Computer did everything right when it started in 1977. The four founders, Paul Magnuson, Robert McCullough, Ray Williams, and Carlton Amdahl, were highly regarded. Using $400,000 raised from private sources, the company built a prototype computer in 1977. Late that year, Fairchild provided $4 million to the new company, a solid infusion of cash. There were no problems with capitalization.

But then the inevitable exodus of the founders-innovators began. McCullough stated that the growing bureaucracy of the company caused everything to get bogged down: "Things didn't get done in time or it became a drag on one's energy to get them done."[28] Amdahl, an engineer, left to join his father Gene's start-up, Trilogy Systems. The adolescent transition for Magnuson came to a head in fall 1978, when the board felt the need for a more forceful business leader. Paul Magnuson resigned as president, and was replaced by Joseph Hitt, formerly vice-president of marketing.

Other personnel problems among top management included a suit charging breach of contract and fraud, filed by a vice-president. Serious production problems began: faulty test equipment, incorrectly sized printed circuit boards, and slow assembly operations. These problems came in cascading series—first a little snag, then something more serious, then a real disaster. The shipment of new models was delayed and some customers went over to competitors. Once the Magnuson computers were shipped, there were problems with field operations. Field service engineers weren't properly trained to repair the new computers. A proposed change in the accounting system had to be scrapped at the last minute, adding to financial woes.

In January 1982 Hitt resigned amidst rumors that the company had failed to negotiate a merger and that the finance page was written in red ink—a loss of $10 million for the fourth quarter of 1981 alone. Faced with this crisis, Charles Cole, a member of the board of directors, assumed the presidency in an interim capacity. Working 80 to 90 hours a week, Cole spent his first three weeks as president assessing the company's problems. For the next two months, he directed negotiations for a financial infusion package consisting of a $5 million bailout from investors. He re-negotiated a loan with the Bank of America. "I have been characterized as sort of a walking sense of urgency," Cole said of himself.[29] He also instituted a very conservative accounting policy. During this turnaround period, Magnuson lost 150 staff, many from layoffs. Five company officers took 10 percent pay cuts. The top officers moved out of their spacious offices to smaller quarters.

In April 1982, Cole turned over the direction of the company to the new president and CEO, Charles Strauch, former president of Memorex. With the financial rescue package negotiated by Cole and with Strauch's management experience, Magnuson might have brought it all together. But the competition dealt the final blow. In late 1982 IBM instituted a program of aggressive price-cutting for its mainframe computers, giving more power for less money. As Magnuson put it, IBM's price-cutting had a "very negative effect."[30] In March 1983, Magnuson announced it planned to reorganize under Chapter 11 of the Federal Bankruptcy Act.

At its peak in 1980, Magnuson stock was selling at $40 per share. At the time of the bankruptcy announcement, the stock was down to $3.

In Silicon Valley some start-ups crash with a big thud. Others just fade away. Both finales remind us that Silicon Valley has losers too.

8

Working

"There's an intensity to it that makes Silicon Valley exciting to work in. I was part of a team that went from watching a water buffalo in a rice field in Penang, to building a producing semiconductor plant in less than eight months. You get kind of cocky. Hell yes, this is the way to do it. You go around with your bony chest sticking out and say, 'If you were from General Motors, you couldn't make it in this Valley.' We're the best there is."

Nick Larsen, technical engineer, 1981

"Silicon Valley is like an individual running around in front of a steamroller. You can outrun the steamroller on any given day. But if you ever sit down you get squashed."

Bob Boschert, President, Boschert Electronics, 1983

TALK to virtually anyone in Silicon Valley and you hear about the long hours. Why? Competition forces them, for one thing. Alan Shugart, originally of IBM, then Memorex, then president of Shugart Associates, now president of Seagate Technology, stated: "You've got to pick out what the market is going to do and go for it. Seven years from now there will be a new technology doing what we do now. Someone will latch on to it. I hope I find it first." And a former Seagate employee now heading a spin-off said: "You get used to running 100 miles an hour while looking back over your shoulder."[1] Or as Karl Harrington, a semiconductor engineer, told us: "There is a real urgency here that is different from old-line industries. For us, the timing is tremendous. Beating a competitor to market by 60 days may be the difference between surviving and going under. Whoever gets to the marketplace first makes a splash."[2]

Some Silicon Valley people simply like to work. They put in long hours and cope with the job-related stress because they like microelectronics better than working in an established industry where they feel most people are bored clock-watchers. Many technical people are motivated by curiosity about how to make a device work, or how to make it work better. Such curiosity is also motivated by knowing that it will pay off in money, often lots of it. Adam Osborne of Osborne Computer said: "Here [in Silicon Valley] it is what you can get done and the faster the better."[3] Al Shugart confesses, "We all work hard because we all want to make a fortune in a hurry."[4]

Not only are the hours long and the pace fast, but Silicon Valley workdays are intense. Rarely do people come to work and sit around chatting about news, weather, or sports. A production manager told us, "I've never had a cup of coffee in our cafeteria. I go to the cafeteria with my peers to discuss problems, but I have never taken a coffee break. I can get coffee and drink it in my office all I want. But there are so many things that have to get done each day that are waiting for you and you have to get going on them. There's a sense of urgency. These are requests from your colleagues and they need it right *now.*"

Ray Brant, vice-president for human relations at National Semiconductor, contracted a rare blood disease that had to be treated with intravenous medication twenty-four hours a day. The disease required hospitalization, but Brant talked his way out of that because of his heavy workload. The semiconductor executive carried his intravenous bottle and pump with him to business meetings and arranged his car so the medication pumped as he drove. "If I backed off work for six weeks, I'd be too far offstream when I came back," he said.[5]

Some of the work intensity is self-induced; perhaps the ambitious people working in Silicon Valley prefer pressure. Nick Larsen commented: "We set the pace ourselves. If the wheel were running at 100 percent, we would spin it up to 120 every morning. Nothing's happening unless you're a little frantic. I've often seen design groups induce this frantic feeling themselves in order to get their juices flowing. There's nothing like a little fear and urgency to force creativity."[6]

It isn't enough just to be hard-working and dedicated. Meritocracy reigns supreme in Silicon Valley and that means knowing what you are doing. It's not who you know, or who your parents were, or where you went to school, or what clubs you belong to. It's *what* you know; intelligence is mandatory. Most who have made it in Silicon Valley have an extensive technical education. Budding entrepreneurs often started working on some technical problem while in college. Engineer Karl Harrington described the talent of employees in his small R&D company: "I report to a fellow who has four other managers reporting to him. Of the four of us, three have Ph.D.s. My boss has a Ph.D. and his boss has a Ph.D. I work with extremely bright and capable people who move quickly, both intellectually and conceptually. I have to use every wily trick I can think of just to survive."[7]

Lee Felsenstein, a Computer Kid and one of the main designers of the Osborne computer, thinks that engineering design work is so much fun that he never wants to leave it to become a manager. He had the title of "Research Fellow" at Osborne Computer Corporation, a similar job description to that of engineer Rod Holt's "Apple Fellow"—and to Ted Hoff's former title of "Intel Fellow." Felsenstein says: "It's fun to design a printed circuit board for a microcomputer. When we were designing the Osborne computer, I worked all three shifts on some days. The difference between tools and toys is not much."[8]

High-tech industry moves so fast that there is never time to relax and consolidate. People who work in Silicon Valley can't settle back and coast. If they do, they coast right out of the industry. Alice Ahlgren, director of communication at Cromemco, described this fast pace and its accompanying stress.[9] Cromemco, a computer manufacturer, had decided to enter the microcomputer market. Their new product, the C-10, was to be unveiled at the National Computer Conference. Just three days before this trade show, Cromemco engineers were still making final adjustments on the C-10. Ahlgren explained that if they weren't ready for this show, the opportunity would not come around again for another year. With three days to go, she balanced her anxiety against the fact that Cromemco had not yet missed a deadline; somehow the product would be ready—it was. Such an edge-of-the-cliff existence doesn't make for nights of easy sleep. But on the other hand, life and work in Silicon Valley never gets dull either.

Frank Vella is a veteran engineer with twenty years in the Valley. He has a paradoxical attraction and distaste for the work ethic: "A young engineer gets a macho thrill in working long days and all weekend. He has heard how everybody works long hours and now he has a chance to do it. He is earning his wings, the right to say 'I'm a bona fide member of Silicon Valley.' Wiser heads set the boundaries on what part of our lives we let work have. I've paid my dues and am interested in other things in my life. I worked my weekends and all those days in a row without a break. The longest stretch I worked was 59 days in a row, when the shortest day was 8 hours and the longest was 17. It simply doesn't turn me on anymore."[10]

How does the work ethic in Silicon Valley compare with other industries? Kleis Bahmann, who had worked in aerospace for 10 years and then switched to microelectronics, explains: "In aerospace the idea was not to get the work done, but to follow the freaking rules. Here we get on with the task; in aerospace you have to fill out the paperwork. People who think of themselves as doers rather than compliers are attracted to Silicon Valley. Hell, if my aerospace boss came over and said, 'You've written 100 engineering orders with no mistakes in the paperwork and that's good,' I would say, 'Any idiot can do that. You can tell me it's great, but both of us know it isn't.' But when you build a computer and get it working, it's obvious that you've done something neat."[11]

The Great Engineering Shortage

The Silicon Valley microelectronics industry sucks up university-graduate engineers. The national shortage of engineers has roots in the public school system, where reductions in the number of qualified math and science teachers occurred as the result of budget cuts.[12] When students from the retrenched public schools reach college, there is a problem of not enough qualified professors. Salaries for assistant professors of engineering average $19,000, while salaries for engineers in industry begin at $25,000.

The U.S. graduates about 60,000 engineers annually. The Soviet Union, with a total population approximately equal to the U.S., graduates 300,000 engineers. Japan, with half the population of the U.S., graduates 75,000 engineers.[13] The U.S. awards about 6 percent of all undergraduate degrees in engineering. Comparable figures are 21 percent in Japan, 35 percent in the Soviet Union, and 37 percent in Western Germany. "Neither the strategic importance of education nor its close link to high technology is widely recognized and understood in America."[14]

In high-tech industry, a B.S. in engineering is a requisite for entry. Yet five years out of college, 50 percent of an engineer's knowledge is obsolete. Working engineers must be recycled.[15] There has been a call for universities to provide off-campus, part-time graduate programs for engineers, and for industry to encourage engineers to spend up to 10 percent of their time in graduate-level classes. The American Electronics Association and the Massachusetts High-Technology Council are collaborating in a campaign to convince 1,500 companies to give 2 percent of their R&D budgets to an engineering educational foundation, amounting to $40 million annually.

Women in Silicon Valley

The Silicon Valley microelectronics industry has been called "one of the last great bastions of male dominance" by the local *Peninsula Times Tribune*.[16] Women are mainly in positions as line-operators, secretaries, and clerical workers. They are under-represented in management and administration. Few women have technical or engineering backgrounds, and they are thought to lack the necessary qualifications for these jobs. However, many men in administrative or managerial positions also lack technical backgrounds. Why there are few women in positions of responsibility in Silicon Valley is complex and puzzling. Until recently the overwhelming majority of engineering graduates were men. Women received only 175 degrees in engineering in the U.S. in 1950, but 6,100 in 1980.[17] Whereas in 1965 less than one percent of B.S. engineers were women, by 1980 the figure had increased to nearly 10 percent.[18] However females have yet to enter the boardrooms or the executive suites of Silicon Valley.

Venture capitalists and entrepreneurs hold a firm grip over Silicon Valley. Most new firms are formed as start-ups with capital provided by venture funds. Scientific and engineering professionals in the finance community and in start-ups are likely to be men; these power-brokers rely exclusively on their personal networks, passing information about job openings, possibilities for expansion, and promising companies to their friends—other men. Women are virtually absent from the power centers of Silicon Valley corporations. Twenty of the largest publicly held Silicon Valley firms listed a total of 209 persons as corporate officers in 1980; only 4 were women. The boards of directors of these 20 firms include 150 directors. Only one was a woman: Shirley Hufstedler, serving on the board of Hewlett-Packard.

While these limitations inhibit the participation of women in decision-making positions in the Valley, there are also opportunities. The need for trained employees exceeds the number of applicants; therefore if you have the credentials, you stand a good chance of being hired. Ann Wells, president of Ann Wells Personnel Services, observed, "Anybody with a technical degree can be placed. A Martian with three heads could find a job in Silicon Valley. So for women with a technical background, it's terrific."[19]

Frances is in sales in a Silicon Valley semiconductor firm. Her story is typical of the experience of many Silicon Valley women. "I majored in French in college, taught for two years, and found I really didn't like it. So I got a job for a distributor in customer service where I learned about electronics. That was in 1972. I worked there for a year and then moved to my present job in semiconductor sales. At that time there were no women in product marketing or sales, so there was no place for me to go. An opening came up in product marketing dealing with the military group, where I could see there would be room for advancement. I got this job in 1979. I was the first woman in our company to get a marketing job. The people I worked for were leery about my ability since I'm a woman. The big problem was traveling. Now there are two women in product marketing. My next goal is to be a regional distributor sales manager. There are no women in this position now. The drawback is that I don't have field sales experience. How do I get it, if they won't let me travel?"[20]

An exception to masculine domination in engineering is Sandy Kurtzig, president of ASK Computer Systems. ASK is an OEM (original equipment manufacturer) that sells software computer programs for accounting, cost-control, and other financial uses to large companies. ASK's software is integrated into Hewlett-Packard minicomputer hardware, so that turnkey (ready to operate) systems are provided to customers. Sandy Kurtzig is a handsome woman but her competitors say there's nothing soft about Sandy Kurtzig when it comes to cutting a hard business deal.

When Sandy and her family moved to Silicon Valley, she enrolled in a master's program in aeronautical engineering at Stanford, while at the same time raising her two young children. At Stanford, she was one of only two women in her class of 250 graduate students.

Like many other women, Sandy Kurtzig wasn't satisfied with just doing domestic chores, so she launched her company in 1974. "I wanted to start in a garage like Hewlett-Packard, but I didn't have one. So I started in the second bedroom of my apartment. But most of the work was actually done on my kitchen table."[21] At first, Kurtzig did sales, bookkeeping, and management of her start-up. As long as ASK had only five or six employees, they worked out of her apartment bedroom. Eventually ASK moved into nearby offices in Los Altos and went into a rapid growth phase. Annual sales reached $23 million in 1982.

Kurtzig believes that one reason for her success was hiring good people. They, in turn, hired other good people. "I told my top managers they had to hire people better than themselves. They wouldn't get promoted until they had their replacement ready." ASK's employees are treated well even by Silicon Valley standards. All get stock options; there is also twice-a-year profit-sharing, averaging about 10 percent of base salaries. In addition, ASK has beer busts every Friday, at which wine is also served ("I don't like beer," says Kurtzig). ASK also has a hot tub and Jacuzzi for its employees.

The key to effective competition in the software field is R&D, a fact that Kurtzig recognizes: "We spent less for R&D last year than H-P spent on coffee and donuts in a week. But then we signed a long-term contract with H-P's main competitor, DEC (Digital Equipment Corporation). So we capitalized on their R&D investment." When asked who her competition is, Kurtzig immediately responds, "IBM." Actually, ASK's sales don't quite rival those of International Business Machines. But when Sandy Kurtzig divorced in late 1982, ASK paid her husband $20 million for his share of ASK stock. That left Sandy Kurtzig with about $54 million worth of ASK Computer Systems.[22]

Immigrant Entrepreneurs

Not all Third World people in Silicon Valley are poor women living in South San Jose, commuting to work as line-operators in semiconductor plants. Kyupin Philip Hwang (pronounced "Hong") arrived in the U.S. 18 years ago with $50 in his pocket and without much grasp of English. Today Hwang owns 69 percent of TeleVideo, the computer company he founded in 1976 and was personally worth about $1.1 billion in June 1983. That kind of money puts the Korean immigrant far ahead of Steve Jobs, and well on his way toward becoming like Dave Packard or Bill Hewlett.

Other Third World immigrants have become success stories in the Valley: Aryeh Finegold, an Israeli, left Intel to start Daisy Systems, a company that makes a computer hardware/software package for scientists and engineers; and Jesse Aweida, a Palestinian, heads Storage Technology Corporation, a firm producing computer data-storage devices.

Phil Hwang was born in what is now North Korea and fled to Seoul during the Korean War. He learned to know hunger. "My father was a mechanic," says Hwang. "We were very poor."[26] After his arrival in the United States, Hwang studied electrical engineering at Utah State University. During the summers he worked 16-hour days at Lake Tahoe as a dishwasher at one casino and as a janitor at another. He saved his earnings to pay his way through college. Later, while working at Ford Motor Company in Detroit, Hwang earned his master's degree, and then moved on to work for several big computer companies. In the mid-1970s he was attracted to Silicon Valley and, with $9,000 of his savings, decided to launch TeleVideo in a Cupertino garage (he was refused venture capital). Hwang went unsalaried for the first two years, while his wife worked as a dietician at a local hospital to support the family.

Hwang's company produces a high-quality, low-priced video display terminal, not an especially innovative product, but it sells and sells. About 200,000, in fact, making TeleVideo the country's largest independent supplier of terminals. The component assembly work is done in Korea, the circuit board stuffing in California, and the final assembly in Puerto Rico. Now the company is producing a microcomputer and it is selling well also. Hwang is the ultimate workaholic, his associates say, regularly putting in 16-hour days. But his tremendous success has sweetened his lifestyle somewhat; in 1982 Hwang purchased a 5,700 square-foot stone house in Los Altos Hills. It cost more than $1 million, and is large enough for Hwang, his wife (who still works at the hospital), two daughters, and has a kitchen that can handle 400 for dinner.[27]

Third World Women

Although women are under-represented in decision-making roles in Silicon Valley, over 75 percent of Silicon Valley's assemblers are women.[23] Most have only a high school education and approximately 40 percent of these skilled manual workers are members of ethnic minorities. Many are recent immigrants: "Minorities used to be black and women . . . now they are Vietnamese and Chinese."[24] The pay for these production workers is low, compared to other U.S. industries.

Clerical and technical support positions are also usually filled by women. According to a survey by Professional Secretaries International (PSI) in 1981, the pay of Silicon Valley executive secretaries is somewhat above the national average: An executive secretary in Silicon Valley earns $1,534 a month, or $18,408 a year. The national average is $1,364 a month, or $16,368 per year. Shirley Martin, president of the local chapter of PSI and secretary to the chairman of American Microsystems, Inc., figures that secretaries in Silicon Valley with at least five years' experience get salaries ranging from $20,000 to $35,000.[25]

Facilities

The egalitarian management philosophy of Silicon Valley is flexible, informal, entrepreneurial, and non-traditional. The goal of rapidly growing large companies is to retain the entrepreneurial spirit of the small company. A favored way is by decentralization, delegating greater responsibility to managers. When a division reaches 1,500 employees at Hewlett-Packard, it becomes a separate administrative unit, and employees are encouraged to identify with the division rather than with the H-P worldwide monolith.

Many observers feel that Silicon Valley firms display a distinctive management style. Compared to established firms in older industries, microelectronics companies believe in treating their workers like human beings, rather than like machines. Being nice to one's employees with financial rewards, exercise facilities, and calling them by their first names seems to be good business sense in Silicon Valley. Perhaps as a result they will remain loyal to the company, rather than leaving for a competitor.

There are no factories in Silicon Valley, only "facilities": modern, low-slung, clean, and quiet. Such buildings are located on a "campus," complete with beautiful lawns, immaculate landscaping, and lots of greenery. If criticism were to be leveled against the Valley's architecture, it might be about the routine sameness of the buildings. Most are one-level "tilt-ups," so-called because the concrete walls are cast on the ground and then tilted up into place. These tilt-ups house the thousands of small Silicon Valley firms that form the backbone of the microelectronics industry. Two-story buildings are the mark of larger companies; most of these are innovative in design and ultra-modernistic in appearance. Multi-story buildings in Silicon Valley can be counted on one hand.

If the buildings are like flat boxes, the landscaping is striking. The Valley's approximately seventy-five industrial parks are created, planted, and manicured by accomplished landscape architects.

Certain companies are famous for their settings. Rolm has hired tour guides to answer questions from the many visitors to their award-winning grounds. A brook meanders through the Rolm campus, rounding patios with umbrella-shaded tables, and gurgling past swimming pools and tennis courts to an outside eating area. Patios adjacent to the cafeteria furnish employees with a luncheon rendezvous. Vine-covered trellises, flower pots, and lush landscaping provides a snatch of serenity in an otherwise intense day.

The interiors of these buildings are an extension of the patios, alive with the vibrant green of plants. Hanging ferns and pot-ted trees are everywhere, houseplants are common, radios play softly, and the walls of the bay seating dividers are covered with colorful, modernistic posters. Areas designed for the public—front offices and reception areas—sport plush modern furniture, posters of fashionable art shows, macrame wall hangings, large plants and trees, and plate-glass windows looking out on green lawns. Coffee or tea is provided for visitors waiting for an appointment.

Stories about corporate recreational facilities are told throughout the Valley. Country club ambience is conveyed by pools, tennis and volleyball courts, parcourses, exercise equipment, and shower facilities. Silicon Valley workers want to stay in shape. The companies are not entirely selfless in providing these highly visible emoluments. They provide a counter to job mobility, and exercise improves health, cutting down on employee sick-days, as a Rolm spokesman pointed out. Rolm's million-dollar sportsplatz may thus be a shrewd investment.

Employees are encouraged to bring their families to use the swimming pools and tennis courts on weekends. Flextime, a policy of allowing employees to set their own hours of arrival and departure from work, is spreading. Rolm, Tandem, and Intel give their employees paid sabbaticals after several years of work. The official explanation is that this is a time of refreshment for the employee, but it also means that someone else is trained to perform the individual's job (and step in, should the employee leave).

In contrast, retirement plans are virtually unknown in Silicon Valley. Most companies have no retirement plans at all; youthful employees do not consider retirement benefits when making a job change. Nobody expects to be with the same company long enough to retire. Silicon Valley employees perceive their current job in terms of months or years, but certainly not in terms of lifetime employment.

The Infrastructure of Silicon Valley

Sunnyvale boasts that it is the only city in the world with eight miles of hydrogen mains under its city streets (along with water

A Day in the Life of a Silicon Valley Engineer

Mike's alarm is set for 6:00 A.M., but he turns it off and dozes for fifteen minutes until he wakes again. He knows that he has to get up or he'll get caught in the worst part of the commute. It's already late. Mike and his girlfriend Angie share a condo in Los Gatos. He heads his Porsche 924 onto the two bumpy lanes of Highway 17, swearing at the on-ramp access signal which always shows red when he is in a rush. At least his car has a good tape system, so he can tune out the traffic during the drive to work.

Today he is concerned about what he is likely to find at work. Yesterday the lead line-operator went home sick and maybe she'll still be out today. Who will run the line if she doesn't show up? Mike's company supplies free donuts and coffee every morning. He looks at the donuts, knowing if he eats one it will sit like a ball of lead in his stomach. He eats one anyway, and 15 minutes later he wishes he hadn't. The lead woman comes in, feeling fine. So Mike stops worrying about the production line, and starts reviewing the features of a vendor's gold ball bonder. He intends to order 100, at $3,000 each, for the Hong Kong plant.

When noon comes, Mike heads for the changing rooms, where he meets the other runners. A core group of men and women jog nearly every day. They head across the industrial park toward the salt flats along the edge of San Francisco Bay. It's a sunny day, and there are dozens of runners out; Mike knows several from working with them at previous jobs. Others he doesn't know personally, but he knows where they work. Everybody yells back and forth, exchanging news and gossip while they jog.

When Mike returns to his desk, he finds a crisis on the line; the bonds are not adhering properly to the die. First he asks the SEM (Scanning Electron Microscope) technician in the lab to inspect the bonds and Mike narrows down the possible causes of the problem. He checks the bonds under an optical microscope. Mike reviews the actual, rather than the prescribed methods, that the line operators use for bonding. Lucky that the lead woman isn't sick today; she's crucial at a time like this. They discuss the trouble with four operators, and decide that the problem must be in the tooling. Mike specifies the modifications to be made, and tells the machine shop to work overtime if necessary. He orders the modifications to be completed, so the line can be going again at noon tomorrow.

It's 7:15 when Mike calls it a day. He's starving and tired, but at least now he won't face the usual commute traffic. Tonight he has agreed to meet Angie for dinner at Steamers. He gets there before she does, and has a drink while he waits. Tomorrow he'll have to get back to the gold ball bonders. Let's hope the shop can handle the design modifications. The line has got to get back on schedule . . . . Ah, tomorrow.

and sewer lines). Cleanrooms, daily deliveries of liquid gas, and local machine shops with tolerances measured in angstroms and microns, are part of the infrastructure of the microelectronics industry. Hundreds of specialized services support this industry:

transportation firms for computers and other delicate equipment, venture capital firms, advertising and public relations firms which understand high-technology, and lawyers specializing in start-up contracts.

But more than any other single factor, local high-tech firms depend on the people who can design the cleanrooms, tool delicate fixtures, and design innovative operating systems. This human resource is placated and wooed. Few other places in the world can offer the pool of experienced, specialized high-tech brainpower of Silicon Valley. Companies have little choice but to locate where these intellectual resource are concentrated. The magnetism of human expertise is one reason for the agglomeration of microelectronics firms in Silion Valley.

Part of the infrastructure that counts dearly is proximity to potential customers and suppliers. Many original equipment manufacturers (OEMs) who use microelectronics in their products have offices in the Valley. With product development often depending on close interaction between the manufacturer and the OEM, dropping by for a daily chat can be critical.

Casualties

Silicon Valley myth implies that success is almost inevitable for engineers and scientists. Although at first the pace will be fast and stress will be high, after a few years of struggling, rewards will accrue. Pay will increase, stock options will produce a substantial profit, a promotion to management will come, the result of job performance and the overall explosion of the industry. Perhaps the company will be another superstar and one's co-workers will become millionnaires too. Life will be pleasant—a comfortable home with a big pool, a new sports car, and money to do whatever one wants.

The Silicon Valley myth is a dream. The proportion of people who have the dream come true is in fact minuscule. Very few articles or books or TV shows are about Silicon Valley casualties.

The standard successes are trotted out for display—attractive, young, bright, and rich. Those who didn't make it aren't mentioned. They are ignored, with hope to fade away, inconvenient reminders that Silicon Valley pressures demand a heavy toll from its workers.

These victims of the Silicon Valley work ethic probably outnumber the successes by a factor of ten to one. No one who lives in the Valley is unaware of its casualties, but no one wants to admit that it happened to him. They avoid remembering failures, being unable to handle pressure, being passed over for promotion, being laid off, or watching a company go under. But casualties exist, even if they are ignored.

Most Silicon Valley workers encounter the caprice of the work ethic via layoffs. It is commonly understood that to be laid off is not necessarily a result of poor job performance, but rather a result of one's particular company or job. For example, a firm's sales department may actually be hiring at the same time production workers are being laid off. Few experienced engineers in Silicon Valley have not been laid off at least once.

Richard was an Intel engineer who experienced the 1975 layoffs. "I was a line supervisor. My boss came to me and said that I would have to lose all the people in my group. So I called them in and said, 'Guys, I know this is really tough, but you've all been laid off.' I walked them out to the parking lot and shook hands. Fifteen minutes later, I was back in my office thinking that was really unpleasant but thank goodness it didn't get me. My boss called me in and asked me if I'd taken care of the layoffs. I said yes, and he said 'I'm really sorry to tell you this, but you yourself are now laid off.' So fifteen minutes later I was out in the parking lot talking to the guys who were still leaning up against their cars, guys that I had just laid off. Fifteen minutes later, here came the plant guards with my boss. They had now walked three levels of personnel out to the parking lot. All of us really cared about the company and wanted to be working there. We were real people with real lives. But now we didn't have a job."[28]

The timing of a layoff is critical. If one is laid off during a Silicon Valley depression like 1971, 1975, or 1982, the prospects of finding another job soon are not good.

Time	*Event*
T minus 3 weeks	I survive the first round of layoffs at my company, and go skiing with my brothers. Come back on Monday, observe the empty desks, and think: "They weren't really accomplishing much anyway."
T minus 2 weeks	I go skiing again this weekend, this time alone. Stay awake until 3:30 A.M. in a cheap hotel room, thinking. I have to make a choice between designing memory boards and doing diagnostic programming. If we were just free of the VCs [venture capitalists], we could cut the deadwood, move into a cheap building, and go for it. Like the old days.
T minus 1 week	I have a conversation with one of the many headhunters swarming like sharks around our company: Headhunter: "Many possibilities if you leave." Me: "I am presently employed and will stay committed." Headhunter: "You should leave while you still have psychological momentum. Get out while you are still on top. Don't let yourself be carried along by situations beyond your control."
T minus 3 days	The big man from the VCs tells everyone there may be a layoff. We know on Friday. Our president is no longer around, due to a "conflict of interest."
T minus 1 day	Conversation with my boss. "This hurts me more than anybody. We had it all—the ideas, the people, the money, the brainpower. It was management problems, pure and simple, that brought us down." This from a man who worked six months of 60-hour weeks to do the initial technical work on the product.
T day	The venture capitalist tells us our company is being dismantled. Thanks us all for our efforts. I feel relief. I can say: "I was hard core, right down to the end. I didn't let anyone down. On a world economic scale, there is no need for another word-processor company. All the effort and resources can go into some endeavor that will amount to something. Anyway it's all over now. Finished."
T plus 1 hour	I walk around our darkened manufacturing floor, turning off the machines running my early version of the diagnostic software. A gesture of finality. Two realizations strike me: It's suddenly unimportant whether or not the machines are tested, and my diagnostic software will probably die, along with most of the other technology, because it's the people that made it go.

T plus 3 hours	By now, 90 percent of the people have left. I clean out my desk last. Say good-by, really sad and depressed. My truck won't start. Very bummed. Remember that I left my lights on in the morning. Have to get a jump. What an exit.
T plus 8 hours	My first impulse after depositing the final $2,200 pay check: Hell with it. Plan A is to head for the snow and go skiing.
T plus 1 day	Jesus Christ! I've got to find a job!
T plus 2 days	A feeling of real emptiness, of not having any meaningful goals. No purpose.
T plus 3 days	First job interview today. This one with a former competitor, arranged by a friend who respected my work.
T plus 21 days	On the sixth interview, I score. This one really looks good. A hefty salary boost. Back to work next week. Think I'll go skiing to celebrate.

Working conditions—competition, the importance of being first to market a new product, peer pressure—encourage marathon "pushes." Mammoth give-it-all efforts to develop a new product are ways a company demonstrates its aggressiveness and validates its claim as a real "comer." Employees can get wrapped up in this team spirit, allow nothing in their lives but work, turned on to being part of a team that makes a supreme effort. They can do it once, maybe twice, but not more than that. Especially if a marathon effort doesn't succeed. Then they burn out, like the circuits with which they work.

Several competing companies will each mount a supreme effort to reach the same goal; only one will be first. For the rest there is questioning of whether the tremendous outpouring of effort and energy was worth it. The cost is burnout of key employees, often at an early age. Charles Peddle, president of Victor Technologies, his fifth start-up in a dozen years, said: "I put my three VPs in the hospital within the past two years, and three of the top four officers in Victor lost their families through divorce in the past year. Suddenly you wake up and realize your kids are two or three years older, and one of them is in trouble. If it costs ten years of your life for every year you are president of the United States, each start-up in Silicon Valley costs you five years."[30]

Three engineers in their mid-thirties discussed "pushes" over salad and a sandwich at an industrial park deli. According to one, "That stuff is for young guys who don't know better. I did it, but

I don't want to do it again. What would I get out of it? More money? Probably not. I can't spend time with my kids and go sailing on weekends if I get involved in a 'push.' It's for young guys who don't have anything else to do."[31]

Burnout can occur in any job in any industry, not just high-tech. But burnout is especially characteristic of work in the Valley. Here it happens fast, hitting people while they are still young. What happens to these people is something of a mystery. The industry is new and there has not been time for the full impact of burnout to be determined, but it is definitely a casualty factor in Silicon Valley.

The final step in many Silicon Valley careers is "dropping off the edge." No one really expects to leave the microelectronics industry, but it does happen. Sometimes a decisive event occurs—a layoff or a merger of companies which leaves some employees out in the cold. More commonly something happens which may not seem that important at the time—assignment to a different job, being moved to a different building out of the mainstream, or getting a new supervisor who is difficult to work for. The employee may attempt to cope with the new unsatisfactory work situation, but eventually there comes a parting of ways. The employee is out of work and must summon the energy to try once again to act enthusiastic about commitment to a company that will probably dump him, or her, when things go bad.

A drop-out pattern occurs that is fairly predictable. First the employee decides not to work full-time. It may be possible to arrange a half-time position with a company, or to work on specific assignments on a part-time basis. But the unsettling gnawing feeling that things aren't working out continues; the job isn't as rewarding as it is supposed to be. A next step is for the employee to become an independent consultant (almost a Valley euphemism for someone who isn't working full-time). Silicon Valley is full of consultants; many are engineers who worked for several companies and are well-acquainted. Some have specialized expertise that is much in demand. Others were laid off some time ago and will consult on almost any issue. They keep active by lining up deals, maintaining old contacts, and postponing the time when, inevitably, they drop over the edge. And then one day you realize that they aren't around anymore.

The long hours and dedication to work required in Silicon Valley make sense in light of the rewards that are offered. But Valley successes share an invisible and powerful contribution from luck. The winners were "there" at the right time; they knew the right people; the economy was ready for their product. The more typical case is someone just as bright and just as dedicated, but one step out of phase with luck. Unlike Steve Jobs, the millions did not flow in for these entrepreneurs. Their dreams did not come true. Why does someone like Jobs or Sanders or Bushnell make it while others do not? To dream great dreams is to invite great disappointments. And Silicon Valley is the land of both.

The Silicon Valley work ethic may be the wave of the future. It is functional in an information society where high-technology plays an increasingly vital role. However if the work ethic that dominates high-tech industry is a model for the future, serious issues with far-reaching implications are raised.

Meritocracy is a positive side of the Silicon Valley work ethic: The single important criterion in determining success is work performance. But there is also a sinister side to the work ethic—one is left with few resources and little self-esteem when one's job is pulled away. The same forces that combined to produce the microelectronics industry, highlighted as the shining example of American innovation and entrepreneurial success, also can produce work-obsessed technocrats with a limited life experience and a stunted human understanding.

9

Lifestyles

"The only important thing is how someone does the job. If she's a good tech writer and plays around, she's a good tech writer. If he's a good design engineer and not interested in women at all, that doesn't matter either. Can she write, can he design, or program, or whatever? That's all that counts."
Mark Larsen, manager, Intel Corporation, 1982

SILICON VALLEY is the home of some colorful characters. Don Hoefler, himself not exactly a colorless figure, calls the Valley "Disneyland North."[1] Flamboyant entrepreneurs, men who lost fortunes and then made them again, and competent executives live alongside computer freaks, hackers, and super-specialists from exotic research worlds.

Silicon Valley is also home for many more people who are completely normal—and about as exciting as old shoe leather. Engineers, essential to the Valley, are neither flamboyant nor are they anti-social. Most are very much "average people," often from the Midwest (for example, Bob Noyce is from smalltown Iowa and Jerry Sanders is from Chicago). When these technologists first came to Silicon Valley, they had short haircuts and a straight lifestyle. California soon begins to have an effect—as the hair gets longer, different lifestyles emerge. The high personal commitment to entrepreneurial activity takes a toll on family life. The basic change, of being married to one's work, brings on a set of alternatives in how people live.

Living together without marriage was at one time an alternative open mainly to young, permissive people. No longer. "Lots of people here are living together and that's fine. We wouldn't look down on somebody for living together. It's normal," says a Silicon Valley observer. While living together is hardly unique to Silicon Valley, what is unusual is the large number of men and women in their thirties, forties, and fifties who choose this alternative. Many have been married, in some cases more than once, and the pain of divorce inhibits them from establishing another formal relationship. General acceptance of living together, without negative sanctions from friends or business associates, opens this alternative to people who would not otherwise consider it. Presidents of companies, executives, and managers are as likely to live with someone as are their college-aged children. Executives elsewhere in the country may want to live with someone, but cannot risk the possible harm to their careers caused by their colleagues' or corporate displeasure. Silicon Valley is highly tolerant of such alternatives.

Another common living arrangement is two or more unmarried people, men and women, sharing a house or apartment. House-sharing is usually a convenient response to the housing crunch and often those sharing the house have limited personal contact and no sexual intimacy.

One might expect affairs to flourish in tolerant Silicon Valley, but most high-achievers bent on success devote their time and energy to work, not the opposite sex. As one engineer observed: "To be honest, I see relatively few affairs among engineers over thirty. There is too damn much work to be done to fool around. You just don't have time for a two-hour lunch with some sweetie. There are plenty of good-looking women and lots of opportunities, but at work you are interested in doing the job, not hustling. And you're always at work."

Rumors abound about certain line supervisors who sleep with women working for them on the line. But generally it is considered poor form to mix sex with work. Personal lives are kept separate from professional lives. Toward others' affairs the Silicon Valley attitude is one of tolerance, as is illustrated by this comment from a manager: "If I learned that the president of our company was sleeping with somebody and had been for years, I really wouldn't give a damn. That's his life. He'd better watch his p's and q's in the corporate area, and I'd better do the same. But if he wants to sleep with somebody, he's a big boy and that's his choice."

Silicon Valley is full of young people, many unmarried. They flock to singles bars, which provide an easy way for gregarious, well-dressed men and women to meet each other. Silicon Valley also has an unusually large number of computer freaks, "space-cadets," and hackers. People who sit at a terminal writing computer code for ten hours are in love with their computer. They don't go to the singles bars and fool around.

A lifestyle alternative not widely accepted in Silicon Valley is homosexuality. In actuality, Valley homosexuality may be widespread, but unlike the tolerance for alternative sexual life-styles involving men and women, there is less approval of the gay lifestyle. A sales engineer in a computer peripherals firm told us that in his work group of thirty people, "There's one guy who might be gay but that's not proven. Even if he were gay, I don't think it would be a big deal. Lots of people are strange in other ways." However, the more common attitude is that being gay in Silicon Valley is a serious career limitation. The wife of a finance manager stated: "A gay executive would not be respected in Silicon Valley. He would not make it. Period."

Silicon Valley accepts change in personal lifestyles, although sometimes with difficulty. Barbara, a personnel representative at Hewlett-Packard, told us: "I was talking to a man in his middle fifties today. He was divorced from his first wife when he was forty and has been living with a second woman for nine years. He was raised a Catholic and although he dated lots of women after his divorce, he said that it really bothered him to be living with this woman. It is hard to get rid of old feelings."[2] Midwestern puritanism fades slowly in trendy California. Silicon Valley people are definitely aware that their lifestyles are changing and they accept the changes, at times reluctantly. However their flexibility regarding lifestyles reflects the dominant Silicon Valley attitude that the only real consideration is work performance. Nothing else matters, unless it affects work.

Divorces outnumber marriages in Santa Clara County today.[3] The divorce rate in Silicon Valley is even higher than the rate for California as a whole, and California's rate is 20 percent above the U.S. average. In fast-growing Silicon Valley firms, people find that keeping up with their work means they have no time for people. Jim, an engineer and divorced, told us: "You have to work at it very, very hard to stay married in this kind of environment because there are so many distractions. Like work."[4]

Betsy's divorce illustrates the family problems resulting from high job mobility. Now in her late forties and the ex-wife of an engineering manager, she explained her reactions toward her husband and his career: "Bob could never hold down a job. As soon as he got one, he started looking around for something better. He was never satisfied. When my father retired he had been with the company twenty-seven years and that's the way it's supposed to be. Bob always said that he would never retire from anyplace. Well, what is he going to do? What were the rest of us supposed to do?" That kind of devotion to work is hard for spouses with a traditional orientation to understand. Betsy said: "A job is something you are supposed to do but then want to get away from. You are supposed to be happy to quit at five and come home. But when five came, Bob just kept on working."[5] For the success-motivated engineer, job performance may crowd out family relations as the most important thing in life. A husband observed: "The man may be getting so turned on to what he is doing at work that it threatens the other person. It's not necessarily sexual, although I'm sure that is there too. Engineers may just find their work more interesting than their spouse."

Many Silicon Valley wives met their engineer-husbands in college or at work soon after graduation. The future wife probably moved to Northern California to work and perhaps had a job for several years before marriage. This usual pattern indicates that most Silicon Valley wives attended college and a large proportion are college graduates. Most do not have family or relatives living in Silicon Valley and as a consequence do not participate in established charities or activities that may have involved their family for generations.

Couples who met in college probably never expected to end up in Silicon Valley. The college coed probably did not take many science courses and almost certainly never studied electronics. Unlike other industries with well-defined and familiar products like automobiles or soap, Silicon Valley companies and their products are mysterious. The technology is difficult to grasp without an understanding of basic concepts of science and physics.

Silicon Valley engineers are busy developing gee-whiz products that were unknown when they or their wives were in college. As the technology becomes more complex, it is increasingly difficult to describe a product or a manufacturing process to wives and families. So many Silicon Valley wives are strangers to the high technology that their husbands love.

Silicon Valley wives often tune out, concluding that the technology is not particularly interesting. Bev is married to a manufacturing engineer now at National Semiconductor, who has worked for four other semiconductor companies in the Valley. As she put it: "Electronics, the technology, is not that interesting to me. The wives really don't understand the product or what it actually does. I don't think it matters." Engineers often state that their wives are not really interested in what they make; therefore it is pointless to talk about the technology. Bev's husband Mike said: "I don't talk about work at home. Bev would not be interested. If I use this dopant, or that dopant, so what? Unless it is something you are interested in, you just don't care."[6]

Many wives, frustrated in their attemps to grasp the technology, turn instead to understanding interpersonal relationships in the company. Many women have developed this skill very well and their insights can be a valuable asset to an engineer-husband. One Silicon Valley wife keeps track of other employees in the company and their current positions, analyzes office dynamics, and knows the general job tasks that her husband performs. She doesn't grasp the technology, but she is very aware of her husband's position in the corporate hierarchy; in many cases she is as knowledgeable as her husband about corporate politics. Often she gives strategic advice to her husband about the best response to a situation. In general wives feel confident of their abilities in interpersonal relations. Bev commented: "Most of us have a really good understanding of things going on in the office. I try to get involved in understanding interpersonal relationships and I think the other wives do too. I am interested in what my husband does each day and how it fits into everything else. For example, is he the man in the middle? Does his boss support him by passing on information to him? Or does he withhold information? I know exactly where he stands."

The high job mobility among Silicon Valley engineers directly affects their wives. As the husbands move from company to company, wives also transfer their allegiance. Like the engineers, no group of wives stays together very long. Knowing all the wives one year means nothing the next. Constant job-changing ensures that virtually every time wives are together, the group of women is different. It is inevitable in an industry where 30 percent of employees job-hop every year.

The only real opportunity for wives to meet each other is at work-related parties. Because of high turnover, many wives do not find these parties particularly fun. People who work together at the office are relaxed and have a good time because they know each other and have work interests in common. Marion is the wife of a regional sales manager for Atari. She stated that at the typical party, "Everybody is trying to be sociable and friendly. And you are particularly trying to be sociable to the wife of the boss. But if the boss changes, it's hard to figure out who the boss's wife is."[7]

A pattern of stages in Silicon Valley marriages occurs so frequently that it is predictable. The first phase begins when an engineer enters the industry, fresh out of college, perhaps newly married. He comes to Silicon Valley in an excited flush of expectancy. The technology he finds is far beyond what he studied in college. He sees a way to apply his theoretical knowledge in new products. He watches others doing similar work, hears stories of fortunes being made, and begins to dream about his own possibilities. His wife also realizes the rich potential in Silicon Valley and wants success. Both husband and wife make a commitment to achieve their goals. But as the years pass, the high cost of this commitment becomes evident: long hours, little time together, stress, a fast-paced life. But the rewards are lucrative, the life is exciting, and they continue in the Valley lifestyle.

The couple matures and reaches stage two. Perhaps fifteen years have passed and they realize just how tough Silicon Valley's demands are. The pressures increase. For the engineer, the thrill of working long hours and of racing to meet imminent deadlines begins to fade. The wife who shared a commitment years ago has since decided that her husband's career is not a sufficient incentive for her to live much of her life alone. The common goals agreed to by husband and wife are no longer common. One or the other decides to leave, they divorce, the wife retains custody of the children for a few years until they are on their own, then it's all over.

Ann is a native of Silicon Valley. She went to school here, met her first husband at San Jose State, was divorced after eight years of marriage, and met her second husband through her work as a Valley sales rep. She is conversant with the technology, knows Silicon Valley like the back of her hand, and shares its ethics and values. Ann notices basic differences between her friends and what she calls "traditional" wives (middle-aged women who came from outside the Valley). A common practice among these "traditional" wives is to prepare dinner but not eat until the husband comes home so that the family can be together. Ann told us: "My attitude is, if he's late, and if he he didn't call in advance to tell me, I go ahead and eat dinner. Some people act as if a basic fact of life is to wait until your husband comes home—whenever that is—and then you can eat. I don't believe in that anymore. It doesn't work here."[8]

Many wives have never been in the building where their husbands work, often because of prohibitions against industrial spying and theft that limit entry to all but a few. "I feel very removed from his job, almost forcibly removed. For example, I cannot go into the facility to say hello because I would have to be signed in. I feel the company wants to keep me and my personal identity out," stated one wife. But there are some advantages to this form of corporate separation. Unlike wives of many American executives, Silicon Valley wives report little pressure from their husbands or from the corporation to conform to established roles. For example, Ellen said: "I have never felt any pressure to entertain. My husband would never ask me to come home from work and start fixing food for a bunch of his business contacts."[9]

A recent survey of wives of corporate executives in American industry at large reported that 75 percent of the wives were 50 years of age or older, more than 80 percent had been married 20 years or more, and only 16 percent were employed outside the home. In contrast, wives of Silicon Valley executives are younger, not married as long, and the majority are working.[10]

Ultimately it is the *time* required by a fast-track career that takes its toll on Silicon Valley families. Many fathers leave the house at 6:30 A.M. to get to work, so there is no contact with the children in the morning. The evening commute can take an hour, so the father may not return home until 7:30 or 8:00. And if there is a drink after work at the Cow Girl Bar, it may be later.

For most families, the only time to be together is in the evening. Ellen and Dennis, a finance expert, have four children. Ellen tries to get the family together for dinner. "I always make the kids wait to eat until he gets home, which is hard on them. Then there is a mad dash to get the kids to take a bath and be in bed by 8 because of school tomorrow. There is never any quiet, peaceful time for us as a family."[11] A more common pattern is described by Beth; she and her husband, a regional sales manager, seldom eat together. "The kids and I eat at our regular hour and Dick's dinner stays in the oven. Then I keep the kids at the table and read to them. Dick comes home about 7:30 and usually is really fatigued. He eats, plays with the kids a few minutes, and then they go to bed."[12] Usually he brings work home with him (as many Silicon Valley men do). So fathers miss important events in their children's lives. According to Beth, "It gets to where he doesn't even know that much about his children, who their friends are, what their interests are. This is a sad situation. He doesn't take the time or make the effort to get to know his own children."

It is not surprising, therefore, that relations between fathers and children are distant. Connie does not have children herself, but her husband Peter has two children from a previous marriage. "He was divorced from his first wife when his daughter was five and his son was three. The break-up with that wife was attributable partly—no primarily—to his work. He has not maintained close contact with his children during the eleven years since the divorce."[13]

Young children may idolize their dads. They are told their father isn't home because he is doing important things at work where people can't get along without him. As young children, they accept this explanation. However, as these youngsters reach adolescence, they form their own conclusions. Ken, the father of a teen-aged daughter, says: "I often spend Friday nights in family-oriented activities. I drive my daughter to games and pick her up. I do family things like this instead of work-related things. On Friday nights."[14]

As a consequence Silicon Valley mothers are expected to be

supermoms. They are involved with the kids' athletics like refer-
eeing soccer games, transporting kids to after-school activities or
to the stables to ride the horse, and to volunteer in school programs. The mother is the mainstay for the family, responsive to
the time demands of Silicon Valley work on her husband. As Ken
recalled, "When I was at Fairchild, my wife used to pack the kids
and the dinner in the car, come down to the office and heat up
the food in the microwave oven there. It was the only way we
could have dinner together."[15]

Silicon Valley women assume roles traditionally assigned to
the father, as well as mother. Ellen, the mother who tries to have
her family eat together, gave an example: "Dennis always gets
home late from work. When I was pregnant with our third child,
I remember sitting on a stool in the front yard, throwing a ball
to our kids so they could practice for soccer. Dennis was never
home before dark, so he never played ball with the kids. He still
isn't around that much."[16]

Not all Silicon Valley fathers are workaholics who rarely see
their children. Some give a high priority to their families. Ken told
us, "My boss has three children and is in his late 30s. He is general manager and could easily spend all his weekends at the office. He doesn't want his kids growing up without him being there.
So he gets to the office at 7, and at 5:30 P.M. he leaves."[17]

The conflict between career success and family life is sum-
marized by Nick, an engineer. "There is plenty of room for a dedicated family man in Silicon Valley, in a small company or in middle management. But probably not in upper management or in a
major firm. When push comes to shove, he won't be there to push
and shove. If you don't give the hours that it takes, you reach a
plateau in the company and you won't go higher."[18]

Two-Career Households

Two-career households are common in Silicon Valley. Over half
of all Silicon Valley women work.[19] Even with the high salaries

paid to engineers, the outrageous cost of housing requires a double income. Sue said the biggest problems with combining two careers is finding time to be together. Her husband and two daughters agree. Tom is a software engineer for National Semiconductor and Sue is a personnel manager at Tandem Computer. They have been married for nine years, a second marriage for both. All four family members have household tasks. The girls clean, help with yard work, and do the laundry. They like the money from two incomes, especially the security it provides in an industry known for layoffs. "We ask ourselves why we're doing it. We take nice trips as a family—to Tahoe, Hawaii, Disneyland. But we don't want to be living like this in ten years."[20] Steve and Marlene Rozett don't go in for the social whirl. Marlene is founder and president of Zyvex Corporation, an electronics subcontractor. Steve is founder and president of Stanford Solar Systems. Their common problem is lack of time. "Our lifestyle is to work, work, work."[21]

When Billye Ericksen, president of Capsco Sales, was engaged to Chan Desaigoudar, president of California Micro Devices, the combined annual sales of their companies were $17 million. They met over work, both were single, and they fell in love. Their firms don't compete; therefore they maintain close business ties. They are on each other's boards of directors and consult on each other's business. They live together in a dream house they bought two years ago. They describe themselves as "fierce competitors" in both business and their personal lives. On a recent golf trip, they played 36 holes of golf every day for six days; Chan ended up only four strokes ahead.[22]

Silicon Valley Kids

Children growing up in Silicon Valley are not typical. In an average U.S. school district of 10,000 students, about twelve children are considered "highly gifted" (IQs greater than 145). One Silicon Valley school district with 12,000 students has more than 500 children in this category,[23] a rate about 40 times the national average. Silicon Valley children come from highly educated families, in which high-tech talk is part of a rich intellectual atmosphere. Most schools have computers in the classrooms. Kids use the family computer at home and are extremely knowledgeable about electronics.

Recently children from first grade through high school submitted 500 projects to the annual Santa Clara County Valley Science and Engineering Fair. The list of projects included the Opto-Acoustic Microscope, submitted by teenager Martin Bodo of Los Altos High School. He got the idea for his project from his summer job at National Semiconductor (a prize he won at the previous year's fair). As Bodo describes his wires, generators, lasers, and rotary drums, "This device has great application for the semiconductor industry. Basically it generates an optical beam, creates a thermal wave, and allows you to look through thin films—like the aluminum layer of integrated circuits—without doing any damage."[24] Bodo intends to be an electrical engineer.

Many children, both boys and girls, seek to emulate their parents. They set high standards and work hard to achieve their goals and be like their parents. Many will make it. For other Silicon Valley kids, success is elusive. Pressure for success grows as they enter adolescence, a time when drugs and alcohol are easily available.

Drinking problems among Silicon Valley teenagers are rapidly growing. According to the National Council on Alcoholism, one in eight teenagers in Silicon Valley has a drinking problem. A 1981 survey of San Jose area teenagers found that 80 percent of students between 11 and 17 consumed alcohol and that 12 percent of students used alcohol regularly. In 1981, 1,357 liquor law violations involved teenagers in Silicon Valley, whereas in 1976 there were only 767 such violations. Of the 1981 violations, 16 were felony drunk-driving violations involving an injury or death.[25] In 1983 the Santa Clara County Chapter of the National Council on Alcoholism and the Junior League of San Jose launched a program to combat alcoholism among children under age 12. Roberta Meter, a pioneer in youth alcohol programs, states that 40 percent of fourth graders have either used or abused alcohol. Program sponsors hope that by starting early, the potential for alcoholism among older adolescents may be reduced.[26]

In 1956 William H. Whyte, Jr.'s book *The Organization Man* was hailed by many as a book of great importance. It described Americans working at jobs in large organizations: the corporation, the university, and government. These jobs provided security and a high standard of living, but required people to relinquish the individualistic hopes and ambitions that had dominated earlier generations.[27]

At the time *The Organization Man* was published, there was no Silicon Valley. High-tech industry had not been born, venture capital was virtually non-existent, and entrepreneurism was dormant. Today, nearly thirty years later, Silicon Valley is the focus of national attention. The contrasts between the life of the Organization Man of the Fifties and the High-Tech Entrepreneur of the Eighties are striking.

Organization Man was family-oriented, with the family defined as a father and mother, married and living together, with three children. They lived in a house in the suburbs, a single-family dwelling, and participated in family-oriented activities on weekends and during free time. Silicon Valley Entrepreneur is likely to choose an alternative to the nuclear family arrangement. Many households are headed by a single parent; other households are headed by married non-parents. The "house" is likely to be a condo or multi-unit dwelling, and, with free time in short supply, family-oriented activities are rare.

Organization Man was dedicated to "groupism," to conforming to social mores. Silicon Valley Entrepreneur shuns conformity and is dedicated to "me-first" individualism. While Organization Man went to lengths to meet the standards important to his peers, Silicon Valley Entrepreneur goes to lengths to flaunt them.

Organization Man was supremely loyal to the organization. If the corporation assigned him to a new task or transferred him to Chicago, if the university urged him to teach different courses, or if the government asked him to enforce new policies, he complied. Silicon Valley Entrepreneur has no loyalty to any company. With luck, he'll spin-off a start-up, or at least get in on the ground floor of someone else's. Everyone is willing to listen to all offers.

Organization Man was mobile. If the corporation transferred him to Keokuk or Tallahassee, he might grumble but would go. If Organization Man did not want to move and was firm about it, the organization found another man. Silicon Valley Entrepreneur stays in Silicon Valley, where everything is happening. Moving to any other location is a big step out of the mainstream. If the company wants Silicon Valley Entrepreneur to move and is firm about it, the Entrepreneur will just find another company.

Organization Man, flying high in the Fifties, has crashed. Will the same thing happen to Silicon Valley Entrepreneur? Some observers think so. Silicon Valley entrepreneurs are classic high-achievers. For this they pay a high personal price. The workaholic disregards basic interpersonal relationships with a wife or husband, children, parents, and friends, and often ignores fundamental issues of purpose. But like it or not, Silicon Valley Entrepreneur is a model for the Eighties.

10

Goodies

"Silicon Valley is absolutely betting on the upside. Most
people do not save money because they don't need to—they
make lots now and will make more in the future. So they
go out and buy expensive clothes and cars and eat out and
party and have a good time. And spending money gives them
something to do besides work."

Stan Thomas, Executive Vice-President for Finance
Hunting Gate Management Company, 1982

AL SHUGART left IBM to form Shugart Associates in 1973, left
Shugart Associates in 1974, and five years later founded Seagate
Technology. When he left Shugart, he was nearly broke and
couldn't sell his stock because the firm was not traded on the public market. He invested in a bar, did some commercial fishing, and
consulted, but mainly he just took it easy. For a time he collected
unemployment payments, but he kept up public appearances by
driving a rented Porsche to the unemployment office. All this
changed in early 1979 when he married Rita, whom Shugart calls
"the ultimate consumer." As he explains it, "I *had* to go back to
work. She has fine tastes. That takes money. Besides, she had
three kids. If we ever move out of this community, the local economy is going to drop."

The day that Seagate Technology went public in 1981, Shugart received $1.2 million for his stock. He spent the money the
same day. He wrote two checks, one to pay off his debts and another to buy Rita a bright red Ferrari. In retrospect, Shugart says

he likes running a high-tech company better than shooting pool. "This is lots more exciting."[1]

John and Toni Manning have been in the Valley for ten years. John, an engineer, has worked at Apple for the last six years. The Mannings have two children and Toni hasn't worked since the birth of their second child. Over the last ten years the Mannings have moved four times, always "moving up." They began in a small condo in Mountain View and now have a rambling four-bedroom house with a pool and hot tub in Los Altos. Things have gone well for the Mannings. Several years ago John took flying lessons and then bought a plane with some friends. When that hobby began to pale, he sold the plane and bought a sailboat, again with friends. Toni is fond of interior design, and has had their house redecorated three times. The family goes to Hawaii or Mexico every year during the winter, and to Tahoe during the summer. They have two stylish cars, a complete set of video games, and a home computer.

John earns a nice income, but even so, how do they manage their high style of living? John explained: "Most of us make lots of money and spend it. We're absolutely betting on the upside. We expect our incomes to continue to increase. In addition to salaries, we try to build up capital through stock options or real estate deals. Jobs are easily available, so we don't need to worry about saving as much as some people."[2]

In 1982 the median buying power in Santa Clara County was $29,239, highest of the 305 metropolitan areas in the United States. The county's per capita buying power was $11,376, second in the nation. Eighteen percent of the county's households had annual incomes of more than $50,000; only 3 percent of households had incomes below $8,000.[3] Eleven major shopping malls of 250,000 square feet or more encircle the non-factories of Silicon Valley, as well as scores of smaller shopping centers. From these malls come the "in" possessions—electronic entertainment equipment, ski vans, waterbeds, motor homes, jewelry, personal computers, and hot tubs.

Although not everyone can rush out and buy a bright red Ferrari, Silicon Valley people purchase lots of goodies, especially high-tech goodies. Cars are a favorite. Some claim that Silicon Valley engineers are overgrown farm boys who long for souped-up hot rods. What they buy instead are exotic cars. Prestige autos with price tags from $55,000 to $110,000 are hot items. Twice as many Lotuses (price: $44,000) were sold by Loose Imported Cars in Palo Alto than at any of the other 35 Lotus dealerships in the United States.[4] According to owner Jim Loose, some car buyers don't write checks or use cash. They purchase their Rolls-Royces by calling their banks and shifting $50,000 or so into Loose's account. The Los Gatos Ferrari dealer was second in sales in the United States (behind the dealer in Beverly Hills), until he went bankrupt in the recession of 1982.[5]

Like other goodies, cars are one way of "keeping score." Nick Larsen, a manager at Exxon Enterprises, tells of the morning he drove down Central Expressway in his Porsche 914 with the top down, feeling like a king. Along came his neighbor, Brad, a manager at Spectra Physics, in his new Targa. Nick good-naturedly relinquished his position of "King of the Expressway" to Brad, who laughed and sat a little more erect in the driver's seat. At the next stop light, up roared Jerry Sanders of AMD, white hair flowing, in his white Rolls Royce. Brad and Nick looked at each other and broke into hysterics. One-up-manship had triumphed again.[6]

Silicon Valley cars can be souped-up sports cars, luxury sedans, or "ordinary" gas guzzlers, but they all have one thing in common: They are loaded with options designed to tug at the heart of gadget-happy technocrats. One wonders whether it is the car or the options that most entice the engineer-buyer. Stereo tape systems, dashboards that look like airplane control panels, antennae that zoom up and down automatically, genteel beepers and raucous buzzers—these cars have it all. Technologists not only like making the goodies, they love to use them.

However the most popular goodies in this high-tech community are electronic consumer products: personal computers, video recorders, home communication systems, video games.

"The Strip" in Silicon Valley is different from the usual notion conjured up by this term. The Strip is a section of El Camino Real, running from Palo Alto to Santa Clara, with the nation's first and longest line-up of computer retail stores. Back in the "old days" of 1975, the first computer stores were basically hobby shops, and the low-rent district was perfect for their low-budget craft-and-hobby customers. But recently, the Strip has gone "uptown," with chain stores threatening to drive the mom-and-pop computer merchants out of business. With at least one computer store in nearly every block on the Strip, competition is fierce.

Consumers along the Strip are likely to be engineers who work with computers all day, and may design hardware or software. Consequently, salespersons in these stores must know what they are selling. Scott Anderson of Jade Computer Products observed that the staff in the Strip's stores are far more knowledgeable than those in the rest of the country. Digital Deli, one of the oldest stores, even has a salesperson who specializes in certain types of software such as real estate property management programs and word-processing programs.[7]

No one knows exactly how many households in Silicon Valley have personal computers, but if demand for computer-related services is any indication, the number is very high, perhaps 20 or 25 percent (as compared to 8 percent nationally). The Santa Clara County Library System lends computer time as well as books. A coin-operated Apple rents for $1 for twenty minutes, and allows patrons to play games, prepare tax returns, and calculate budgets. The computers are rented from Micro Timesharing, a firm founded by 18-year-old Kim Cohan and his 17-year-old partner. Cohan built his first computer when he was 13, and said that the waiting list for his computer installations stands at 170 libraries across the country.[8]

If you don't want to go to the library to use a computer, or if the status of having your own computer at home is tempting, you can rent a computer by the month. Don Bartel, founder of Rent-A-Computer in Palo Alto, hopes that renting a computer will become as popular as renting cars or vacation condos. He has more than 100 Apples available for monthly rental and the demand is so high they are always booked.[9] Or, if you don't want to go to the store, it will come to you. Computer parties, similar to Tupperware's, are the latest fad in which a company makes a sales presentation for a personal computer in your home to you and your friends.[10]

With all these home computers, it should come as no surprise that community computer networks are springing up at a phenomenal rate. In early 1982 there were an estimated thirty networks connecting computer owners in Silicon Valley. Many provide electronic message centers with want ads, messages for specific people, questions, or general comments. There are also special interest networks: Micro Smut gives X-rated messages; there are two networks for gays; and Winer's Living Bulletin Board users are writing an interactive novel about Dripkin, a slightly retarded young man who lives in a world of adventure. Some users form friendships through these computer networks. J.Q. Johnson, a Stanford student, has "a good working relationship" with Don, a San Diego computer scientist whom he has never met in person. Steve Garber, a computer consultant who has "met" many people through computer networks, said: "You'll find that what is on most people's minds is nothing but high-tech."[11]

Not all the networks are fun and innocence. One network in Santa Clara—8BBS—was raided by the FBI and police. The network was allegedly used by individuals in different parts of the country to make toll-free long distance calls and for breaking into computer systems. The operator of the network wasn't surprised at the raid: "I knew the FBI and telephone company security were logging on our system regularly. I would see mention on other bulletin board systems that the line was under surveillance, which was fine with me."[12]

Status symbols in high-tech culture are not the traditional American symbols. In some ways, this discrepancy between old and new characterizes the difference between the established industrial society and the emerging information society. According to *Washington Post* columnist Diana McLellan, some of Washington's status symbols are a chauffeur at taxpayers' expense, a bugged phone, home computers, use of a Presidential box at Kennedy Center, and a Top Secret security clearance. *San Jose News* columnist Leigh Weimers pointed out that in Silicon Valley, "Having a home computer and a security clearance are ordinary in the extreme. Status symbols in the Valley include an earth station [antenna] for satellite TV reception, lights on your tennis courts, playing video games before their public release, a 10-year-old mortgage, and not having to drive to the office (chauffeured or otherwise) to do your work."[13]

Housing—Outrageous!

One image of Silicon Valley is that it is a land of plentiful jobs, mild climate, sleek cars, beautiful people, and lots of goodies. This dream of the good life is very attractive, and people are migrating to Northern California in increasing numbers. The population of Santa Clara County quadrupled in three decades from 290,547 in 1950 to an estimated 1,256,200 people in 1980.

As the population grew, the demand for housing increased along with it. Initially, housing needs could be satisfied by sacrificing the thousands of acres of orchards, vineyards, and fields in the then agricultural Valley. In 1950 there were only 78,000 housing units in the county and lots of space. By 1980 some 466,000 housing units had been constructed and still the need for housing was not met.[14] Jobs are generated at such an explosive pace that housing construction lags far behind. The diminishing supply of both land and sewer capacity thwarts new housing construction. By 1990 the number of people working in Santa Clara County but unable to live there will be over 100,000.[15] Lots of people and the severe shortage of housing create Silicon Valley's major problem: The Great Housing Dilemma.

Housing, in a word, is outrageous! The average price of a single family home leaped from $43,000 in 1974 to $101,000 in 1979, an increase of 300 percent. Average monthly payments have gone from $230 to $880.[16] Within 20 miles of the microelectronics job centers there is not a house available for under $120,000.[17] The most affluent engineers and executives live in the foothills of Los Altos Hills, Saratoga, Monte Sereno, and Los Gatos. These cities average about one dwelling per acre; Los Altos Hills averages about two acres. The houses are virtually all single-family homes, and the median family income in these four cities is 50 percent higher than the Santa Clara County average.[18] In general these homes are large luxury houses with such features as "innovative bathrooms, the vast ones with spa tubs and adjoining private sundecks; tennis and racquetball courts; exercise rooms; lots of closets; a three-car or better garage; and building design aimed at effortless entertainment and plenty of floor space."[19]

In response to the continuing demand for housing, one major homebuilder in Silicon Valley has moved to the construction of "economy" homes to ease the price of buying a house. These economy homes are detached dwellings of 1,200 to 1,700 square feet, placed on smaller than usual lots. The average price of the economy home is $175,000,[20] considered cheap in Silicon Valley.

In order to recruit employees to Silicon Valley today, firms must pay housing-related inducements. A 1982 survey of CEOs of Silicon Valley microelectronics firms disclosed that 22 percent of the firms paid $50,000 or more in relocation assistance beyond normal moving expenses. Four percent of the firms paid over $100,000. For middle managers, 73 percent paid from $10,000 to $50,000. Even technical personnel received from $10,000 on up from 57 percent of the firms. At those rates, even the most successful companies can't afford to relocate very many individuals to Silicon Valley. That's the basic reason why present-day expansion of the Silicon Valley microelectronics firms is mainly occurring elsewhere in the United States.

Gold in the Garbage

Electronics firms flush their wastes down the drains like other companies. However, debris from these companies is not like other industrial waste. The precious metals that this exotic garbage contains can be valuable, a fact not lost on several Silicon Valley cities. In 1979 Palo Alto began a waste-recovery program, figuratively going through the garbage with a fine tooth comb. Sewage sludge is incinerated and metals are recovered from the ash. A firm was hired to extract gold, silver, and copper from the garbage. About four ounces of gold and ten ounces of silver are recovered daily. After the program had been in effect for three years, gold going down the drains of electronic firms had given the city $1.5 million in revenue.[21] Where else could that happen but in Silicon Valley?

Spare Time, What Spare Time?

Legends of the Valley's early days describe the bashes where everyone who worked together would go to someone's apartment for a party. A relative old-timer (now in his forties) reminisced: "The parties were full of young people and it seemed like college. Three or four people in their thirties and the rest younger. Everyone in the department would be invited. It tended to be young secretaries, often divorced, young professionals, and engineers, and then a few older people who were bosses. There were kegs of beer and food. Spouses and families were never included. There was one wife who came every Friday, though, because she didn't trust her husband. It was fun—something to do on a Friday night. Things have calmed down a lot since then. The industry is older, and so are the people. There aren't the rowdy parties there used to be."[22]

Private parties are still the favorite, but now official company parties are common, one for the Christmas holidays and usually a summer picnic. Large corporations rent an auditorium, hire a band or two (usually rock bands, since that is what the largely young crowd prefers), and serve dinner followed by dancing and entertainment. The president and vice-presidents make the prescribed rounds, going to all the tables and shaking hands. In the summer the company rents a park and holds a family-oriented picnic with games for the kids and hot dogs and soft drinks. Some companies own their picnic spot; for example, Hewlett-Packard has a 200-acre park in the Santa Cruz Mountains for its employees.

With the industry's demonstrated respect for individual technical ability, putting in an appearance at a party is not as important as in other industries. Engineer Karl Harrington commented: "In manufacturing we have lots of going-away parties and after work we go to the local bar and wish someone luck. That happens about once a month, but attendance is up to you. It's no big deal if you don't go."[23]

One of the few distinctions drawn in the normally egalitarian Valley concerns the party habits of the highly gregarious salespeople versus the parties of all others. Salesforces have the reputation of throwing grandiose parties that make the parties of other groups pale in comparison, especially those of the more "brainy" designers, who prefer smaller groups. A group of thirty design engineers is a BIG party, but sales is something different, thanks to generous entertainment budgets and the intrinsically outgoing nature of salespeople.

Mark Larsen is in sales at Intel, and he described a surprise birthday party thrown for his boss two levels up: "The party was a Western party, and there was a country band. There were about seventy people, but it wasn't crowded because the house was big. There was an open bar and a big buffet. People wore whatever they wanted, but everyone was casual. All the people at the boss's level were invited, and all the people who worked for him for two levels down. I never know for sure who all the people are because they come and go so fast."[24]

Life in the fast track can become addictive and slowing down is not necessarily a pleasant kind of decompression. Judy Wheeler, a sales representative at Signetics, mused: "There are times on the weekends when I get bored because I don't have lots of things planned. I tell myself, this is ridiculous. I'm used to the Valley's fast pace, and I enjoy it. When things slow down, I really go nuts."[25]

None would agree with this statement more than the local travel agencies and vacation planners. Predictably, Silicon Valley people prefer active, sports-oriented vacations, often with some kind of physical challenge. Scuba-diving, tennis camps, and skiing are popular; golf isn't considered active enough. Vacations usually are short and fast—a week at a time, two weeks at the very most. Mini-vacations of three or four days are increasingly popular, especially when they are combined with a business trip. The ultimate mini-vacation is a quick trip to Europe (on company expense).

The workaholic's one-dimensional focus is one reason why individuals don't go on longer vacations. Mark Larsen of Intel gave another reason: "They don't go on long vacations because they consider themselves indispensable. And in some cases they are. I know people unable to take vacations because there isn't anybody they can turn their job over to. In some ways, it's guaranteed job security. If you don't let anybody know what you do, then nobody else can do it. There's a lot of that. Intel put a sabbatical policy into place for exactly this reason. It will force everybody to have someone trained who can do their job. It's really important for the company that our people not be indispensable."[26]

Hobbies are not all that popular, perhaps because there is

not much leisure time. After a full workday, some engineers head for an exercise class or a game of handball. Others just collapse. Jim, a thin-film engineer for National Semiconductor: "It's not unusual for people to put in so much energy that they are drained at the end of the day. My boss talks about having a real high energy level at the start of the week and by Wednesday he's slowing down. When I get home, I'm just plain tired. I watch TV, a lot of dumb shows. I'm usually so tired and hassled from dealing with people all day, I want to have some stupid thing coming at me where I don't have to pay attention or think."[27]

The most popular leisure-time hobbies are electronic. Karl Harrington commented: "I know guys who build computers all day for a living and then go home and build computers for pleasure all night. My friend Jim knows everything there is to know about software. For fun he built a computer by soldering all those little wires, which was completely strange and kind of wonderful for him. A hardware person thinks it's dumb to solder wires, but exciting to do the programming. A software person thinks its crazy to do programming, but fun to solder wires. It just depends—the grass is always greener."[28]

"Engineers are a special breed. They like to work with their hands, to design machines that work. That's where engineering departs from science. We make things that *work.* So, understandably, when an entrepreneur becomes a millionaire, he often builds himself a pretty nice little shop in his home. Dave Packard has a shop that is fabulous," said Les Hogan of Fairchild.[29]

For some technocrats, inventing in a home workshop is a means of relaxing from a workday of inventing at the company. Silicon Valley has the only subject-classified patent library outside the U.S. Patent Office in Washington, D.C. The patent library in Sunnyvale allows patrons to trace a patent by topic instead of by number, a feature that helps inventors check the originality of their ideas. Patronage of the library runs at 1,400 users per month.[30] The grass roots California Inventors' Council attempts to protect fledgling inventors from potential pitfalls. This coalition of volunteers provides the naive inventor with access to a local network of professional inventors who know the ropes. They advise on how to protect an idea, provide a list of recommended patent attorneys, and answer inventors' questions.[31]

High-Tech, Veggies, and Fitness

Silicon Valley people—men and women—are very concerned with their figures. The men complain about their bulges and paunches as frequently as women, and everyone watches what they eat. The stereotype of a corporate official as an overweight, florid, balding man smoking a cigar and downing a third martini at lunch is not part of Silicon Valley. Wine is much more common than booze, and meat, potatoes, and gravy are shunned in favor of fish, Oriental food, or half a sandwich and salad.

Next to work, physical fitness is the biggest thing in Silicon Valley. Everyone is involved, men and women. Carol Bogert tells about a sales convention that she attended: "At the meeting in Phoenix they had a 10K run at 6:30 in the morning. I wanted to try because everybody else did. There were fifty men and three women. We all ran the race. Some of the people ran only 5K and then dropped out, but most of us finished. It was great, a really big deal."[32]

The mild climate and emphasis on outdoor life account for the hoards of runners that take over the streets of the industrial parks during lunch hours. Many companies and industrial parks have specially designed jogging trails, but the number of joggers quickly exceeds the trails, and they overflow into every street. A common corporate activity is the running club, however loosely formed, and its annual race. An example is the Silicon Valley Striders, formed by a handful of employees at National Semiconductor who were interested in running and physical fitness.[33] Every year they sponsor a one-mile and a 10K race. So do most of the other clubs, with the result that nearly every Sunday morning a group of runners winds its way through an industrial park.

Physical fitness is so important to employees that exercise programs have become a pawn in recruiting. Jerry Beavers coordinates a YMCA exercise program attended by thousands of Silicon Valley workers. "Companies are offering fitness programs to help recruitment. There is peer pressure." More than 4,500 employees participated in Beavers's program last year. The size of his program may be surprising in Silicon Valley where many companies have on-site athletic facilities. But the firms don't have enough space or time to meet their employees' needs. Rolm Corporation, with one of the most elaborate facilities (gymnasium, two racquetball courts, two swimming pools, and two tennis courts, all costing $1.5 million) is a case in point. According to Sam Medford, Rolm's recreation director, there are only eight running classes a week for the 3,000 employees. "We don't have the time or space for more classes; our facilities are full." The YMCA program is provided through five local Y's, and the sessions are scheduled during lunch or right after work. Most classes meet two or three times a week and last from six to ten weeks.[34]

Culture, Or Lack of It

In a hard-hitting editorial, the *San Jose News* stated: "To all outward appearances, Silicon Valley corporations inhabit the 21st century, with the sleekest offices, the smartest computers, and the slickest managerial talent. But when it comes to supporting charities or the arts, the attitude is more what one would expect to find in the executive suite of Ebenezer Scrooge Enterprises, Ltd."[35]

On the average, Silicon Valley firms donate only three-fourths of one percent of their pretax profits, compared to a national average of 1.1 percent. The United Way of Santa Clara County ranked 49th among the top 60 chapters nationwide in donations per capita (with $9.31). It lagged behind such economically depressed areas as Pittsburgh ($16.96); Akron ($14.05); and Newark, N.J. ($10.25). Tandem Computers of Cupertino denied United Way permission to make presentations to its employees. Although Tandem "informed" its employees about the United Way campaign, its 1,000 employees in Santa Clara County gave only $2,700 in 1981. Apple Computer made a corporate donation of $20,000, but only 87 of its 1,354 employees pledged support.[36]

Perhaps the me-first, get-rich-quick mentality that pervades

Silicon Valley is the culprit. Individuals (and corporations) are nouveau riche, flaunting their conspicuous consumption, preening to impress others. With employees and corporations espousing a chew-em-up and spit-em-out attitude, charging after success and profits, many do not consider their obligations to the community. Perhaps corporate giving and community involvement require a maturity that comes only with age. Hewlett-Packard, Santa Clara County's leading contributor, is one of the oldest electronics firms. But there are other mature companies such as California Microwave and Siliconix that don't give to the United Way.[37]

Thomas Vias, executive director of the United Way, says many electronics executives and professionals are blind to community needs. "We have a lot of professional people who live in middle and upper-class neighborhoods like Saratoga and Los Gatos. They drive on well-paved roads to well-landscaped buildings. They don't see blighted areas or come into contact with disadvantaged people."

While in general Silicon Valley's record of corporate giving is negligible, there are bright exceptions. Far ahead of the pack is Hewlett-Packard, the county's largest corporate United Way donor with a gift of $636,907 in 1981. In 1982 H-P donated $15 million throughout the country, $11 million of it in equipment. In addition, the William and Flora Hewlett Foundation donated $13 million. Bill Hewlett, co-founder of H-P, says he really doesn't know why he is a philanthropist. "Maybe I got involved because it is a distinctly American phenomonon. We've got to do it. It's in the national interest." Other high-tech firms with glowing records of giving include Amdahl, Atari, Measurex, IBM, and Syntex.[38]

With minimal civic concern, perhaps it should come as no surprise that cultural activity is also sparse in the Valley. With a population of well-educated, wealthy professionals likely to patronize the arts, it seems strange that an active artistic program is lacking. Possible explanations are the lack of corporate support, competition from nearby San Francisco cultural activities, a general cultural ignorance among engineers and technocrats, and the pull of outdoor activities.

Corporate largesse toward the arts usually involves Silicon

Valley firms with a reputation for philanthropy. In 1982 a furry life-sized Pac-Man walked up to Mayor Diane Feinstein of San Francisco with a donation of $1 million. Atari, manufacturer of Pac-Man video games, thus presented its donation to the Save-the-Cable-Cars campaign.[39] In a less spectacular manner, IBM gave the San Jose Museum of Art a gift of $250,000, and Santa Clara's Triton Museum of Art received a grant of $90,000 from the David and Lucile Packard Foundation.[40] So there are exceptions to the general stinginess of Valley companies regarding the cultural arts.

Silicon Valley individuals express an almost complete lack of concern for social, civic, or charitable activities. An engineer observed: "I don't know anybody who is a member of a political party, or if they are, they never say anything about it. We never talk about politics." The wife of a corporate president commented: "I can't think of anyone among our friends who does community work. But in the typical family where both people are working, there isn't time left over for that sort of thing." The Volunteer Bureau of Santa Clara County reports that their pool of volunteers is very small: "People don't have time anymore. They are all working."

According to some, the one topic discussed even less than civic affairs is religion. Church membership and regular church attendance do not appear to be a high priority for most Silicon Valley families. As one engineer put it: "People don't talk about it. I think most people believe in God or something like that, but they don't go to church. It's just something you don't talk about."

Silicon Valley's Art

With limited artistic activity in Silicon Valley, the most interesting events often occur in non-traditional forms. The Teatro de la Gente and the San Jose Black Theatre Workshop raised the issue of computers and culture in their production of "Electrobucks," a comedy centering on working in an electronics plant.[41] Pat Pfeiffer won an award for her play, "The Feeding," the story of a Silicon Valley family caught up in the race for technological success at the expense of human emotion.[42]

During the late 1970s, pop art showed up in many Silicon Valley publications. Annual reports and advertisements were collected not for the information they contained, but for their art. AMD (Advanced Micro Devices) has long been known for its imaginative promotional campaigns. In 1975 Lawrence Bender designed an abstract circuit tree for the cover of AMD's annual report. It was so attractive that AMD had Bender remove the lettering and create both posters and a limited edition of signed prints that were given as executive gifts. According to Bender, high-tech firms offer graphic designers a degree of freedom unusual in the business world. Much of what the high-tech firms are selling is abstract, something the consumer can't see. As a result the designer is free to use imagination and creativity.[43]

Verbatim Corporation of Sunnyvale, producer of flexible disks for computers, established a $100,000 fund in 1983 for the San Francisco Museum of Modern Art to purchase paintings. In addition to the display of the originals at the museum, Verbatim reproduces 20,000 poster versions of each, to be distributed free to office workers to adorn the walls of their cubicles.[44] Now, when workers look up from a computer terminal, their eyes can rest on posters from the Verbatim Collection.

The Sunnyvale Community Center was among the first to recognize the cultural by-products of the microelectronics industry and highlighted this avant-garde movement in their show, "Tribute to Silicon Valley." The gallery became "a collage of form and functions, symmetry and software, dance and double-density floppy disc drives."[45] David Kroos displayed his silkscreens based on circuit boards given to him by friends in the industry. "The way this industry has been growing and expanding it's only been ten years and already I'm working with antiques." In another room the newest computer graphics were demonstrated by Bryan Ehlers of Apple Computer. He explains that the graphics system is for the person who wants to "free-hand draw, for the design professional to use with space planning. But for fine art? I'm an engineer, and I really don't know."[46] The Helen Euphrat

Gallery at De Anza College in Cupertino also organized a show, "Crossover: An Artech Exhibit," with the purpose of exploring the crossover between art and technology.[47]

So in Silicon Valley, even art (what there is of it) is high-tech. Perhaps that's the way it will be in the information society of the future.

11

Problems in Paradise

"If engineers are the artisans of high-tech society, production operators are its migrant workers."[*]

"Freedom in a commons brings ruin to all."[†]

SILICON VALLEY corporations were a chamber of commerce dream: non-polluting, handsome in appearance, attracting high-income engineers and managers. Until a few years ago Silicon Valley microelectronics companies seemed the ideal kind of industry to have as a neighbor. But in the 1980s cracks began to appear in this happy picture. The quality of life in Silicon Valley was deteriorating. On some days a brownish-orange cloud of smog hung over the southern part of Santa Clara County, created by the auto emissions rising from the jammed traffic on the expressways below. In addition to pollution problems, the theft of semiconductor chips reached major proportions. Further, it became evident that the Valley was a community characterized by extreme socioeconomic inequality. "North County," the jobs belt, is where the high-tech firms are concentrated, where engineers and managers live in nice homes on spacious plots. "South County," centering in San Jose, is home for the skilled manual workers in the microelectronics plants. They are paid low salaries to do monotonous, sometimes dangerous work. Many are Third World women. When viewed from their perspective, Silicon Valley doesn't look idyllic.

*Robert Howard, "Second Class in Silicon Valley," *Working Papers* (1981): 20–31.
†Garrett Hardin, "The Tragedy of the Commons", *Science* 162: (1968): 1243–48.

Crime: Domestic Theft and International Espionage

Semiconductor chips are so diminutive that a handful can easily be slipped into a pocket or a lunchpail and taken right out the door of a fabrication plant. The net result is an estimated $20 million per year in crime. Some of these losses occur by the truckload. In addition to domestic crime, the illegal international trade in stolen silicon chips is a matter of the gravest concern to U.S. federal authorities. Often Russia is on the receiving end of a criminal chain that reaches back to Santa Clara or Sunnyvale, threatening America's electronics defense position. It seems that the Silicon Valley Garden of Eden contains a number of evil serpents.

"The semiconductor firms have their security policies because they are extremely vulnerable to theft. The product is so small and lightweight that it frequently gets stolen. There is a lot of 'shrinkage' in this business. The chips just disappear. Then they show up in the grey market," said Don Hoefler, editor of *Microelectronics News* and a veteran observer of Silicon Valley.[1] Some semiconductor houses give the impression of electronic fortresses: squadrons of armed security guards, televison cameras trained on the company parking lot, paper shredders,and infrared cameras. For instance, Intel has 100 security officers and an annual security budget of $2 million for the 5,000 people employed in Silicon Valley; Amdahl spends $1 million annually and has a security staff of 39 for 3,600 employees.[2]

The Sheriff's Department of Santa Clara County has set up an Organized Crime and Intelligence Unit in order to investigate grey market chips. The county's deputy district attorney, Douglas Southard, confirms the estimate that more than $20 million a year in microelectronics technology and products are being stolen.[3] This figure is undoubtedly conservative because many companies do not even know when a theft has occurred or do not want their customers or the public to know that their security system has been violated. A county task force on high-tech crime has been formed, with each city in the county having its own high-tech crime specialist. In addition to investigating the theft

---

Thanksgiving at Monolithic Memories[9]

The four-day 1981 Thanksgiving vacation had been uneventful for Irwin Federman, president of Monolithic Memories, Inc. On Thursday he ate turkey dinner with thirteen guests at his Saratoga home. On Friday, Federman guided his out-of-town visitors around San Francisco. On Saturday, he did yardwork around his home. Sunday, Federman relaxed watching the San Francisco 49ers defeat the New York Giants on TV. "I thought it was an uneventful weekend. I found out Monday how wrong I was."

Over the Thanksgiving weekend, 529,000 semiconductors worth $3.2 million were stolen from Monolithic's warehouse in Sunnyvale. This theft set a record for semiconductor crime in Silicon Valley. Even though the chips are each very tiny, half a million of them weigh 1.5 tons. Placed end to end, they would be 10 miles long. The chips were state-of-the-art and Russians were immediately suspected of being involved in the crime.

The robbery at Monolithic's Building 3A stumped criminal investigators. The missing semiconductors were packed in 100 boxes, each weighing 30 pounds. They were stored in a chicken-wire cage. The cage was hooked to sophisticated cameras and motion detectors and was tightly locked. A security guard on duty at all times sat 50 feet away, watching two television monitors that took pictures of the area every two seconds. An alarm system was electronically geared to go off if any door of Building 3A was touched. Yet no physical evidence of a break-in was evident to the 30 FBI agents, county sheriff's staff, or city police on the Monday morning after the theft.

The Thanksgiving caper at Monolithic Memories seemed to be the perfect crime. Six months later authorities were able to solve this bizarre theft, when they recovered the 529,000 chips in a storage space at South Lake Tahoe.[10] A Monolithic security guard, Ron Washington, had helped two armed burglars steal the semiconductors by shutting off the electronic alarm system. The boxes of chips were loaded on carts, pushed to a loading dock, placed in a rental truck, and driven off to Lake Tahoe.

All three criminals went to jail and the chips have been returned to Monolithic. Washington said he was "overcome by temptation," and stole the chips because he needed money. His role in the Thanksgiving crime was detected when police were tipped by an informant. They then set up an elaborate sting operation, which caught Washington.

The lesson of the Thanksgiving holiday at Monolithic Memories has not been lost on Silicon Valley. Since 1981 much stricter security measures have been instituted at most companies.

---

of integrated circuits and other high-tech components, the specialist is trained in dealing with theft of information from computer data banks.[4]

Theft in Silicon Valley involves an active "grey market," a system of middlemen, both legal and illegal, who distribute chips from the semiconductor houses to small quantity buyers such as certain computer and other firms (large customers like Intel, National, and Fairchild buy directly from the semiconductor manufacturers). Sometimes the small buyers are in a hurry to buy chips, or are anxious to get a cut-rate price. These are conditions that foster the theft of semiconductors; as they pass through the grey market, the chips may lose their source of origin, thanks to cooperative middlemen who conveniently overlook it. Thus a lot of money can be made—and lost.[5] Sometimes the grey market chips are rejects that failed quality-control tests which have been mislabeled and sold. Later in the process these defective chips may show up and fail in a vital piece of electronic equipment. Defective semiconductors have been found in a heart pacemaker, in a kidney dialysis machine, and in the on-board components of a NASA space-shot computer.[6] The grey market of Silicon Valley can lead to some very serious consequences.

Stolen, counterfeited, or defective chips may be mixed in small quantities with large batches of good semiconductors, making the illegal chips difficult to detect. Santa Clara County deputy district attorney Doug Southard estimates that 100 to 200 grey marketers exist in Silicon Valley. Many are legitimate, but "even the most honest brokers will turn their heads from time to time and purposefully be fooled."[7] How do Southard and other authorities catch the chip thieves? One of the best ways is to monitor the grey market and when an unusually low-priced sale occurs, the police investigate it. Southard says that 30 to 40 successful prosecutions of illegal grey marketers have been made.[8]

Listening Post on Green Street

A few years ago, a fisherman off the coast of North Carolina picked up a Soviet sonar buoy, designed to track the movement of U.S. submarines. When disassembled, the Russian device was found to contain precise replicas of state-of-the-art semiconductors from Silicon Valley. The discovery sent a shiver down the neck of U.S. national security experts.

Since then the U.S. government has greatly escalated security measures to prevent the leakage of high-technology information to the Russians. Because America is considered far ahead of Russia in semiconductors, computers, and telecommunication, Silicon Valley has come to be regarded as the most important U.S. military resource in the world. More than 600 firms in the Valley perform security-classified work, mostly in satellites, missiles, radar, and computers.

It is estimated that each year the Russians get more than $1.5 billion worth of high technology through dummy companies, espionage, and simple theft. The U.S. Navy's top intelligence officer, Rear Admiral Edward A. Burkhalter, Jr., said that Soviet spies have stolen more than two-thirds of Russia's military technology from U.S. companies, many of them in Silicon Valley.[11]

The process by which U.S. microelectronics technology moves from Santa Clara or Sunnyvale to Russia is directed from KGB headquarters in Dzerzhinsky Square in Moscow. The Komitet Gosudarstvennoi Bezopasnosti (KGB), or state security committee, combines the functions of the CIA, FBI, and military intelligence in the U.S. The KGB's "First Department" runs operations in the U.S. and Canada, its "Service T" concentrating on high technology. The main outpost for Service T is the Soviet Union's consulate at 2790 Green Street in San Francisco. An electronic forest of antennae protrudes atop the roof of the consulate building. Some antennae transmit and receive messages from the Soviet embassy in Washington, others are capable of instant contact with Moscow. Yet other antennae are aimed south toward Silicon Valley where the high-tech firms send messages, often via satellite, to their offices and plants around the world. Green Street ears are often listening in on these conversations, hoping to pick up valuable trade secrets. In the Soviet consulate are a staff of KGB agents, at least eight of whom are experts in high technology. These activities on Green Street are all perfectly legal.

Much of the technology that flows to Dzerzhinsky Square is obtained from public sources: trade publications, computer shows, and from other information activities of an open society. Occasionally technical information is obtained by the KGB from American collaborators, motivated by greed to divulge company secrets, some of a confidential or classified nature.

Inequality: The South Side of Silicon Valley

Silicon Valley has a two-class structure, with almost no mobility across class lines. The upper-class segment, the highly paid engineers, reside in North County. The other half of Silicon Valley's population lives in South County, concentrated in San Jose and its suburbs of Milpitas and Gilroy. The skilled manual workers of Silicon Valley's microelectronics industry live here, the proletariat of the information society. These workers make up almost half of the total Silicon Valley workforce. The 1980 median family income in San Jose was $22,886 and in Gilroy, $19,139, compared to a median family income of $48,000 in North County.[12] About 7 percent of South County residents live in poverty; they are most often families headed by single mothers.

Historically Silicon Valley began in the Stanford Industrial Park and gradually spread south toward San Jose. The North County communities of Palo Alto, Mountain View, Sunnyvale, and Cupertino got first choice of the microelectronics firms. It was like an industrial development smorgasbord, with each city filling up its plate. Gilroy and San Jose were at the end of the line and what was left was to house the manual workers. From the viewpoint of a city's property tax base, providing housing for the poor is a losing proposition; costs of government services like education, welfare, police and fire protection are high relative to taxes paid per person. In short, North County profits at the expense of South County due to the segregation of Silicon Valley.

The lower-class resident will not see much of the fabled Silicon Valley lifestyle ballyhooed in the mass media. "For the production workers who make up half the electronics industry workforce, Silicon Valley means low-wage, dead-end jobs, unskilled, tedious work, and exposure to some of the most dangerous occupational health hazards in all of American industry. It is a dark side to the sparkling laboratories that neither barbecues, balloons, nor paid sabbaticals can hide."[13] Race and gender are part of the proletarian lifestyle of South County people. To simplify, white males in Silicon Valley hold the engineering and managerial positions with the highest incomes and greatest power.

Non-white men (Hispanics, Vietnamese, Filipinos, and blacks) and white women fall lower in the socioeconomic status hierarchy of Silicon Valley. Minority women are at the bottom of the occupational structure.[14]

The salary for assembly-line workers is the lowest in the industry. Starting pay is $4.50 per hour, close to the minimum legal wage. Because electronics jobs usually do not require English language ability and because of the high turnover rates (about 50 percent a year), these jobs are relatively easy to get. Therefore companies can pay low salaries, but be assured, by the pool of cheap labor available in South County, of a constant supply of employees who want jobs.

To most electronics executives unionization is anathema. Presently none of the Silicon Valley firms are unionized. Companies often warn their employees about the dangers of labor unions, anti-union literature is distributed, and managers and executives are given training courses (by the American Electronics Association, for example) on how to prevent unions from gaining a toehold. The last union election in Silicon Valley was held in 1980 at Raytheon's semiconductor plant in Mountain View; the International Brotherhood of Electrical Workers lost.[15]

A union organizer told of cases of harassment against organizing efforts. An employee in one firm passed out union literature to her co-workers and she was fired immediately, charged with slashing the tires on her supervisor's car parked in the company parking lot. The pro-union employee claimed this was a trumped-up accusation.

At a 1982 public hearing of disgruntled Fairchild employees which was conducted by the Santa Clara County Commission on Human Relations, a Filipino stated that she had been fired for reading a union leaflet, printed in English, to a Tagalog-speaking fellow worker (who also was fired).[16] Several other ex-Fairchild employees at this hearing described anti-union activities by their supervisors and managers.

Nevertheless, the threat of possible unionization may have the indirect effect of causing improved working conditions and better treatment for Silicon Valley's manual workers. The American Electronics Association's anti-union seminars preach that a preventive approach to union busting is the most effective. Silicon Valley firms treat their employees to generous benefits and give their workers a good deal of respect and responsibility. In part this policy coddles brainpower, the scarcest resource in Silicon Valley. The other reason for treating employees like human beings, particularly important regarding manual workers, is to prevent unionization.

Bob Noyce of Intel said: "Remaining non-union is an essential for survival for most of our companies. If we had the work rules that unionized companies have, we'd all go out of business. This is a very high priority for management here. We have to retain flexibility in operating our companies. The great hope for our nation is to avoid those deep, deep divisions between workers and management, which can paralyze action."[17] The captains of Silicon Valley are convinced that unionization is an enemy only slightly worse than Japanese competition in microelectronics. As long as these leaders are so convinced, Silicon Valley firms will continue to treat their employees with a high degree of paternalistic care.

About 2,000 Filipino immigrants work for National Semiconductor, one-quarter of National's total workforce in Silicon Valley. Similar concentrations of Third World nationals are found in other companies—for instance 4,000 Vietnamese work at Hewlett-Packard. Filipinos are dominant on the AMD semiconductor assembly lines, and Spanish-speaking workers are numerous at several other Silicon Valley firms. These ethnic concentrations in various companies stem from the interpersonal networks through which people find jobs. A Filipino working at AMD encourages her cousin, newly arrived in San Jose from Cebu City, to apply at the AMD personnel office. This cousin, once hired, can speak in Tagalog with her supervisor and fellow workers in an AMD cleanroom.

As a rule the newest ethnic group to arrive in Silicon Valley is closest to the bottom of the occupational class structure. Currently this group is Vietnamese refugees. Several hundred new immigrants arrive in San Jose each month, many "boat people." South County is one of the two main concentrations of Vietnamese in the United States (San Diego is the other).

There are certain disadvantages to ethnic diversity among the line-operators in Silicon Valley companies. One problem is communication among different minority groups. At its wafer fabrication plant in Mountain View, which is so old it practically has a dirt floor, Fairchild Semiconductor achieves a very high yield of about 70 percent (that is, about 30 percent of the semiconductor chips must be rejected). But at its spiffy new wafer fab in San Jose, Fairchild's yield hovers around 10 percent.[18] The difference in quality of production seems to be due to the diversity of languages and cultures at the San Jose plant—most line-operators are Vietnamese refugees, Taiwanese, or Mexicans. Company orders and instructions in English are not understood by many workers.

A Day in the Life of a Semiconductor Line-Operator

Maria wakes at 6:00 A.M. so that she has time to prepare breakfast for her three children and get them dressed before leaving for work. Driving up Highway 101 from her apartment in East San Jose, she drops her smallest child, a baby of six months, at a day-care center run by her aunt. Then back into the slow-moving traffic to Mountain View, a 15-mile commute requiring 45 minutes in the morning rush. By the time she pulls her old 1968 Buick into the huge parking lot behind the semiconductor fabrication plant it is almost 8:30. She arrives breathless at the locker room, where she hurriedly changes into her cleanroom bunny suit.

Maria then faces a seemingly endless line of silicon wafers which she checks for defects under a microscope. By her 10:00 coffeebreak, Maria's neck and shoulders hurt. She knows that by the end of the workday, the pain will have settled into a dull ache. But complaining to her supervisor does little good, and anyway the plant has recently announced threatened layoffs. A semiconductor fab worker would have a difficult time getting a new job.

So Maria copes as best she can. She complains to Isabella, her co-worker at a neighboring microscope. As the workday wears on, they talk, *sotto voce*, about what they saw last night on TV, their fellow employees, their children. The company provides a volleyball court, swimming pool, and sauna, but their 30-minute lunch break hardly allows an opportunity to use the facilities. At 4:30 Maria heads her old Buick (she affectionately calls it "Blunderbuster") back down 101 toward home, picking up her baby on the way.

She fixes dinner for the kids, and then talks with a neighbor (another single parent) while half-heartedly watching Spanish-language TV. By 10:00 Maria is yawning. As she goes to bed, she thinks, "Now, if I just don't get laid off."

The Black Market Garage Operations

One often associates Silicon Valley garages with such successful entrepreneurs as David Packard and William Hewlett, or Steve Jobs and Steve Wozniak. But garages today also have another association, one which is illegal, unsavory, and illustrates the exploitation of Third World women.

"Beneath Silicon Valley is an underground of cheap labor in which housewives, aliens, refugees, welfare recipients, and others struggling to make ends meet earn less than the minimum wage and do without Social Security and workers' compensation benefits."[19] These "sweatshops" take advantage of the thousands of illegal aliens, many of them recent immigrants from Mexico or Vietnam, who cannot accept legal employment. The black market garages operate in a cash market, thus eliminating the 10 percent of labor costs that would otherwise go for payroll deductions, and the 15 or 20 percent ordinarily paid by the employee as income tax and Social Security. Thus a Silicon Valley company contracting with a sweatshop can get a $9-an-hour job done for only $6 or $7 per hour.[20]

Board-stuffing is a kind of work that is easy to subcontract to a garage-type operation in Silicon Valley. Let's say that a microcomputer firm wants 50,000 circuit boards stuffed, and will pay fifty cents per board. The boards and the semiconductors that are to be inserted are delivered in an unmarked car via an intermediary (who is likely to extract a 10 percent fee). Nothing is put in writing and all transactions are handled in cash. The garage sweatshops are not a small-time operation; knowledgeable sources say that thousands of people and millions of dollars are involved. One Silicon Valley executive estimates that 200 sweatshops are presently assembling circuit boards.[21]

As with any illegal operation involving weaker sectors of the population, exploitation occurs. A state investigator for the California Division of Labor Standards said: "Most people who work at home are not paid the minimum wage. The laborers suffer. It also creates unfair competition. In home work, the pervasive violation of minimum wage and overtime laws is chronic."[22] In some cases, illegal aliens from Vietnam must pay an "entry fee" of $150 to $200 in order to get jobs as black market home assemblers. Kickbacks are also paid by sweatshop bosses to company officials who direct business their way.

The cutthroat competition of the Valley, which encourages using any means of reducing labor costs, and the quick service sweatshops provide, ensure their existence. Consider the following: In a rundown section of San Jose, a Vietnamese woman invites two well-dressed men into her home. Soup bubbles on the stove and children play in a back room. Using hand signs and fractured English, a deal is concluded in which the woman, her aged relative, and a woman down the street will assemble printed circuit boards for fifty cents apiece. "We work faster, we get more. Slower, we get less," says the sweatshop boss.[23]

Why don't state and federal officials crack down on the garage sweatshops in Silicon Valley? In the first place they are hard to identify. Everyone involved cooperates in hiding their location. Most are operated by ethnic minorities, and their neighbors and friends (fellow Mexicans or Vietnamese or Filipinos) will not inform government authorities. But everyone knows they exist and do a flourishing business. The sweatshops are part of the seamy side of Silicon Valley, operating outside the law as part of the information economy's underground.

Assembly Operations in the Third World

In addition to the garage operations in Silicon Valley are the semiconductor assembly plants in Asian nations, employing hundreds of thousands of young women. "Wages vary from about 5 percent of the U.S. norm in Indonesia to nearly 25 percent in Hong Kong."[24] Almost every major semiconductor firm in Silicon Valley, and many of the computer companies, own "offshore" assembly plants in Asia.

This unique international assembly line got started when Fairchild Semiconductor built an assembly plant in Hong Kong in 1963. In the 1960s the final testing of silicon chips was done

in Silicon Valley. Companies shipped the chips to the offshore locations in Asia, they were assembled and encapsulated in plastic
protective cases, then airfreighted back to California for final
testing. Now most off-shore facilities are self-contained, carrying
out all operations through final test and "mark and pack."
The original engineering design work is all done at the companies' headquarters in Silicon Valley.[25] Fairchild alone operates assembly plants in six Asian nations, plus Brazil and
Scotland.

During the 1960s and early 1970s the Silicon Valley semiconductor companies became a worldwide industry. Asian governments invited these corporations into their countries with hopes
of gaining technological expertise, obtaining foreign exchange in
U.S. dollars, and providing employment for their huge and growing populations. The U.S. semiconductor industry is highly competitive and one can hardly blame it for seeking to cut labor costs,
although the transfer of assembly operations to Asia means fewer
jobs in the U.S. Labor is much cheaper in Asia compared to the
1983 average Silicon Valley microelectronics worker's wage of
$9.20 per hour (including fringe benefits). In Mayalasia it is 60
cents per hour; the Philippines, 50 cents; and in Hong Kong,
$1.20.[26]

During the past five or six years, Silicon Valley firms have
opened newer production facilities in a dozen or so locations
around the U.S. These newer "Silicon Valleys" share one important characteristic with the offshore locations in Asia: the availability of relatively cheap, non-unionized labor. The majority of
this workforce is young women between the ages of 15 and 25,
mostly unmarried, and fresh from the countryside.

Silicon Valley as an Unhealthy Place

According to the California Division of Labor Statistics and Research, the electronics industry has illness rates much higher than
those of U.S. industry as a whole.[27] On the surface, the microelec-

tronics plants look startlingly attractive. But inside Silicon Valley, important health problems occur.

One of the most visible and talked about problems in Silicon Valley is air pollution. Because the area is a kind of geological valley, pollutants become trapped. The chief source is auto exhausts. As Silicon Valley exploded into its present crowded condition, no one thought much about how people would transport themselves to work. Today everyone pays for this negligence. The main expressways connecting the South County workforce to the North County places of work are congested daily with traffic jams. The worst cases of mile-long "parking lots" take place heading north in the morning and south in the late afternoon. About 90 percent of Silicon Valley residents go to work by private auto; no one thought to plan for mass transportation by bus or commuter train. The average auto commute of 15 miles today will go up to 22 miles in the next few years, an increase of 50 percent.[28] The trend is to longer home-to-work travel as the North County/South County separation of the workforce from its employment places becomes more pronounced. The time wasted while sitting in a car stalled in traffic continues to increase; today average commuting time approaches 46 minutes per day.[29] If one has a mental picture of Silicon Valley that only includes the manicured campuses of the high-tech firms, the miles-long "parking lots" of the main expressways should also be part of the picture.

What can be done about the traffic problems of Silicon Valley? The construction of new freeways between North County/South County is not feasible, as previously available space is gone. Improved bus service, light rail (that is, modern streetcars), and commuter trains could help, as could the organization of more carpools. Silicon Valley firms could contribute to a public transportation tax, levied on the basis of number of employees, as has been proposed recently by the City of Palo Alto. Flexible working hours already have been instituted by many companies. They help somewhat, but the basic transportation problem goes deeper, back to the 1960s and 1970s when the Silicon Valley complex was dividing into a North County and South County.

Also guilty of causing pollution problems are the microelectronics firms. Even though these are presumably "clean" industries, not characterized by belching smokestacks, Silicon Valley's semiconductor firms blow 25 tons of precursor organics into the air each day. These materials chemically react with sunlight to form smog.[30] A recently implemented regulation requires the semiconductor firms to filter (or "scrub") their exhaust fumes to remove the pollutants, at a cost of $37 million over the next 10 years.

Silicon Valley can be a dangerous place in which to live, especially if one has a semiconductor company as a neighbor. This realization began to crystallize on December 4, 1981.[31] Workmen were digging a hole for a new water tank at the South San Jose plant of Fairchild Semiconductor. They noticed strange, rust-colored earth around a chemical storage tank that had been in use since 1977. They dug deeper and found that industrial chemicals were seeping through the bottom of the old fiberglass tank. The gauge that was supposed to measure the volume of liquid in the tank had failed. The stain in the earth was extensive, and Fairchild notified the Great Oaks Water Company, whose wells were nearby, that there might be a problem.

The well nearest the leaky tank, about 1,500 feet away, was contaminated with 1–1–1 trichloroethane (TCA), with concentrations nearly 29 times higher than levels considered acceptable by the state health agency. About 40,000 gallons of TCA had leaked out of the defective underground tank beginning in May 1980.[32] The well was closed the next day, but neither the water company nor Fairchild disclosed the problem to the public for 50 days.

Housewife Lorraine Day opened the *San Jose Mercury News* on January 20, 1982, and read about the leak. She could look out her window and see the Fairchild plant, within a quarter mile of her home. Her family got its water from the Great Oaks Water Company. Her smallest child had multiple congenital heart defects, had almost died, and needed open-heart surgery. Ms. Day recalled that her neighbors had complained that their water tasted funny. Within the past three years on her block, four children had been born with birth defects, two miscarriages had occurred, and one stillbirth had happened. Lorraine Day wrote to the president of the water company, demanding an investigation. Her action attracted considerable media attention; the *San Jose Mercury News* wrote an article about her and she began receiving phone calls from the Associated Press and the *National Enquirer*. Within days 31 birth disorders were reported to the Great Oaks Water District. As the alarm about the water supply spread 36 other leaks of hazardous chemicals were found in the Bay Area, 7 in Santa Clara County that involved chemical solvents used by semiconductor plants such as Intel, Hewlett-Packard, Signetics, and AMD. Leaks at other Fairchild plants in Los Altos, Mountain View, and Santa Clara were also found.[33] Suddenly, Silicon Valley did not seem to be such a healthy place in which to live. Eventually 11 tanks were found to be leaking chemicals.[34]

Lorraine Day and 265 of her neighbors sued Fairchild, Great Oaks Water Company, and various government agencies, charging negligence. Lawyers for the accusers expect about a hundred more people to file suits. While legal actions are still pending, the TCA incident set off public concern about the handling of chemicals used in the semiconductor industry. Fairchild has removed the faulty tank and is digging up its other underground storage tanks and placing them in cement storage vaults that will contain future leaks if they occur. The company has spent $12 million in excavating contaminated soil and has sunk more than 100 wells in the area around their plant site to pump out the contaminated water.[35] Health authorities are investigating the water pollution problem, monitoring chemical leaks, and developing a code to prevent such problems from happening again.

Perhaps the TCA incident and its attendant publicity have raised the consciousness of industry officials, government figures, and the public. They will no longer be lulled into complacency about the seeming "cleanliness" of the semiconductor industry in Silicon Valley.

Housing and traffic have been acknowledged as Silicon Valley problems that got out of control, a lesson of history. Ironically, the same thing is likely to occur again, but this time it will be energy and water that are in such short supply as to limit further activity in the Valley.

For computer and electronics manufacturers an absolutely essential element is the availability of reliable electrical power. Any fluctuations in voltage or the temporary loss of power will shut down a computer and dump its data, or will cause interruptions in the thin-film manufacturing processes of semiconductor chips. Erosion in the quality of electrical power represents a serious financial threat to high-tech manufacturing. According to Intel's Gordon Moore, "We're very susceptible to power interruptions. As the area gets near to maximum generating capacities, the chance of rolling blackouts increases and they just scare the heck out of us."[36]

One of the most far-reaching exposés of 1982 involved plans for the San Jose sewage treatment plant. While plans for sewage treatment plants are usually not at the top of most people's concerns, treating chemicals produced by Silicon Valley manufacturers is hardly a typical problem. The cost of improving the sewage treatment plant in San Jose alone is estimated at more than $138 million.[37] Chemicals used in high-technology companies must be flushed down a drain or carried away somehow, and indeed they are—in large amounts. Waste removal and treatment are serious problems in Silicon Valley. Avoiding repeats of chemical leaks from underground tanks and limiting the discharge of potentially dangerous chemicals into water and air is an issue likely to gain even greater importance in the next decade.

The Tragedy of the Commons

The problems of Silicon Valley might seem to be separate and distinct. Actually, they are all interrelated to the way in which high-technology industry developed in the Valley. There are sixteen local governments involved; each looked out for itself over the past twenty or thirty years, encouraging firms to locate within city limits, but at the same time pursuing policies of self-interest regarding housing of company employees. Palo Alto, Mountain View, Sunnyvale, and the rest of the North County cities re-zoned residential area for industrial use. The net result was a severe housing shortage, a lengthy commute by workers, and creation of a bimodal North County/South County workforce characterized by socioeconomic inequality.

Unfortunately this pursuit of municipal self-interest means

that no one, or at least no one with any clout, looked out for the overall welfare of Silicon Valley as a total system. Each city, each firm, and each entrepreneur looked out for good old Number One. Unfettered free market forces in Silicon Valley worked to the considerable advantage of the strong and powerful, but unfortunately most of the benefits obtained were at the cost of creating disadvantages for the poorer and weaker sectors of the system. Lack of a strong and public-spirited centralized government in Silicon Valley meant a vigorous knees-and-elbows kind of industrial development that ignored public benefits, creating a socioeconomically unbalanced high-technology system. Today we belatedly realize there are many problems in the "paradise" of Silicon Valley. The other "Silicon Valleys" springing up around the United States want to avoid these problems. How can they?

The recent decades of Silicon Valley history represent a classic case of "the tragedy of the commons." This concept was coined by Garret Hardin, an ecologist, to describe the situations when what an individual wants to do conflicts with the needs of the social system to which the individual belongs.[38] If individual independence is maximized in these situations, the common good is sacrificed to the detriment of the system, and ultimately, of its individual members. The tragedy of the commons derives its name from the historical case of the commons pastures in medieval England. The tragedy occurred because each farmer increased the number of his cows grazing in the commons pasture of his village, leading to disastrous overgrazing and eventually to erosion and the demise of the commons. Each herdsman acted rationally in adding yet another animal to his herd because he figured that the additional cow would only be a small increment to the total herd grazing on the commons. The societal tragedy occurs because each herdsman does not consider the societal consequences when his individual actions are aggregated for the system.

"Each man is locked into a system that compels him to increase his herd without limit—in a world that is limited. Ruin is the destination toward which all men rush, pursuing his own best interests in a society that believes in the freedom of the commons."[39] We see contemporary examples of the commons tragedy on all sides: overpopulation, industrial pollution, and the global military race. A lack of concern for the welfare of society has a very high cost. The bottom line is the kind of social problems that exist today in Silicon Valley.

As a much-envied center of microelectronics high technology, Silicon Valley is, and will be, much copied. Those who mimic Silicon Valley owe it to themselves to learn a crucial lesson from the experience gained in the past thirty years: *That the same factors and forces encouraging the individualistic entrepreneur, if not understood and managed effectively, can lead to the tragedy of the commons evinced today by Silicon Valley's problems.* This is a sobering, cautionary lesson, one that has not received much attention in previous accounts of the Silicon Valley story.

If Silicon Valley had been better planned there would be more high-rise housing in downtown San Jose and along the central transportation corridor, which would carry a mass transportation system with feeder buses, designed to move commuters to and from jobs. Taxes might be shared among the individual cities, which would cooperate with each other in planning a logical combination of housing and industry. Certainly there should be a strong regional government looking out for the overall welfare of the entire system, a counterbalance to the greedy, self-serving forces of the sixteen communities, the thousands of companies, and the legions of on-the-make high-tech entrepreneurs. The microelectronics firms would pursue enlightened policies of social responsibility, thinking of the system and society as well as of their net worth and annual profits.

The Cost of Paradise

The problems in a high-tech paradise are to some extent inevitable; some may even be functional. In a free enterprise system, manufacturing looks for a base of cheap labor. The availability of cheap labor in Silicon Valley attracted high-tech industry to the area. The problem—a large group of low-paid workers—is symbiotic.

Other problems are also inevitable accompaniments to paradise. The pervasive wealth of Silicon Valley is an invitation for crime. When the valued object is as small and light as a chip, and when security is more cavalier than secure, the only question is how long until the next heist occurs. Considering the amount of wealth in Silicon Valley, both personal and corporate, crime is actually rather low. The point is that one cannot separate the benefits of Silicon Valley's microelectronics industry—like wealth and employment—from the disadvantages of crime, pollution, and inequality.

Some of Silicon Valley's problems are shared by other metropolitan areas. The absence of coordinated regional planning has resulted in traffic congestion and accompanying pollution, as well as housing dilemmas, in other American cities and cannot be attributed to high-tech industry alone. But the problems happened more quickly in Santa Clara County than elsewhere. Other problems have an obvious link with the get-rich-quick, exploitative approach of the aggressive entrepreneur. Black market board-stuffing operations exist because profit sheets encourage them; computer crime flourishes since companies don't want to invest adequate resources to hinder it; patent violations continue as long as almost everybody benefits.

Perhaps the greatest threat of all—which continues to be ignored—is the single-minded devotion to self-interest at the expense of the common good. Unless high-tech industry and Silicon Valley acknowledge this tragedy, it may end up being the problem that destroys paradise.

PART III

THE TOMORROW

OF

SILICON VALLEY

THE VALLEY faces a major threat today, the most serious since it began thirty years ago: Japanese competition. Unless the U.S. semiconductor and computer companies can cope with this technology race, Silicon Valley will not have much of a future ten years from now.

Ironically, Silicon Valley is also today a place and an industry that has become a state of mind. High technology culture is spreading to a dozen other locations around the United States. In a few decades, high technology may become the American way of life.

Information technology from Silicon Valley is now impacting on American society: office automation, home computers, video games, and microcomputers in schools. Will the effect be to create a cadre of computer hackers who are alienated from society? Will it increase unemployment? Or will high technology be the route to curing the economic health of the U.S.?

12

Growing Competition: The Japanese

"We're at war with Japan, not with guns and ammunition, but in an economic war with technology, productivity, and quality."
    Charles Sporck, president, National Semiconductor Corporation, in a speech to his employees, 1981

"Unless the U.S. government takes steps to counter the Japanese market penetration, Silicon Valley is going to be a wasteland."
    Robert Noyce, vice chairman, Intel Corporation, 1982

PERHAPS the birth of the information society really began in October 1973 when the Yom Kippur War broke out and the Organization of Petroleum Exporting Countries (OPEC) shut down the world's supply of crude oil and the price skyrocketed.[1] OPEC's decision to cut oil supplies escalated the cartel into world consciousness. This phase-change in international trade marked the end of the unlimited cheap energy assumption on which the industrial era rested. After 1973 Japan, the U.S., and other rich nations of the North began to look to information, not energy, as the vital ingredient on which society runs. To a certain extent, information could substitute for energy as a nation shifts from being an industrial society to becoming an information society. The Japanese were most immediately and fully aware of the information/energy equation. The *shockku* of 1973 was a telling lesson for Japan, a nation the size of California but with more than half the U.S.'s population and almost no natural resources.

The Japanese government and its business leaders had foreseen the end of the industrial era. By 1971 MITI (the powerful Ministry of International Trade and Industry) had adopted a policy aimed at gaining greater control of world sales of computers, which are the heart of an information society. That meant taking on IBM. And MITI knew that to be a leader in computers, Japan would have to first reach a dominant position in semiconductors. Silicon Valley lay directly in the path of Japan's progress.

Recently a top executive of a U.S. high-technology corporation said: "Japan beats us in any field that they choose—radios, televisions, zippers, automobiles, you name it. They overcome us in quality and in lower price. Now they are beating us in innovation. There is no defense against them. Soon the United States will just be a supplier of food and raw materials to Japan and a purchaser of their manufactured products. Japan is rapidly making the U.S. into a Third World nation."

During the 35-year period following World War II, the Japanese economy increased 55-fold. Today Japan accounts for 10 percent of the world's economic activity, although it occupies only 0.3 percent of the world's surface with only 3 percent of the world's population. Japan's economic recovery from the low point of its military defeat in 1945 is indeed a "miracle," as it so often has been described.

How did the Japanese do it? A key factor is imported technology, much of it from the United States. For instance, Sony paid $25,000 in 1953 for a license to manufacture transistors. Japanese companies followed a similar strategy in the semiconductor field, copying a U.S. design and then producing the product with higher quality at a lower price. Such technology transfer was encouraged in the post-World War II era, when the U.S. thought Japan was weak. Only in recent years have U.S. businesses begun to limit the flow of technological innovations to Japan. As one American business executive put it: "Now we want to sell more milk and fewer cows."[2]

The U.S. aided Japan's economic recovery in another way—guaranteeing Japan's defense, in part by stationing 45,000 troops on her islands. Japan spends only 1 percent of its gross national product on defense, compared to five times that amount for the U.S.

Americans are hooked on Japanese consumer products: 15 percent of motorcycles in the U.S. are Japanese made, 60 percent of television sets, and 20 percent of automobiles. Japan earns about $50 billion in the U.S. each year and even though Japan is America's biggest overseas market, the U.S. suffers from an $18 billion annual trade deficit.

A factor in the Japanese economic miracle lies in its special relationships with the U.S. But most of the credit should go to the Japanese people. They have a hard-work ethic, a high level of education, and a spirit of group cooperation that translates directly into business success. These traits may stem from Japan's traditional rice-growing culture, a way of life that requires group consciousness and working together. These qualities also happen to be ideally suited to the needs of a modern information society.

Japan has enjoyed political and economic stability for several decades; the liberal Democratic Party has reigned for 28 years. Government and private industry work together hand in glove, leading to a type of collaboration called by Americans, "Japan, Inc." The Japanese government's vision of its nation's future is to lead the world in microelectronics.

All things considered, it's understandable that Silicon Valley executives live in mortal fear of Japanese competition. Watch out, world, here come the Japanese.

Nowhere is the Japanese threat to the Silicon Valley microelectronics industry better illustrated than in the case of the 64K RAM, the basic chip of the microelectronics industry. A noted observer said: "The American semiconductor industry, that bastion of innovation and enterprise, is reeling under its first major defeat, . . . a defeat that came upon it with blinding speed."[3] The defeat concerns the 64K RAM.

The 64K Random Access Memory (RAM) will be the central product of the semiconductor industry for at least several years, and is destined to become the largest selling single chip in dollar volume in the history of the industry[4] (Figure 12.1). This product represents the vanguard of microelectronics technology. Whoever controls the manufacture of the 64K RAM will have enormous commercial power in the near future. Their strategic position will be enviable for the push, already underway, to the 256K RAM.

The 64K dynamic RAM is a chip containing over 64,000 memory cells—65,536 to be exact. Random access memory (RAM) means that each of the memory cells in the semiconductor chip can be reached independently, rather than having to start at the beginning and procede sequentially until reaching a desired cell. So each bit can be accessed at random. A dynamic RAM needs to receive continuous charges of electricity for it to operate. So when information in the memory cells of a 64K dynamic RAM is no longer needed, new information can be entered to replace the data already there. In popular terms, the memory cells can be recycled.

The most important application for the 64K RAM is computers. Memory chips store data, and when combined with data-processing logic chips like microprocessors, RAMs provide the "brains" of a computer, missile, robot, or other microelectronics product. The U.S. "defeat" in 64K RAMs is that it controls only 44 percent of the world market for this product, while the Japanese firms have 56 percent.[5]

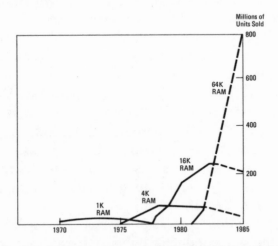

Figure 12.1.   Annual sales of random access memory (RAM) chips. The amount of memory that can be incorporated on a chip is defined in bits of information: 1K stands for 1,024 information bits: a 64K chip stores over 64,000 bits of information. Development of next-generation chips occurs by increasing memory by a factor of 4. Memory chips have moved from 1K to 4K to 16K to 64K. The next generation, 256K, is in production. The sequence is cumulative; a firm cannot easily produce a 256K RAM unless it first manufactures 64K RAMs.
SOURCE: Dataquest

How that happened was that during the 1973–75 recession U.S. semiconductor firms lost a third of their employees and cut investment in plants and equipment in half. When the economy rebounded, U.S. companies were unprepared. By 1978 Japanese semiconductor firms controlled about 40 percent of the 16K RAM market. This market share was a tremendous jump over Japanese production of 1K and 4K RAMs. The 16K RAM success alerted Silicon Valley semiconductor firms to the Japanese competition. They began to see what was coming—and it wasn't good.

U.S. firms led with the 1K RAM and continued ahead of Japan through the 4K and 16K. In each case the basic innovation was introduced by U.S. firms, then picked up and perfected by Japanese semiconductor companies. However, present Japanese dominance of the 64K RAM market, and their introduction of the 256K RAM in market quantities, suggests that the old pattern is changing. Yesterday's technological followers have become today's leaders. The five companies selling 256K RAMs in 1983 are Fujitsu, Mitsubishi, NEC, Toshiba, and Motorola. Only Motorola is an American firm.

Some observers feel that U.S. dominance of the RAM market may have ended with the 64K RAM war, although prospects are still bright for other microelectronics products like custom-designed chips and microprocessors. The U.S. is also strong in software. However, semiconductor memory is basic to the entire microelectronics industry. If U.S. innovation in RAM technology is lost, perhaps other areas will be overtaken, such as computers. Loss of the dominant position in 64K RAMs by U.S. firms is also important in simple economic terms. Although more than 10 million 64K RAMs have been sold to date, this amount represents less than one-half of one percent of all 64K RAMs that will ever be sold.[6] By 1985 64K RAM sales will reach $2 billion, about 10 percent of all semiconductor sales expected for that year.[7]

The 64K RAM defeat for Silicon Valley semiconductor firms makes Bob Noyce, Jerry Sanders, and their peers grit their teeth and search for new ways to compete with the Japanese. In October 1981, Intel and AMD agreed to jointly develop new semiconductor products and to manufacture certain of each other's chips. The Intel-AMD agreement, linking two American firms, signals a change from fierce competition within the U.S. microelectronics industry to collaboration.

A second conspicuous reaction to the Japanese 64K RAM victory by U.S. semiconductor companies and computer firms is a move toward joint R&D. In a closed-door meeting in February 1982, officials of fifty American firms called for cooperation in basic research. "Our microelectronics and computer industries are suffering from enormous duplication of research and development. For every corporation to rediscover what all others have already learned represents waste of the most pernicious sort."[8] U.S. semiconductor producers and computer firms are now contributing funds and personnel toward several collaborative R&D programs.[9]

The learning curve phenomenon gives a financial advantage to being first to market with a new semiconductor product. As the supply of a chip increases, the price drops. In the case of the 64K RAM the price drop has been precipitous. In 1982, 64K RAMs sold for $5 each, compared to $50 in 1981. When the price of the 64K RAM dropped so rapidly, Motorola asked the U.S. government to begin an investigation of Japanese pricing policies, claiming that Japanese firms might be selling 64K RAMs at a loss in order to corner the market. U.S. semiconductor companies want the government to provide protective tariffs and to change legislation so that American firms can cooperate more closely. After decades of a suspicious attitude toward Washington when Silicon Valley firms preferred to act unencumbered by the U.S. government, Japanese progress in semiconductor memory drove microelectronics firms to ask for government assistance. Thus the Japanese threat helped cause the politicization of Silicon Valley.

Theory Z: Japanese-Style Management

Dr. William G. Ouchi is a management professor at the UCLA Business School who wrote an extremely popular book, *Theory*

Z: How American Business Can Meet the Japanese Challenge. [10] It was on the *New York Times* best seller list for 22 straight weeks, something of a record for an academic volume. Undoubtedly one reason for *Theory Z*'s popularity was timing; Detroit was crashing just about the time the book was published and many Americans wanted an explanation of Japanese superiority in autos, videocassette recorders, and other products.

Ouchi's book said the answer lay in the nature of Japanese management style. The book argued that a set of U.S. firms were already successfully following a kind of Japanese-like American management style, called "Theory Z," showing that many aspects of the superior Japanese management could be applied to American conditions. Most of Ouchi's examples of Theory Z firms came from high-technology firms, many of them in Silicon Valley. Indeed, most of Ouchi's research was conducted in firms like Hewlett-Packard, while he was a professor at the Stanford Business School, prior to his move to UCLA.

In Japanese-style business management the main elements are lifetime employment, seniority, and extensive welfare benefits. The consequences of lifetime employment mean that in-service training programs for employees are justified because the workers will be retained by the firm for a longer time. But in order to provide lifetime employment to their workers, Japanese managers must effectively cope with the economic uncertainties of the up-and-down swings of the economy.

In comparison to the typical U.S. firm, a Japanese firm is much more important to its employees. Most of an individual's contacts with other people are made at work. Co-workers spend more time together outside of work hours; for example, fellow employees regularly eat and drink together after work at a restaurant. Japanese who work together feel they are part of a family and to socialize outside of working hours seems perfectly natural to them.

Japanese firms are characterized by extensive horizontal communication and by decentralized decision-making. A morning assembly of four or five minutes at the beginning of the workday is customary in many firms. Making decisions through participatory discussions with lower-level workers is common for Japanese bosses. Such bottom-up communication makes the leader's role that of a harmonizer, an orchestrator, and builder of consensus.

The general theme of Ouchi's book on Theory Z is not arguable: Treat your employees like human beings, invite their participation in company matters, promise them a long-term future with your firm, and they will do more work of higher quality. This management style in turn will make the company more profits and earn the loyalty of the employees, who will not leave for your competitors.

Theory Z fits the unique conditions of high-technology firms in Silicon Valley and a number of microelectronics firms are already following their own version of it: Intel, Apple, IBM, and Tandem, for instance. Not that they were influenced to do so by Ouchi's book.[11] Perhaps it's surprising that more high-technology companies in Silicon Valley do not practice Theory Z management. Some firms, like National Semiconductor, for example, are decidedly not Theory Z. At National, massive layoffs occur with any downswing in the semiconductor industry, which are then followed by equally massive hirings when business goes up again.

A few Silicon Valley spokespeople feel that Theory Z is just puffery for Japanese superiority. "Theory Z is like the Scarsdale diet book of the electronics industry," charged AMD's Jerry Sanders. "It's nothing more than a cheap promotion to capitalize on the belief that Japanese management is superior to the U.S. approach. That's a myth."[12]

Some Silicon Valley officials acknowledge that while there may be something to Theory Z, it cannot be applied in its entirety, due to Japanese-U.S. cultural differences. "Treating people with respect and dignity is as American as apple pie, but to many people, lifetime employment seems like lifetime slavery," said Fred Zieber, vice-president of Dataquest, Inc.[13] Nevertheless, Silicon Valley firms are displaying much more interest in learning about management from their Japanese competitors than a few years ago, before the 64K RAM competition.

Major Japanese electronics firms affiliate loosely with other firms in a *keiretsu*, or business group, a collection of companies with interlocking boards of directors and cross-ownership of stock. A *keiretsu* usually includes only one firm in each major industry; for example, the Matsui *keiretsu* includes Toshiba (microelectronics), Toyota Motors, and so on. There are several advantages to membership in a *keiretsu:* it is easier to acquire capital, an internal market for products is provided, advertising expenses may be decreased due to use of a common name like Mitsui or Mitsubishi[14], product planning is assisted, and access to foreign markets is aided because each *keiretsu* includes a trading company within its structure. Each microelectronics company in Japan[15] is a longstanding member of a business group whose member firms are bound by financing, buying-selling relationships, and management, with the heart of each group a bank.

In contrast to the spinning off of new semiconductor firms in Silicon Valley in the 1960s and 1970s, an entirely different pattern of founding semiconductor firms occurred in Japan. The six or seven main semiconductor "firms" are divisions of larger electronics companies, which in turn are members of business groups. A special advantage of such vertical integration is that a semiconductor division has close contact with its market. A similar advantage is achieved by the semiconductor divisions of U.S. electronics corporations like IBM, Texas Instruments, and Hewlett-Packard, but not by most of the Silicon Valley semiconductor firms, which are not part of a larger electronics company.

MITI and Japan, Inc.

The Ministry of International Trade and Industry (MITI, pronounced "meetee") is housed in a dull-grey, eleven-story building in downtown Tokyo, a few blocks from the Imperial Palace. MITI's squarish building is filled with dark-suited, brainy young men, many of whom are the elite graduates of the law school or the school of engineering at the University of Tokyo. They are crowded into cramped offices along with stacks of paperwork, the accommodations anything but elegant.

MITI is the greatest concentration of brains and power in Japan; its jurisdiction ranges from control of national betting on bicycle racing, to setting electric power rates, to planning national industrial policy.[16] It rose in the post-World War II era out of the wartime Ministry of Munitions and today plays a critical role in coordinating Japan's current semiconductor/computer "war" with Silicon Valley. MITI influences Japanese private firms through a complex set of formal and informal relationships; the term "Japan, Inc." is often used by Americans to refer to this closely coordinated government-industry partnership.

Several decades ago MITI encouraged the Japanese steel industry with the slogan, "Steel Is the Nation." Soon Japan was producing high-quality steel at the lowest cost in the world. About a dozen years ago MITI decided that the future lay in the computer industry, particularly the semiconductor industry on which it is based. So computers/semiconductors became a "targeted" industry, as steel had been before it. Future generations of semiconductor chips were referred to by MITI as "the rice of industry," meaning that they were the basis for the emerging information industry.[17] In the late 1970s, MITI contributed $130 million of the $320 million for a collaborative government-industry research center on semiconductors—over 1,000 patented innovations resulted. This research program helped Japanese semiconductor companies catch up to and, in certain areas, surpass their Silicon Valley counterparts.

MITI is powerful because it represents a national consensus that technological innovation in microelectronics is the priority direction for economic growth. MITI decides economic policy in Japan. The Diet, the Japanese legislature, and the courts function mainly to intervene when (and if) the bureaucracy goes too far.[18] MITI influences the Japanese microelectronics industry through "administrative guidance"—gyosei shido—by giving priority to semiconductor and computer firms, setting forth the national vision of the future they are to obtain, and providing capital, tax breaks, and R&D assistance. As a result, the Japanese microelectronics industry is much more highly integrated, interconnected, and coordinated than is its counterpart industry in Silicon Valley. These differences between the U.S. and Japanese semiconductor industries are in part a reflection of dominant cultural values—independence and competition in the U.S. versus Japanese values on collectivism and coordination.

The nature of government/industry relationships in Japan is markedly different from the United States where the microelectronics industry has only a little influence, and almost no help, from federal agencies. Unlike Japan, the U.S. government maintains a remote stance from microelectronics firms. In Japan, government and industry are mutual partners in a joint endeavor. Their relationship is an alliance; in the U.S. that relationship is often adversarial. Interaction between government and industry in Japan occurs in an organized way, through formal associations, and via informal relationships. An industry association composed of the firms in the microelectronics industry sponsors collaborative research programs in Japan. Funding for the industry research institute comes from membership fees paid by association members and from a special government tax, coordinated by MITI, assessed on betting in the national bicycle races (about $10 million is thus contributed to R&D each year).

Thus MITI and private industry are interconnected in a network of influence relationships leading to a consensual process of decision making about industrial policy. MITI acts as a coordinator and an orchestrator of this process. One Japanese semiconductor executive remarked: "Government should be half a pace ahead of industry, but not a full pace." In contrast, Silicon Valley leaders insist: "We don't want to get in bed with government bureaucracy." An industry leader stated: "We insist on preserving the right to fail." Perhaps the essence of U.S./Japanese differences in industry/government relationships comes down to the fact that America has no policy for high-technology industries and MITI does.

Just as Silicon Valley firms fear their Japanese counterparts, the latter are apprehensive about the U.S. giant of the computer industry, IBM. Japanese computer companies control only 10 to 15 percent of the world market at present, while IBM alone controls 50 percent. Japan hopes to win a market share of 30 percent by 1990, moving first into increased sales in developing countries, especially Asia, and then into the U.S. market.

Japan is beginning its attack on IBM with serious disadvantages. Chief among them is the Japanese written language, consisting of over 2,000 *Kanji* characters, each an ideogram, that are extremely difficult for a computer to handle. Imagine a computer or a typewriter keyboard with 2,000 keys—finding the right key would entail a lengthy search process. In order to help overcome this serious language problem, R&D priorities go to optical character recognition and to voice recognition. Japanese computers are able to do amazing things by way of recognizing the spoken word or written characters. However English is still the worldwide language of computing.

MITI has taken the lead in planning the computer catch-up race with IBM through two collaborative research programs: the Fifth Generation Computer Project; and the National Superspeed Computer Project, commonly called the Super Computer Project. The first is a 10-year program begun in 1982 and funded at $400 million. The objective of the Fifth Generation Computer Project is to create a new breed of computers that are much more human-like in their functioning.[19] The fifth generation computer should be easy to use as it is designed to learn how to solve problems on its own, gaining lessons from its experience as it goes. The new computers will incorporate recent work in artificial intelligence (AI) in order to mimic human recognition and will process non-numerical information like pictures and graphs. MITI created a new organization, the Institute for New Generation Computer Technology (ICOT), to run the Fifth Generation Computer Project.[20] ICOT includes MITI, Nippon Telegraph and Telephone (NTT), and Japan's eight leading computer firms. MITI asked each company to contribute funds, as well as its brightest computer engineers under thirty-five years of age.[21] A hoped for result of the Fifth Generation Computer Project is to create a corps of elite computer designers, who will represent the cream of technologists in the information society.

The other major thrust being planned to overcome IBM's world domination in computers is the "Super Computer Project," funded at $140 million during the 1980s. MITI's objective is to produce a computer that is more than 1,000 times faster than present computers.[22] To attain such high speed the Super Computer Project will replace semiconductor chips of silicon with those made of gallium arsenide. This collaborative R&D activity involves MITI and Japan's leading computer firms.[23] As in ICOT, each firm contributes funds plus its talented R&D workers. The super computer is intended for such science applications as nuclear fusion simulation, meteorological forecasting, and aerodynamic analy-

How Japan Did It in Autos

Detroit is on everyone's mind in the microelectronics industry as far as Japanese competition is concerned. A recent analysis of the U.S. auto industry shows that its cost of production is much higher than for its Japanese counterpart, while U.S. quality is lower.[24] When U.S. consumers were asked if they would buy the same make or model again, 77 percent who bought a domestic subcompact said yes, compared to 92 percent for those who bought imported cars. Today, every fourth car sold in America is made in Japan.

In 1960, 8 million autos were built in the United States, 48 percent of world production. Japan produced only about 3 percent. 1980 was the turning point in which Japan achieved supremacy in world auto production with 28 percent, the U.S. dropping to 20 percent. American automobile factories ran at only half capacity and the industry lost $4.2 billion, an all-time record for any industry. The Detroit disaster continued and worsened in the 1980–82 period. Many observers thought that the U.S. auto industry simply had to switch to producing small cars, but when this change was made, the small U.S. autos did not sell as well as Japanese minicompacts.

It costs Detroit $2,203 more than the Japanese to produce a subcompact car. The major Japanese cost advantages are (1) lower labor costs, mainly because the Japanese put an auto together with only 60 hours of labor, compared to 120 hours in the United States, $550 less; (2) lower parts inventories, $550 less; (3) better management of labor, $478 less; (4) better quality control, $329 less, and (5) all other factors, like more advanced technology, lower absenteeism, et cetera, $296 less.[25] Shipping and related costs eat up $485 of the Japanese advantage of $2,203, which still means that a Japanese car can sell for $1,718 less than a similar American car in the United States, or earn Toyota or Datsun an extra profit of $1,718. The Japanese use of advanced production technology (like robots, computer-aided design, et cetera), high quality assurance, and close labor-management cooperation creates this difference.

Much of the Japanese technology came from the U.S. General Motors Chairman Roger Smith told his company's 500 top executives: "Never again can we let them [the Japanese] take over technology and beat us at our own game."[26] GM and other U.S. auto companies are now carefully studying Japanese factories to see what they can copy or adapt, while company executives are lining up deals with Japanese auto firms. GM has agreed to import Suzuki and Isuzu minicompacts which General Motors cannot produce economically in its own plants. In early 1983 General Motors and Toyota agreed to produce small cars at a GM plant in Fremont, California. The car will be a Toyota design, have a Toyota engine and transmission, and the plant manager will be Japanese. U.S. auto companies are buying back technological innovations that they had given away, while acquiring the fruits of Japanese management and work ethic.

The Japanese victory over Detroit in autos was a humbling experience for U.S. car manufacturers.

sis. Thus the super computer is expected to be a scientific tool for creating future technological innovations in a variety of fields. The world's first super computer was used by the U.S. Department of Defense to calculate the dynamics of airflow around a rocket engine. The task took 18 hours. The planned Japanese machine will do the job in 10 seconds.

MITI orchestrates the R&D activities of competing computer firms in a joint research program like the Super Computer Project. The R&D largely represents work the participating firms wish to do anyway and their collaboration helps prevent unnecessary duplication of R&D activities. The participating firms also get first crack at any inventions resulting from the Fifth Generation Computer and the Super Computer Projects. In this way individual competition among Japanese computer firms is encouraged, even while they cooperate in MITI-sponsored projects.

American microelectronics firms claim that Japan, Inc., represents an unfair type of competition. Certainly the unique assistance provided by MITI to Japanese firms is a considerable advantage, although Japanese government/industry relationships are not the only reason why Japan is catching up to Silicon Valley in technological innovation. U.S. firms are free, at least within the limits imposed by anti-trust laws, to form collaborative R&D programs. In fact several have been created in the 1980s as a response to Japan, Inc. The U.S. government could also coordinate American high-technology companies by formulating long-range national policies, but at present it has not done so.

Does IBM need to worry about competition from Japan, Inc.? A recent visitor to MITI's collaborative research projects likened them to a band of revolutionaries planning a guerrilla attack, implying that IBM has little to fear. Perhaps not, but that's also what General Motors said a few years ago.

Quality

In an old skit, Bob Hope pulls a pistol from his pocket, and tries to fire it. The trigger clicks repeatedly, but the pistol does not fire.

Hope inspects the pistol, then says with a sneer, "Made in Japan!" For many years, "Made in Japan" was a synonym for shoddy goods. But no longer. Japanese firms produce semiconductors of higher quality than do U.S. firms.

One of the semiconductor industry's major problems is the rejection of large numbers of chips on the basis of poor quality and reliability. A rejection rate of about 50 percent is common by the producing firms. Further, each semiconductor is subjected to further testing, called quality assurance, by the company that purchases the chip for use in its products, like computers.

The quality superiority of Japanese semiconductors exploded like a bombshell on March 25, 1980, at a conference of the Electronics Industries Association of Japan, held in Washington, D.C. Richard W. Anderson, general manager of Hewlett-Packard's Data Systems Division, showed a slide comparing semiconductor quality for U.S. and Japanese firms. During 1979 Hewlett-Packard purchased 16K RAMs from three Japanese and three U.S. firms. The highest quality domestic firm's product had *six times* as many failures as the lowest-quality Japanese firm.[27] When the slide was projected on the screen, you could hear the audience's collective jaw drop. Hewlett-Packard would not identify the vendors, but a knowledgeable observer said the Japanese firms were Fujitsu, Hitachi, and Nippon Electric Corporation (NEC), and the U.S. suppliers were Intel, Mostek, and Texas Instruments.[28]

The immediate reaction to the Anderson presentation by Silicon Valley semiconductor firms was outrage. Then they set about raising their quality of chip production, presumably just what Anderson had hoped would happen. Half a year later, Anderson reported that U.S. firms supplying H-P had approximately doubled the quality of their 16K RAMs.[29] But the best U.S. performance was still worse than the worst Japanese firm. Japanese competition has had a beneficial effect on Silicon Valley semiconductor firms, pushing them to place a higher value on quality.[30] In part, this push for quality comes from customer demand.[31]

In the U.S. quality control is usually a synonym for strict and frequent inspection as part of the production process. In contrast, the Japanese approach is mainly preventive—in the initial planning process for a new semiconductor product, its configuration is designed to reduce the probability of defects occurring. Much effort is also given to the human side of quality control, by motivating workers to display craftsmanship so that each employee becomes, in effect, a quality control expert. The Japanese experience shows that much improvement in quality can be brought about by the workers themselves. QC (quality control) circles were established in Japanese firms, each composed of about a dozen co-workers. The QC circle meets regularly, usually for about an hour per week, to discuss ideas for improving performance and the circle's leader sends their proposals to supervisors for decisions to reject or implement them.

The Japanese approach to quality control began to be admired throughout the world during the 1970s, a result of awareness that Japanese products sell well because of their high quality, in addition to their competitive price. In a few decades Japanese quality went from being a joke to becoming admired and copied.

How Japan Obtains U.S. Technology

Until recently, Japanese firms bought U.S. microelectronics technology. For instance, Japan's NEC has technical assistance agreements with Intel and Texas Instruments, Hitachi has a technology licensing agreement with Motorola, and Fujitsu has a pact with AMD. These technology-for-sale deals, needless to say, were made prior to Silicon Valley's awakening to the Japanese threat.

Within the past five or six years Japanese firms have utilized another strategy to tap Silicon Valley know-how: They have established what are disparagingly referred to as "spy shops."[32] NEC in 1977 purchased Electronic Arrays, a semiconductor company in Mountain View, California. NEC Electronics U.S.A., Inc., the American arm of its Japanese parent, now has 600 employees in the heart of Silicon Valley. One of their tasks, in addition to making chips, is to pick up technical information and convey it to Tokyo. Other Japanese microelectronics firms also maintain listening posts in Silicon Valley; Toshiba bought Maruman Semi-conductor in 1979 and Fujitsu owns 36 percent of Amdahl Computer. A joint venture, such as that involving Toshiba and LSI Logic, Inc. (in Santa Clara, California), is yet another way to tap Silicon Valley technology, in addition to providing entry to the U.S. market.

As technological information trickles back from Silicon Valley to Tokyo, it is carefully sifted and evaluated. Certain of the data thus obtained are coordinated through MITI, which has been referred to by one Silicon Valley critic as "an industrial CIA." The image conveyed is one of scores of Japanese technologists pouring over U.S. magazines and journals, culling articles with useful information.

None of these technology acquiring strategies is illegal. Other strategies which Japan uses to acquire U.S. technology may be. The most famous case, described in Chapter 5, occurred in 1982 when Hitachi and Mitsubishi Electric were accused of trying to illegally buy IBM technology secrets.

Inside Entrepreneurs

A popular saying in Japan is: "The pheasant that flies gets shot." University graduates who enter the large electronics firms are admonished: "The nail that protrudes gets pounded down." In a culture where collaboration with peers is rewarded while individualistic thinking is punished, one would not expect Silicon Valley-style entrepreneurial fever to burn very brightly and it does not. Venture capital is almost nonexistent in Japan. It isn't needed, as start-ups and spin-offs seldom occur. The hotshot young electrical engineering graduate of the University of Tokyo looks for employment in MITI or in electronics companies like NEC, Toshiba, or Fujitsu. The last thing in his mind is to start his own small company. As Intel's Bob Noyce observed: "Japanese kids go into a rigid mold in school when they are four years old, and never come out of it. So Silicon Valley can excel in entrepreneurial activity. That's been the backbone of the U.S. microelectronics industry."[33]

"Silicon Island" is Kyushu, the southernmost of the main islands in the Japanese archipelago, an area of surplus labor and pure air and water. In recent years, Silicon Island has become the center for semiconductor wafer fabrication plants of NEC, Toshiba, and the other major electronics firms. In this sense, Silicon Island is like Colorado Springs; Austin; Portland, Oregon; and the other "Silicon Valleys" where U.S. firms are now locating their new production facilities. Like them, Kyushu does not have entrepreneurial spin-offs. But unlike them, Kyushu probably never will.

However Japan's entrepreneurship can be expressed in another, quite different way: by invention and innovation *within* a large firm. Individuals taking the lead as such "inside entrepreneurs" are being strongly encouraged as Japan seeks to compete successfully with Silicon Valley in technological innovation. To keep their innovation entrepreneurs within the company the Japanese firm may allow the individual to continue to work part-time on a promising new idea, even if the firm decides not to exploit it as a new product. Japanese firms have started to encourage somewhat greater individualism, at least in their R&D operations. For example, NEC now provides limited venture capital to "spin-off" activities within the firm. Two new divisions, one in laser technology and one in industrial microprocessors, have arisen within NEC and one new company has been formed, entirely owned by NEC.[34] Toshiba also allows its R&D workers to pursue "voluntary research" of personal interest but which the firm does not feel will have much payoff. Such voluntary research can be conducted with Toshiba's facilities but cannot interfere with an R&D worker's assigned research duties.[35]

Some Japanese firms seek to attract creative individuals whose originality may prevent them from fitting into lifetime employment with a large, established company. For example, Namco Ltd., a video game producer, advertises for reformed juvenile delinquents and C students to apply for employment. Namco's president, Masaya Nakamura, explained: "For game designers the knowledge acquired in school is not so helpful. I want people who think in unusual ways, whose curiosity runs away with them, fun-loving renegades."[36] One of the C students attracted to Namco by its unique ads was Toru Iwatani, who designed Pac-Man.

National culture affects the way in which innovation is encouraged. Entrepreneurial spin-offs around a technological innovation are the crucial event in the individualistic culture of Silicon Valley. But in collectivistic Japan a comparable or superior rate of technological innovation may be achieved within existing firms, whose large size and industrial structure give them certain advantages over their Silicon Valley competitors. To accomplish certain large-scale R&D objectives, the collaborative industry-government programs coordinated by MITI may be uniquely advantageous. Such a collaborative approach, perhaps involving government assistance, is a new game for Silicon Valley firms, but one they now realize they can play as well as the Japanese.

The Politicization of Silicon Valley

Until recent years Silicon Valley captains of industry perceived the U.S. government as crabgrass in the lawn of their life. But as the Japanese threat in microelectronics became stronger, the California entrepreneurs have increasingly looked to Washington for solutions. Politics has become a growth industry in Silicon Valley.

Most executives in Silicon Valley firms are conservative Republicans; they have "made it" as engineer-entrepreneurs and, quite understandably, believe that the capitalist system in which they have excelled is inherently right and good. To think otherwise would cast doubt upon their own success. Often these industry leaders carry their general belief in free market forces to self-defeating extremes. For several years they hesitated to appeal to the U.S. government for solutions to the growing problem of Japanese competition in semiconductors and computers. Indeed, there is still not a consensus in Silicon Valley about whether it is appropriate to involve the federal government in the technological struggle with Japanese electronics. Such appeals to government mean that bureaucrats may have some say in how Silicon Valley firms operate, a notion that is anathema to entrepreneurs. It simply does not fit in with the value they set on free market forces as the final judge in competition.

Tom Skornia, formerly an executive at Advanced Micro Devices, now a venture capitalist in San Jose, recalled the early history of Silicon Valley's politicization.[37] In 1973 the Western Electronics Manufacturing Association (WEMA, now the American Electronics Association) favored a U.S. law allowing tax-free reimportation of products assembled abroad. This law was essential to the off-shore assembly of semiconductors by U.S. firms, although it meant fewer jobs in the U.S. Labor unions opposed the law, feeling that it contributed to unemployment. WEMA was invited to send representatives to testify on the electronics industry's position before the House Ways and Means Committee. When WEMA initially balked at this, Bob Noyce (Intel), Charlie Sporck (National), Wilf Corrigan (then at Fairchild), and Jerry Sanders (AMD), met for lunch at Ming's Restaurant in Palo Alto. They were alarmed by the fact that Japanese firms had already captured 5 percent of the market for 4K RAMs. By the time the fortune cookies were served, these four semiconductor leaders decided to form the Semiconductor Industry Association (SIA). In order to give the association a geographically broader focus, they invited Motorola (headquartered in Phoenix) to join next. A Motorola man, Tom Hinkelman, became the executive director of SIA. Today the Semiconductor Industry Association consists of 33 U.S. firms, banded together against "Japan, Inc."

At first SIA narrowly concentrated on semiconductor trade issues with Japan. Only gradually, over the next three or four years, was the SIA able to assemble much of a financial war chest. There is still resistance to the SIA thrust of sending influential spokespersons like Bob Noyce to Washington. Some executives in Silicon Valley still feel that the further they stay away from the federal government the better. But in the past couple of years the SIA has become a more and more influential pressure group. SIA's legislative activities have motivated the American Electronics Association (AEA) to devote more of its actions to lobbying, as its nemesis, the SIA, has shown that a high-tech industry association can command influence in Washington. Grudgingly, Silicon Valley business had to admit that the U.S. government is a necessary partner for success in competition with Japan.

Another reason for the recent politicization of the U.S. microelectronics industry is the rise of a powerful Japanese lobby in Washington. In 1977, 17 lobbyists for Japanese interests were registered with the U.S. Justice Department; today there are over 140. The Japan lobby annually spends $30 million in fees and retainers on such powerful figures as former Senators J. William Fulbright, Frank Church, and John Tunney; former Reagan campaign manager John Sears; and Democratic National Chairman Charles Manatt. The Japan lobby has quietly become the largest and best-funded foreign contingent in Washington. In comparison, the Semiconductor Industry Association and the American Electronics Association look rather puny. "The Japanese have learned how to buy their way into the U.S. political system."[38]

In the meantime Silicon Valley executives throw their weight behind political candidates, both Republicans and Democrats, that profess sympathy for the special problems of high-technology firms. The concentration of microelectronics firms in the 12th Congressional District, which includes Silicon Valley, weakens the political power of the semiconductor/computer industry.[39] But as a dozen other "Silicon Valleys" spring up around the United States, the political base of the microelectronics industry will broaden. Coupled with the high profits earned by these firms—which can translate into political contributions—the political clout of microelectronics companies is due to increase in the near future. And a popular issue like the threat of Japanese competition to Silicon Valley has wide appeal.

A sign of the times in Silicon Valley is the political conversion of Charlie Sporck, chief at National Semiconductor. Until the early 1970s, Sporck dug in his heels against any type of political activity by semiconductor firms. Gradually he came to realize that National, despite its power as one of the leading U.S. semiconductor producers, could not cope alone with Japanese technological competition. Sporck's was one of the first Silicon Valley firms to start a PAC (political action committee) to feed campaign funds to politicians that would represent high-technology interests. And a new high level of political contributions and personal testimonials for candidates (especially for Senator Pete Wilson, his opponent Jerry Brown, and for Congressman Ed Zschau) were made by Silicon Valley leaders in the 1982 election.

From Competition to Collaboration

An external threat can often serve to unite the members of a system that were previously locked in competitive conflict. The new forms of collaboration in Silicon Valley include technology-exchange agreements among semiconductor firms, the sponsorship of cooperative R&D programs, and joint activity through industry associations to promote engineering education.[40]

The 1981 Intel-AMD agreement called for both companies' R&D engineers to sit down together and design new semiconductor products. AMD began to manufacture two of Intel's popular microprocessors, the 8086 and the 8088. An obvious advantage to both firms was avoiding duplication in their R&D activities. The agreement united the most innovative semiconductor company, Intel, with the premier marketing firm in the industry, AMD. Jerry Sanders, president of AMD, declared: "The semiconductor industry is undergoing a very significant attack on its profitability by the Japanese devastation of the memory market. The purpose of the agreement is to bring more technology to market for a given amount of R&D."[41]

U.S. semiconductor companies invest about 9 percent of their total sales in R&D, while all U.S. industries invest about 3 percent. But the 9 percent figure should be taken with a grain of salt—in a sense almost every employee in Silicon Valley is an R&D worker, constantly on the lookout for technological innovation.

In the past, almost all microelectronics R&D was conducted individually by each of the semiconductor firms. But in the face of increasing anxieties about Japanese dominance, Silicon Valley firms in 1982 began to consider the obvious advantages of certain types of collaborative research. One result is the Center for Integrated Systems (CIS), formed in 1981 at Stanford University to conduct research on "very large systems integration," a next step in the design of semiconductor chips. CIS is funded by 18 industrial sponsors (including such "biggies" as IBM, Intel, and Hewlett-Packard), each of which made three-year commitments of $750,000 amounting to the tidy sum of $40.5 million. The U.S. Department of Defense has provided another $8 million in research contracts.[42] CIS is headed by Professor John Linvill, former chairperson of Stanford's Electrical Engineering Department. An annual output of CIS will be 100 master's graduates and 30 Ph.D.s. The 18 industrial sponsors will have first opportunity at hiring them, as well as getting an early peek at the research conducted at CIS. Each firm can also post several of its key R&D employees at CIS for one-year periods so they can actually participate in the research program.[43]

Joint R&D centers in the U.S. are significant signposts of the new feeling of collaboration in the microelectronics industry. But MITI officials need not lose much sleep worrying about them. In comparison to their Japanese counterparts, the U.S. collaborative R&D programs lack the unity of purpose represented by, say, the Fifth Generation Computer Program. When it comes to collaboration, competitive America still has much to learn from integrated Japan.

Can Silicon Valley be saved from Japanese competition? First consider whether the U.S. microelectronics industry should be saved.

While Japanese competition poses a very stiff challenge for the U.S., it also provides several beneficial aspects: prices of semiconductors, and of computers and other electronics products in which semiconductors are a component, are lower than they would otherwise be; technological innovations have been brought rapidly to the marketplace; and Japanese competition has influenced U.S. semiconductor firms to improve their quality of production. Further, Silicon Valley leaders have moved into politics with a different attitude toward government, and have changed from a belief in pure competition toward supporting some limited kinds of collaboration.

One view of U.S.-Japanese competition is that if Japanese firms can manufacture microelectronics products of higher quality and lower price, then let them. All consumers, including those in the U.S., will benefit directly. Let NEC, Fujitsu, Toshiba, and the rest dominate memory chips and, perhaps in the future, computers. Let U.S. firms do what they can do best—computer software and, perhaps, microprocessors. If one belives in free market forces, this scenario would be a logical conclusion to the present competition.

Unfortunately this let-each-do-what-they-do-best reasoning could make America a second rate nation. So let's assume that American society is committed to saving Silicon Valley from the Japanese, and see what can be done.

The first step is to understand how serious the Japanese competition is in microelectronics. Silicon Valley business executives have been fully aware of this problem for at least five years, but most of the American public is yet uninformed. They think of Detroit and autos, but not of Sunnyvale and semiconductors. Everything else equal, semiconductors and then computers will be the next to go. The public must recognize the likelihood of this event if it is to be prevented.

A second strategy for coping with the Japanese threat in microelectronics is to learn from their strengths. Certain elements of Japanese-style management, modified to Z-style in the American setting, can be advantageously adapted by U.S. firms, as shown by the experiences of Hewlett-Packard, Tandem, and others. The Japanese electronics firms may also have shown us the crucial importance of government as a coordinator of long-term planning—as a facilitator of joint R&D programs, and for pointing an industry toward a vision. Maybe the U.S. needs its own MITI if it is to survive. Finally, Silicon Valley companies grasped the crucial importance of quality production from the Japanese. Moving quickly down the learning curve is not the only way to profits for a microelectronics firm. Starting later in producing a new semiconductor chip or an innovative computer can be advantageous if quality is emphasized.

A third goal for Americans should be to understand the Japanese as well as the Japanese understand Americans. To misunderstand one's competitor is a fatal weakness. Japan represents a blind spot for Americans. We do not know their language and culture. Admittedly the Japanese language is difficult for foreigners to grasp, but as a result U.S.-Japanese business negotiations must be conducted in English, even when they are held in Tokyo. English is the required second language for all Japanese school-children and most Japanese businessmen have at least some ability in our language. This means they can monitor U.S. technical publications and keep abreast of U.S. technological innovations. Since the reverse seldom occurs, when U.S. microelectronics officials go to Tokyo on a business trip, they are more likely than not ignorant of the broader context of their specific negotiations. The American operates with a different set of cultural rules than his Japanese counterpart, whose culture he does not understand. The result is a tremendous one-way advantage for the Japanese.

Consider the Silicon Valley business official who goes to Japan on a two-week, round-trip ticket, expecting that ten business days are more than enough to close the deal. The American does not comprehend the importance to the Japanese of forming a long-term, trusting relationship. He returns to San Francisco discouraged. The basic reason is not the terms of the deal, but a lack of understanding of Japanese cultural values.

If Silicon Valley is to be saved, it must build upon what it does best: entrepreneurship. This spirit may be America's greatest resource in the microelectronics competition with Japan. It can lead high-technology activities into yet unrealized directions, where Japanese firms can only try to follow. A continued faith in entrepreneurship is fundamental to American success. Federal government policies that would diminish entrepreneurial drive (such as higher tax rates on capital gains, which act to limit venture capital) are thus a long-range mistake.

13

The Spread of
"Silicon Valleys"

"As long as we maintain the practices that have made us
what we are today, there is no limit to the longevity of this
situation."

Fred Terman, 1974*

IS SILICON VALLEY a one-time-only phenomenon, or can lessons derived from its experience be applied at other times, in other places? The basis for an answer comes from a synthesis of parallel experiences at several locations in the U.S. and abroad:

1. Three planned attempts to create other "Silicon Valleys" at Research Triangle in North Carolina, the University of Utah Research Park in Salt Lake City, and at RPI (Rensselaer Polytechnic Institute) in Troy, New York. In each of these cases, a research university and/or a state government took the lead in development.
2. Another set of "Silicon Valleys" are emerging around Dallas and Austin, Phoenix, Minneapolis-St. Paul, Colorado Springs, Portland (Oregon), Seattle, and Orange County (Los Angeles). These complexes typically spring up in the form of manufacturing facilities for microelectronics firms headquartered in Silicon Valley. There is not enough space left on the San Francisco Peninsula and skyrocketing housing prices preclude further expansion. Hewlett-Packard, Intel, AMD, Apple, and other large firms have based their new production facilities in Texas, Colorado, Arizona, and Oregon.

*In Gene Bylinsky, "California's Great Breeding Ground for Industry," *Fortune,* June 1974.

The fact that mayors, governors, and other officials flock to Santa Clara County, then return home to nickname their aspiring high-technology area "Silicon Prairie," "Silicon Mountain," or "Silicon Valley East," shows the degree to which they accept Silicon Valley as the model for what they are trying to create. The Silicon Valley model has not only spread over the U.S., but has gone worldwide—to France, Germany, and Japan.

Factors in Silicon Valley's Success

Proximity to a Research University

What Silicon Valley, Boston's Route 128, and North Carolina's Research Triangle have in common is they all have at least one research university.[1] Stanford for Silicon Valley, MIT for Route 128, and the triad of the University of North Carolina, North Carolina State, and Duke University in Research Triangle. Each of these research universities has policies that facilitate technology transfer through close industry-university relationships. Each university is strong in engineering, and engineering professors took the lead in spinning off new high-technology firms. Today computer science and biomedical professors are also increasingly engaged in entrepreneurial activities. Engineering, computer science, and biomedicine are all highly applied university fields; they do not exist as academic disciplines without commercial firms to exploit the advances in basic knowledge that are made by university scholars.

It is worth noting that Harvard and Berkeley, universities near MIT and Stanford, respectively, did not play much of a role in Route 128 and Silicon Valley. They are excellent academic institutions, but Berkeley and Harvard lack an ethos favorable to technology transfer from university scientists to private firms. Neither Berkeley nor Harvard is particularly strong in engineering.[2] Instead their strengths are in more basic sciences and fields like the social sciences and humanities. There are only two important spin-offs from Harvard University on Route 128: Wang Laboratories, begun in 1952 by Dr. An Wang of Harvard's Computer Lab; and Polaroid, launched in 1937 by Ed Land. There were almost no Harvard spin-offs during the 1960s and 1970s, while MIT engineers were busy getting Route 128 going.

The California Institute of Technology in Pasadena is an outstanding engineering school, certainly in a class with MIT and Stanford. It has one special kind of spinoff, the Jet Propulsion Laboratory (JPL), which does high-technology work in aeronautics, space, and energy. But other than JPL, Cal Tech has not helped create a high-tech complex in Pasadena. It's as if any entrepreneurial spark that might be generated at Cal Tech gets suffocated in the smog of the Greater Los Angeles Basin.

In an information society the university (particularly the research university, where the production of Ph.D.s and the conduct of scientific research is a main activity) is the central institution, much as the factory was in the previous era of the industrial society. It is not an accident that most high-technology systems in the United States are centered around a prestigious research university. A nearby source of well-trained graduates for work in high-technology firms, plus a steady flow of research-based technologies, are important contributions by the research university to a "Silicon Valley."

Since the founding of the Stanford Industrial Park in 1951, eighteen other university-related research parks have been created in attempts to attract industrial firms. All eighteen were modeled after Stanford's. Research parks at Rensselaer Polytechnic Institute (RPI) in New York State and at Research Triangle Park in North Carolina look promising, as does the University of Utah's Research Park. Some university research parks have been complete failures; the University of Miami's research park was unable to attract any industrial occupants.[3] Another university research park in Georgia, launched with much fanfare a few years ago, has only been able to attract one occupant, the university nursery school for faculty children.

Infrastructure

A newborn firm is necessarily very fragile in its dependence on suppliers, financiers, markets, and other parts of its infrastructure. Logically, start-ups are most likely to be formed and succeed in an area where the infrastructure already exists. Infrastructure is a basic reason for the principle of agglomeration, the tendency for firms in an industry to gather together in the same area.

Venture capital is a crucial aspect of the microelectronics infrastructure because of its importance to start-up firms. About one-third of the available venture capital in the U.S. today is concentrated in Silicon Valley; most of the rest is in New York or Boston. Almost none of it is in the "Silicon Valleys" springing up around the U.S.

An astute observer of other "Silicon Valleys" in the U.S. is Intel's Bob Noyce, who said: "Venture capitalists from here are willing to go to Boulder to look at a new opportunity. Or Minneapolis. Or Cedar Rapids, Iowa. But there isn't the local sophistication of what it takes to succeed with a new business. There is suspicion of the venture capitalist who comes out from a big city to Boulder. The entrepreneur doesn't have someone at his side to help him talk to venture capitalists. Today I get more and more calls from someone in Podunk asking me who could help them write a business plan."[4]

Climate and Quality of Life

Most of the "Silicon Valleys" are located in the Sun Belt areas of the United States. A pleasant climate helps attract engineers and other technicians and holds spin-off firms in the same area, contributing to agglomeration. Sometimes a sunny climate helps attract an already established company; an example is VisiCorp, a leading microcomputer software firm that was launched in Cambridge when its founder was an MBA student at Harvard. But at the first opportunity, VisiCorp's founder left the winters of Boston and moved his fledgling company to sunny San Jose.

Everything else being equal, people who can work anywhere usually prefer to reside in an area with a sunny climate. Why wear overshoes and overcoat when you don't have to? But sunshine is not the only location preference factor. More important is quality of life, indicated by the availability of beaches, ski areas, theaters, and other cultural amenities. In the U.S. such quality-of-life attractions usually come with access to a nearby metropolitan center. While Route 128 is strictly second fiddle to

Silicon Valley in sunshine, Boston area residents are justifiably proud of their other quality-of-life resources, as those who have attended the symphonies, witnessed New England's fall leaves, or who have enjoyed Cape Cod beaches will certainly attest. Even frigid Minneapolis has its summer lakes.

Bob Noyce pointed out that, "In the 1960s, you could hire anybody in the country to work here in Silicon Valley. They would get up and leave for the San Francisco area at the drop of a hat. But that's not true today. There are lots of other attractive places to live in the country today. . . . So we'll see a dispersion of high-technology industries, and that's a good thing. We'll see lots of little 'Silicon Valleys.' "[5]

Entrepreneurship

The most important single factor in the rise of a "Silicon Valley" is entrepreneurial fever. It is doubtful that its spirit can be taught in formal classes, although several universities now have courses on entrepreneurship. Entrepreneurship is best learned by example. When individuals know of successful role models like Steve Jobs, Bob Noyce, Bill Hewlett, Dave Packard, and Nolan Bushnell, they naturally begin to think, "If he did it, why can't I?" Once an entrepreneurial climate becomes established in an area like Silicon Valley, individuals are attracted to seek work there in order to step into an entrepreneurial role. Entrepreneurial fever is concentrated in an area both by modeling, and by selective migration.

"Most communities and states attempting to establish a scientific complex seek transplanting growth and appear to be ignoring the importance of growth from within through the formation of new firms."[6] Instead of trying to seduce other cities' companies, officials wanting to start a high-technology complex should be thinking about their own spin-offs. But a steady stream of city, state, and national officials come to Silicon Valley, seeking to woo California firms to their area by offering tax breaks, cheap land, and other inducements. Most of these trips are futile.

An agglomeration of spin-offs in the same neighborhood as their parent firms is why a high-technology complex builds up in a certain region. The chain reaction of spin-offs from spin-offs is a kind of natural process, once it is begun. Setting off the initial spark is key.

The thousands of engineers and managers in Silicon Valley represent a sizeable workforce. Each technologist represents 16 additional jobs. Since engineers and managers usually comprise 20 percent of the total workforce in a high-technology firm, the rest are clerical and skilled manual workers, about four for each engineer or manager. In addition, each engineer and manager in a high-technology firm typically creates 12 additional jobs in supporting service industries. It is this 1 to 16 multiplier effect that makes high-technology industries so attractive as a force for economic growth in a local region.

Yet an even higher ratio is that of the entrepreneur to jobs created. This ratio may be 1 to 500, or 1 to 1,000. Each new spin-off, if it grows to any size, may create jobs for hundreds, if not thousands, of employees in the new firm. And some of those employees typically will spin off to launch additional companies. Thus entrepreneurship is the yeast of high technology.

Route 128

The Route 128 complex around Boston is the second largest microelectronics heartland in the world, second only to Silicon Valley. The geography of Route 128 is distinctive in that the major firms are scattered along access roads just off a main highway (instead of in a more compact valley, as in Santa Clara County). Route 128 is an eight-lane highway that was built in the 1950s in a semicircle around Boston in a radius 10 miles from the city. Originally it was designed to keep long-distance traffic out of Boston; instead it brought an economic renaissance. Route 2 and the Massachusetts Turnpike connect the private firms along this highway with Cambridge and with the intellectual resources of MIT.

There are two layers of the Route 128 complex. Furthest from Boston are the newer firms built along Interstate 495, another circumferential road about 10 to 15 miles further out from Boston than Route 128. Among them are Wang Laboratories at Lowell, Digital Equipment Corporation (DEC) at Maynard, and Data General (DG) at Westboro, word-processing and minicomputer firms that rose to prominence in the 1970s and 1980s. Closer to Boston along Route 128 an inner layer of military electronics firms includes Mitre, Raytheon, and Itek, built in the earlier era of the 1950s and 1960s. Between the foundings of the two bands of high-technology firms was the economic catastrophe of the early 1970s, when thousands of Route 128 engineers were fired or out of work.

MIT was the savior of the Massachusetts economy. The history of Route 128 goes back a bit further than that of Silicon Valley. Several spin-offs from MIT research laboratories occurred prior to World War II: Ionics, High Voltage, and EG&G, for example. Carl Taylor Compton was president of MIT during this era and he encouraged his engineering faculty and staff to become involved in area private firms. In his view the high-technology start-ups represented an important kind of technology transfer in which innovations coming out of MIT research labs would be commercialized by for-profit companies. The net result was that MIT faculty were not just allowed to engage in consulting with these local firms, they were encouraged to do so. The MIT policy of close industry-university relationships was unique for the 1930s, almost heretical in its day. But to the great advantage of the local economy in the Boston area, it worked. Today about one-third of Massachusetts' manufacturing workforce is employed in high-technology firms, most of them along Route 128 and Route 495. Almost all of these companies have either a direct or an indirect connection with MIT. Without MIT there would be no Route 128 complex.

Route 128 pioneered a different kind of building in the New England area, as well as a different kind of industry. There was plenty of space out on "The Road," as it came to be called by Bostonians, so two-story construction was used. Instead of moving heavy objects up and down by elevators, these new firms moved materials horizontally with fork-lift vehicles. Route 128 buildings represented a sprawling type of construction, with lots of grass and trees around them. A pastoral setting was preserved: "A scientist likes a quiet office with a blackboard, a window, and a tree outside, and better still if the tree has a squirrel in it."[7] There are plenty of trees, and squirrels, on Route 128—flying over it or driving through it, one sees a peaceful-looking forest. But there is a beehive of activity inside it.

MIT President Compton did not stop at pushing his faculty into working with local firms, he also realized that the new high-technology companies had to have venture capital in order to start up. He took the lead in founding the American Research and Development Corporation (ARDC), obtaining the money from Boston-based insurance companies. Indeed the original board of directors of ARDC included four MIT department chairmen.[8] This venture capital firm, headed by Georges Doriot, bankrolled the early high-tech companies in the Boston area. Its most famous start-up was Digital Equipment Corporation, an MIT spin-off that was to begin several years later, after World War II.[9]

The first little acorns that were to grow into the Route 128 oak forest were planted by President Compton, but the high-technology complex did not really sprout until massive federal funding for wartime research began in the early 1940s. That is when the basic formula for Route 128 began to fall in place: Federal government monies went to MIT research laboratories, which spun off engineer-entrepreneurs who took a "hot idea" for a technological innovation from the banks of the Charles River out to Boston's western suburbs on Route 128 in the form of a new company. MIT saw this movement as a contribution to society's progress. The entrepreneurs were chasing dollars and enjoying the innovation game, while some of their profits flowed back to MIT. The high-tech industries helped revitalize Massachusetts' wornout economy, making its political leaders look good.

Route 128 shifted into a high-growth stage from 1955 to 1971, a period when the number of firms jumped from 39 to 1,200, a result of defense and aerospace contracts. Following this boom a serious decline set in as the economy went sour and government contracts were cut back. Suddenly 12,000 engineers and technical people were out of work.[10]

The second coming of high-technology on Route 128 is another example of the principle of agglomeration: A region with a headstart in a particular industry will grow faster than other regions. Due to the Boston area's stock of skilled engineers left over from the military electronics era of the 1960s, a pool of born-again capitalists was ready to launch the minicomputer push in the late 1970s. MIT played a pivotal role, again demonstrating that a research university is the key institution in an information economy.[11] Digital Equipment Corporation, founded by Ken Olsen in 1957 as a spin-off from MIT's Lincoln Laboratory has been parent to at least 20 spin-offs, the best known of which is DEC's rival, Data General.[12] Olsen developed the TX-O computer at MIT under a military contract, and then commercialized it as DEC's first minicomputer. In 1982, DEC had 42 percent of all minicomputer sales, and Data General cornered 11 percent. So minicomputer means Route 128.[13]

A two-way exchange of social technology has occurred, first from MIT to Stanford in the 1940s, and then from Silicon Valley to the Route 128 complex in the late 1970s. Fred Terman engineered the first transfer when he returned in 1946 from his sojourn in Cambridge with a vision of creating a West Coast high-technology electronics complex around Stanford University. Terman synthesized the main principles of industry-university relationships during his World War II years at MIT.

Thirty-five years later Route 128 was to profit in return from the Stanford-Silicon Valley axis. Ray Stata, president of Analog Devices in Norwood, Massachusetts, is considered "Mr. High-Tech" of Route 128. In 1977 he visited Silicon Valley and was impressed with the way in which the California electronics firms collaborated in solving common problems. Route 128 firms were physically more scattered than their counterparts in California and, while each executive might complain bitterly about state government corruption and the resulting high taxes, he did not band together with others to solve these problems. So Stata and several other executives formed the Massachusetts High-Technology Council.[14]

The second economic spurt on Route 128 following the 1970–75 recession helped convince many political and business leaders to think of the high-technology firms as essential to Massachusetts' economy.[15] High-technology executives have a lot of clout when they act together. The Massachusetts High-Technology Council today has as members 124 companies that employ 115,000 workers. Although some large firms such as Raytheon, Polaroid, and General Electric have not joined, the Council is widely regarded as the powerful voice of Route 128.

The political strength of the Massachusetts High-Technology Council was demonstrated in November 1980 when Massachusetts voters overwhelmingly approved Proposition 2½, a local tax reduction referendum patterned after California's Proposition 13. The High-Tech Council funded a media blitz supporting the proposition, and is credited with convincing the public to vote for it. Taxes are high in "Taxachusetts," as the electronics executives claim. Prior to Proposition 2½, state and local taxes consumed an average of 18 percent of personal income, a figure that the Massachusetts High-Technology Council claimed put their state at a marked disadvantage in competing with high-tech areas in other states.

Proposition 2½ in Massachusetts limited local property taxes to 2½ percent of the value of a property; statewide, property taxes were reduced by about 9 percent.[16] One result was a 14 percent school budget reduction (which included the effects of inflation) in 1981–82, leading to the firing of 7,000 teachers and other school staff, with several thousand more dismissed in fall 1982.[17] A study of seven Route 128 school districts (Newton, Lexington, Waltham, et al.) found that 60 percent of the math and science teachers were planning to leave or expected to be laid off. The teachers indicated widespread demoralization due to low salaries and the Prop 2½ budget slashes. A math teacher said: "Working conditions are deteriorating. I want to leave Massachusetts and its anti-education attitude."[18]

Perhaps the Massachusetts High-Technology Council has killed math-science education in the state as a result of its pushing for Proposition 2½. The Council gave $229,000 to the campaign in 1980, 60 percent of its total budget. Council officials admit that without their last minute funding of the media blitz, Proposition 2½ would not have passed. Route 128 entrepreneurs have long complained against high taxes, which they felt made it impossible for them to recruit engineers from outside the area. The local businessmen expected that the new law would prune peripheral programs in local schools, like courses on "the mystery novel," but not effect science and math teaching. The high-tech executives blamed school inefficiency on administrative problems and graft, not on inadequate finances.

Teachers resent the effort by the Massachusetts High-Technology Council to turn their schools into technical trade institutes. One teacher remarked: "Around here, high-tech is a nasty word."[19] The Route 128 firms depend on a highly educated labor force and they did not foresee the full ramifications of Proposition 2½. Understandably school teachers and officials in the Boston area are antagonistic toward the Route 128 firms, which they feel are only concerned with immediate profits and not with long-term social responsibilities.

In the long range of twenty to thirty years from now, the United States will certainly see a major role for scientists and engineers in top policy-making positions. Perhaps engineers will someday occupy the high positions in Washington that economists now hold. This trend toward more political power for engineers and scientists may be a mixed blessing for society. Some critical observers fear that the social narrowness of some engineers poses a danger when these technicians rise to high positions in society. For starters, the Massachusetts High-Technology Council's role in Proposition 2½ does not bode well for putting technologists in charge of society. However, engineers are often fast learners, and maybe they will learn a useful lesson from the deterioration of Massachusetts education in the early 1980s.

North Carolina Renaissance

Unlike Silicon Valley, Research Triangle was designed, planned, and created by government officials, especially Luther H. Hodges, a former textile executive who became governor of North Carolina in the 1950s, then went on to become U.S. Secretary of Commerce under President Kennedy.[20] Hodges followed Silicon Valley's lead by launching a university research park in order to create a high-technology complex. And he did it in a most un-likely place, a little-known area of three university cities in the South. Research Triangle was very slow to start, but now it shows signs of becoming dynamic.

Research Triangle is a high-technology complex in the Ra-leigh-Durham-Chapel Hill metropolitan area. The complex began in 1960 with the founding of the Research Triangle Park, a 6,000-acre R&D center that presently contains 40 private and gov-ernment R&D organizations in such fields as electronics, pharma-ceuticals, and air pollution research. An early boost to Research Triangle was provided by IBM's 1965 decision to locate one of its R&D operations there; now it has about 8,000 employees in the Triangle, more than a third of its total workforce.

Three nearby universities, Duke, North Carolina State Uni-versity, and the University of North Carolina, helped fuel the rise of Research Triangle along with the instrumental persuasive charm of former Governor Hodges.[21] Until 1960 North Carolina ranked near the bottom of the U.S. in per capita income and aver-age industrial wages. That's quite different now, thanks to the Research Triangle.

In addition to the brainpower represented by the three uni-versities, Research Triangle offered low taxes, freedom from unionization, and a pleasant climate. The Southern small-town atmosphere had a certain charm to visiting industrialists from the North—Chapel Hill has a population of only 32,000 (plus 20,000 students), and Raleigh, the largest of the three cities, has about 150,000 residents.

Total employment at Research Triangle Park is now about 20,000, with an annual payroll of $500 million. By Silicon Valley standards not much, but there are unmistakable signs that Re-search Triangle is starting to gather steam. The population of the three-county metropolitan area grew by 26 percent from 1970 to 1980, while the national population increased 10.5 percent. Per-sonal incomes rose locally by 143 percent during this decade, and the number of manufacturing jobs went from 29,000 to 43,400. The local unemployment rate was only 4.7 percent in 1982, the fifth lowest of all metropolitan areas in the U.S.[22]

In the past few years Research Triangle has concentrated on microelectronics. North Carolina Governor James B. Hunt, Jr., convinced his legislature to put up $24 million for the Microelectronics Center of North Carolina (MCNC), a research and training facility in Research Triangle Park. These are promising developments; however as yet Research Triangle doesn't have venture capital, nor any entrepreneurial spin-offs.

Bionic Valley: Mormon Entrepreneurship

With nurturing from the University of Utah, a promising high-technology center has been growing in the metropolitan area around Salt Lake City. Three-quarters of Utah's 1.5 million population are concentrated here next to the Great Salt Lake in an area that is the heartland of the Church of Jesus Christ of Latter-Day Saints (Mormons). This religious group prizes making money, formal education, and large families. They approach the building of a high-tech complex with the zeal of missionaries, as it provides opportunities for young Mormons to remain in, or return to Salt Lake City, and also turn a handsome profit, 10 percent of which ideally goes into church coffers.

"Bionic Valley" is a center for biomedical engineering research for the health industry. The University of Utah (locally called "The U") is a leading research university in the medical field, especially in the field of artifical organs. Dr. William Kolff, developer of the artifical kidney and a professor at The U, has spawned as the result of his research, several private firms now working on artifical hearts, artifical limbs, and other organs. The man behind high-tech in Salt Lake City is James Fletcher, who became president of The U in 1964 and immediately began lobbying for federal research funds. Taking a leaf from Fred Terman and Stanford, Fletcher offered his faculty start-up facilities in rundown wooden buildings on campus. In 1970 he launched the University of Utah Research Park on 320 acres next to The U and it now leases to 35 firms with 1,700 employees.[23] Firm activities run to microelectronics, geological/mining research, and biomedical engineering.

The pioneer firm in Utah Research Park was Evans and Sutherland Computer Corporation, a computer graphics firm that specializes in military work. E&S's founder is Dr. David Evans, a 44-year-old Mormon whom President Fletcher persuaded to return from Berkeley in 1966 to become chairperson of the University of Utah's Department of Computer Science. Evans in turn recruited Ivan E. Sutherland, then only 30 and the inventor of computer graphics (a computer system that displays pictures as well as words and numbers on a computer terminal screen). Evans and Sutherland Computer started up in 1968, the same year as Intel and Data General (DG), in an old building at The U. Soon it moved nearby to the Research Park and began to grow to 700 employees.[24] Although not nearly as successful as Intel or DG, Evans and Sutherland is like them in being state-of-the-art in its field. Evans pays himself around $600,000 a year, thus setting a good entrepreneurial model for young Mormons at The U.[25] "Evans is the David Packard of the Wasatch Range," says Mark Money, director of the University of Utah Research Park.[26]

Although Bionic Valley is just getting underway, it has a lot of things going for it—a beautiful setting, a research university, cheap labor, reasonable housing, and Mormon entrepreneurial spirit.

Silicon Valley East

Another high-tech center now on the make, is "Silicon Valley East" in the Troy-Albany-Schenectady area of upper New York State. The sparkplug in this recent development is George M. Low, president of Rensselaer Polytechnic Institute (RPI). Low is an RPI alumnus who returned as president after twenty-five years with NASA. Drawing lessons from the entrepreneurs of MIT and Stanford, Low thinks that the way to put his engineering school on the academic map is to create a neighborhood high-technology complex.

Troy was one of the nation's first industrial cities, pioneering in new methods of iron making, railroad car building, and textiles in the mid-1800s. The steel rails produced at Troy led to the city's downfall (its population fell from 76,000 eighty years ago to only 56,000 today) as railroads moved mills and factories to the West and South.[27] Dr. Low wants to reverse this industrial decline by building an electronics complex: "The area's ripe for high technology and to create that environment, we will build it." One of Low's first moves was to launch an Incubator Space Project by providing two vacant campus buildings at RPI for fledgling firms at low rent. Each start-up also receives 50 hours of free computer time on the RPI computer plus expert advice from RPI professors. RPI in essence acts as a special kind of venture capital company, taking equity in a start-up in lieu of rent.

In 1981 Low inaugurated Rensselaer Technology Park, a 1,200-acre site at nearby North Greenbush. This facility has yet to receive its first high-technology lessee, but it lies waiting as a potential encouragement to aspiring entrepreneurs. In addition to RPI, nearby is the State University of New York at Albany, an important research university with 50,000 students. Neighboring Schenectady has General Electric's R&D Center. Housing in the tri-city area is reasonable in cost and residents boast of their quality of life. But frigid winters are a negative factor.

Silicon Valley East represents an important test of whether an industrial economy on the skids can recoup through a planned "Silicon Valley." It's now too early to tell whether George Low and RPI can turn around the decline of Troy.

Silicon Prairie

Some call the area around Dallas (especially on the northern side toward the airport) "Silicon Prairie" because of the high-technology interests that are growing there, mainly in the form of spin-offs from Texas Instruments. TI originally began as a producer of oil discovery instruments and evolved into an electronics firm during World War II. Silicon Prairie is dominated by gigantic TI, employing over half of all the electronics employees in the Dallas metropolitan area. One usually thinks of Dallas in terms of oil, cattle, and big spenders wearing expensive suits and cowboy hats like "J.R." on the popular television series. Indeed these stereotypes exist in Dallas, but so do shirt-sleeved engineers and a growing number of electronics firms. In addition to TI, the Dallas-Fort Worth area is the home of Tandy Corporation, which operates Radio Shack, a national chain that sells microcomputers and other electronics, and Mostek, an important semiconductor firm and TI spin-off.

In recent years the Dallas area has been challenged by Austin as a microelectronics center. The state capital and site of the University of Texas, Austin is now home for production plants of AMD, Intel, Tandem Computers, Rolm, Lockheed Missiles and Space, TI, and Motorola. From 1965 to 1980, Austin's manufacturing employment jumped from 5,000 to 30,000, and its current unemployment rate is half the national average.[28] Housing prices in Austin are about half those in Silicon Valley, which is one reason why new plants are locating in this area. But spin-offs have not occurred in any great numbers. A boost to the Austin area was the 1983 decision to locate the Microelectronics and Computer Technology Corporation (a joint venture of twelve major U.S. high-tech firms) in the Texas capital.

Silicon Prairie is mainly a high-tech production center whose entrepreneurial fever and capacity for technological innovation have not yet been fully developed.

Silicon Mountain

Until a decade ago Colorado Springs was characterized mainly by military employment at the Air Force Academy and at some nearby Air Force and Army bases. The city fathers were anti-industry.

Now this has changed as electronics firms have located their plants in the Colorado Springs area. Hewlett-Packard and Ampex

Corporation, two Silicon Valley regulars, arrived there in the mid-1960s. Rolm, Micro Mask, Ford Aerospace, DEC, TI, Honeywell, Inmos, Mostek, and several others followed. These electronics firms presently employ about 8,500 workers, three times the number in 1975. Subcontractors and other support services have also come in, but few spin-offs have occurred. Colorado Springs is a 90-minute drive down Highway I-25 from Denver, where the closest major airport is located. "Silicon Mountain," as the area is known, lacks a symbiotic relationship with a local research university. However there is some R&D on the part of the microelectronics firms located around Colorado Springs: Hewlett-Packard is decentralized in divisions, so H-P conducts R&D locally for oscilloscopes, graphic displays, and logic development systems; DEC designs, as well as manufactures, computer disc drives; and Inmos and Mostek (both semiconductor firms) conduct R&D on Silicon Mountain.

Silicon Valley North

In the early 1970s an Oregon governor announced: "Come and visit Oregon. Just don't stay." The state saw itself as an ecological paradise and economic growth was considered anathema. Oregon's present governor says: "Oregon is open for business." Especially electronics business, because local planners decided that an alternative was needed to Oregon's boom-or-bust forest products industry.[29]

The major newcomers to the Willamette Valley, south and west of Portland, are Hewlett-Packard and Intel, spilling north from Silicon Valley. These firms join such home-grown electronics firms as Floating Point Systems (computers) and Tektronix (electronics instruments) to form a "Silicon Valley North." Tektronix with 20,000 workers is Oregon's largest employer. About three-fourths of all the electronics workers in the state are located around Portland, attracted by low housing costs (about half that of Santa Clara County), and a high quality of life. If one likes rain, Portland is an ideal place to live. About 20 electronics firms have plants in Oregon and the industry accounts for 20 percent of all manufacturing employment, about four times that of 20 years ago.[30]

There are limits to future expansion of microelectronics in Silicon Valley North: Portland lacks a research university, venture capital, and there is a small local base of qualified workers so many must be imported from elsewhere. Further, the eruption of Mount St. Helens in 1980 may have caused some uncertainty on the part of microelectronics firms about locating in the area.

Table 13-1 shows a comparison of twelve "Silicon Valleys" around the U.S. Each high-technology complex is rated on the main factors involved in the rise of Silicon Valley.

In addition to the seven "Silicon Valleys" described in this chapter, Table 13-1 includes four other high-technology centers:

1. Phoenix (sometimes jokingly called "Silicon Desert") which is dominated by Motorola, a major electronics firm and semiconductor producer. Honeywell, IBM, DEC, Intel, National Semiconductor, and other electronics firms have located production facilities in Phoenix, but the entrepreneurial fever has not yet warmed up; spin-offs are still few.
2. The Minneapolis-St. Paul area has been a mainframe computer center for some years, with Sperry, Control Data, Honeywell, and others located there. Around 40 percent of Minnesota's workforce is employed in high-technology. However minicomputers and microcomputers are centered elsewhere; entrepreneurial spin-offs have been more difficult in the mainframe industry. The frigid winters of Minnesota have not proven attractive to high-tech start-ups. The Minneapolis-St. Paul region does have a research university and perhaps venture capital and the other requisites for a high-technology complex will develop.
3. Seattle is known as the home of Boeing and specializes in aircraft and aerospace technology. But when heavy layoffs occur at Boeing, as happened in the 1982 recession, new electronics firms spring up (10 start-ups began in the 1980s).
4. Orange County, a fast-growing area just to the south of Los Angeles, is different than most of the other second-tier cities in the microelectronics industry today because it is not a site for the production facilities of firms headquartered elsewhere. Instead Orange County is characterized by many small firms that apply semiconductor chip technology (with chips purchased from Silicon Valley firms). So there is much entrepreneurial activity in Orange County although venture capital is sparse and its local university, the University of California at Irvine, is not a major research center. However, Irvine does have strength in engineering and computer science. The proximity of Orange

TABLE 13.1.
A Scorecard Comparing "Silicon Valleys" in the U.S.

High-Technology Complex	Was the High-Tech Complex Spontaneous or Planned?	Research University	Is Venture Capital Present?	Is Entrepreneurial Spirit Demonstrated by Spin-Offs?	Climate and Quality of Life	Prognosis
1. Silicon Valley	Planned somewhat	Stanford	Yes	Yes	Sunny climate; high quality of life	Will remain the leading hi-tech complex
2. Route 128	Planned somewhat	MIT	Yes	Yes	Good quality of life	Second only to Silicon Valley
3. Research Triangle	Planned	Univ. of N.C., N.C. State, Duke	No	No	Good	Rising gradually in prominence
4. "Bionic Valley" (Salt Lake City)	Planned	University of Utah	Little	Some	Good	Off to a promising start
5. "Silicon Valley East"	Planned	RPI, SUNY Albany	No	No	Cold climate	Just getting started
6. "Silicon Prairie" (Dallas-Austin)	Spontaneous	University of Texas at Austin	Some	Some	Good	Shows potential

High-Technology Complex	Was the High-Tech Complex Spontaneous or Planned?	Research University	Is Venture Capital Present?	Is Entrepreneurial Spirit Demonstrated by Spin-Offs?	Climate and Quality of Life	Prognosis
7. "Silicon Mountain" (Colorado Springs)	Spontaneous	None	Little	Few	Good	Shows potential
8. "Silicon Valley North" (Portland)	Spontaneous	None	No	No	Good	Shows potential
9. "Silicon Desert" (Phoenix)	Spontaneous	Arizona State	Little	Few	Hot climate	Shows potential
10. Minneapolis-St. Paul	Spontaneous	University of Minnesota	Little	No	Cold	Some potential
11. Seattle	Spontaneous	University of Washington	No	Some	Good	Some potential
12. Orange County (Los Angeles)	Spontaneous	UC Irvine	Some	Yes	Smog	Good potential

County to Los Angeles gives it certain advantages, like a pool of talented technologists and airports, and some disadvantages, like smog.

The Future of Silicon Valley

Given that Silicon Valley is spreading across the U.S., what is the future of Silicon Valley in Santa Clara County? Is there an ultimate limit to the future of Silicon Valley? Many observers think so. The direction of the microelectronics industry is toward further miniaturization of semiconductor chips, thus achieving lower and lower prices for greater and greater computing power. But the chips sooner or later will reach an ultimate barrier to further miniaturization. Ted Hoff, inventor of the microprocessor, foresees this limit occurring within about 20 years.[31] He feels that Silicon Valley's microelectronics industry will mature; R&D will become less important. Perhaps labor unions will be organized and firms will lose their present freewheeling independence and flexibility. Silicon Valley will resemble Pittsburgh, Cleveland, and Detroit today. The center of high-technology will move away from Silicon Valley to other parts of the U.S., to Japan, or elsewhere.

A more optimistic perception of the future is that the great collection of entrepreneurial talent in Silicon Valley will overcome the ultimate barriers to chip miniaturization. Perhaps California's technology entrepreneurs will invent an alternative to semiconductor chips as we know them, as the basis for the future information society. Maybe some kind of hybrid of the bioengineering industry and microelectronics will develop. In any event, the optimistic view banks on Silicon Valley's innovators to keep inventing new technologies, thus staving off decay of their industry and their high-tech complex.

Obviously established firms in Silicon Valley are maturing with every day that goes by. Their engineers and other key employees are getting older.[32] The firms are growing in size, a manifestation of their financial success. The space for new production facilities in Silicon Valley is gone. These forces propelling the microelectronics industry in Northern California toward maturity are indisputable.

But these trends do not necessarily mean the demise of Silicon Valley. The entrepreneurial spirit is firmly implanted and will not go away in the future. New companies will find their niche and exploit it. The manufacturing function of Silicon Valley represented, for instance, by wafer fabrication plants, will continue to move out, starting new "Silicon Valleys" around the U.S. Silicon Valley in the future will become more and more the essence of an information society, gaining the status of the R&D capital of America and of the world. In this sense, Silicon Valley will clone itself.

14

The Impact of
Silicon Valley

"Radio Technology Update, broadcasting from Silicon
Valley, world headquarters of the 21st century."
Radio station identification, San Jose, 1982

THE INFORMATION REVOLUTION of today is different from
the industrial revolution that preceded it. One difference is that
the present revolution is happening much faster. Instead of the
several generations required for the industrial transformation,
the information revolution is occuring in the period of just one
generation. Another difference is that we recognize the information revolution as it is happening. A hundred years ago few residents of Manchester or other English industrial towns knew what
was occurring in their society, in part because it was such a grad-
ual change.

An indication of the rapid speed of the information revolution is the number of computers in use. By 1984 computers were
becoming ubiquitious as Silicon Valley made them increasingly
smaller and cheaper. In the decades since ENIAC (the first computer) launched the computer revolution in 1946, the number of
computers went from one, to 600 in 1956, to 30,000 in 1966, to
400,000 in 1976. By 1984 there were over 6 million. In 1990, 50 percent of U.S. households are expected to have a microcomputer.
By then the computer revolution will have conquered American
society.

Microelectronics is such a widescope technology that semiconductor chips and computers can be applied to almost every situation. Consider farming: a modern dairy farm is equipped with microcomputer-controlled feed devices, triggered by a magnetic key worn by each dairy cow on a chain around her neck. The key serves to determine the amount and type of feed given that cow each day. When a particular cow passes through the milking parlor, a minimum-cost ration is instantly computed and fed to her individually. If her milk production drops, the microcomputer notifies the dairy farmer and cuts the cow's ration, giving her less of the higher priced protein supplements and larger amounts of roughage.

In the past we thought of each communication technology as a separate entity—telephones, for instance, and radio and TV. Today this distinction is disappearing. Due to the computer, each of these communication media are being integrated into a single communication network, which some call "compunications."[1] Such integration occurs when a television news program like Ted Turner's 24-hour news is beamed by satellite to your local cable TV system which then sends it to your home. If your system is interactive, you may respond with a signal to the headend of the cable system, indicating your like or dislike of the news program. Your vote and others are tabulated by a computer and the results flashed on the TV screen. This communication system consists of an integrated network of satellite, cable TV, and computer technologies. Similar integration is happening in the modern office, where a computer terminal on your desk provides a word-processing function, and also links you to other offices to which you can send electronic messages. These instantly transmitted messages can be printed out by the receiver or stored in a computer file—thus the paperless office.

Tool technology is an extension of man's physical powers. Communication technology is the extension of perception and knowledge and enlarges our consciousness. In this sense communication technology is basic to all other technology, as the computer is basic to the new communication technologies. It is computing capability that makes the new information technologies interactive. Interactivity in mass communication systems makes them two-way instead of one-way, as were radio and TV broadcasting and the press. Such interactivity of communication changes the nature of who controls a mass medium. Instead of a handful of TV network executives or a few newspaper moguls deciding what you receive, each individual user of an interactive system has a large degree of control in choosing what information to request and what to avoid. Computers make possible interactive communication, allowing the individualization of information systems.

Office Automation

The "office of the future" is today. At the heart of office automation is the word-processor, essentially a typewriter connected to a computer. The reason so many organizations rush to buy these expensive machines (the average price for a stand-alone word-processor is $12,000) is the jump in productivity they provide. An office secretary can usually raise typing output by about 20 percent with a word-processor, because editing and retyping are so much easier. Text can be corrected without having to retype the parts of a manuscript that are not changed. The more expensive word-processors can justify the right-hand margin of the page, print in a variety of type faces, and generally make the typed page look like a thing of beauty.

By 1984 there were about 800,000 word-processors in operation in the U.S. with 100,000 of these machines sold during 1983. Yet there is more to office automation than just word-processing. Electronic mail transmits memos and letters from computerized office to computerized office, usually via telephone lines. The advantage is that messages are conveyed instantly and correspondence can be "filed" and retrieved in the computer's memory. Not only can the automated office store correspondence, but it can also store reams of data, putting it, on command, into graphic display on the computer screen.

Given the advantages of the computer in the office, one would expect a rapid rate of adoption. On the contrary, even though office automation got off to a fast start, and is the subject of a great deal of discussion among business executives, the actual rate of adoption today has slowed.[2] It's expensive for one thing. Further, the introduction of office systems often has not been carried out smoothly, as problems of implementation have occurred. The extent of anticomputer feeling often was overlooked when computers first came to the office. Honey was poured into computer terminals in the Minneapolis Post Office and a computer at Metropolitan Life Insurance Company was attacked with a screwdriver. In Denver, car keys were fed into a disk drive, and in Bell, California, a police station computer was shot with a revolver by a policeman.[3] Such extreme cases of frustration with computers are rare, but telling.

One reason for resistance to office automation is the effect of computers on employment. If an office computer can improve a typist's efficiency by 20 or 25 percent, that means that an organization can lay off 20 or 25 percent of its typing employees. Secretarial work represents one of the most important occupations for women and about 35 percent of the typical secretary's time is spent typing. Office automation threatens to add to unemployment rates.

There is another effect of office computers on employment. *Deskilling* is a process of job simplification by means of computer technology so that less skilled, lower paid workers can be substituted for more educated, higher paid employees. Office automation can lead to deskilling if secretarial work is broken down into keyboarding on a word-processor versus other duties where shorthand dictation, accurate typing, and editing skills are required. Another example of deskilling by computer occurs at grocery check-out stands, where the new technologies no longer require that the operator be able to operate a register. Deskilling is obviously an advantage to employers, but not to the skilled workforce.

Office automation can also change the nature of supervision and control in the office. Computers capable of monitoring, for instance, employee lateness or absence records as well as daily productivity information could easily run a company more "efficiently" than a softhearted human boss given to overlooking employee weaknesses.[4]

A Day in the Office of the Future[5]

Scene: 8:05 A.M. in the order-processing office of a major corporation. Late for work, Frank hurries down rows of computer terminals already blinking in response to the flying fingers of their operators. He slides hurriedly into his chair and logs on to his terminal.

YOU ARE SIX MINUTES LATE, FRANK. THIS IS YOUR THIRD TARDINESS THIS MONTH AND THE TWENTY-FOURTH TIME THIS YEAR. SEE YOUR SUPERVISOR AT THE MORNING COFFEE BREAK.

"Damn," mutters Frank, "now I'm in trouble." With a sigh, he begins entering a stack of customer order forms into his terminal.

Two hours pass.

YOU ENTERED 215 CUSTOMER ORDERS SO FAR TODAY, WHICH IS LESS THAN YOUR AVERAGE OF 231. WHAT IS THE MATTER, FRANK? SEE YOUR SUPERVISOR DURING THE COFFEE BREAK.

Frank's headache intensifies as he walks down the aisle toward his supervisor's cubicle. His mind returns to his scheme for sabotaging the corporation's computer system.

Robots

The word "robot" brings to mind an anthropomorphic machine that walks about on two legs, talks, and sometimes harbors sinister intentions. In reality, most present-day robots work in factories and most of them work in Japan. Industrial robots bear little resemblance to humans. They look more like exotic insects, somewhat like the oil pumps dotting the Texas countryside. Some industrial robots resemble a human arm, with an elbow and a clamplike hand (called the gripper). A robot possesses intelligence in the form of a computer (usually a microprocessor) programmed to control the robot in a series of repeated activities. The auto industry is the single most important application for industrial robots, where they work on assembly lines doing such tasks as spot welding, drilling, sanding, and cutting. Robots work a 24-hour shift and perform especially monotonous and/or dangerous tasks. A few manufacturing plants in Japan are almost completely robotized.

Computerized robots provide a means to replace labor with highly capitalized information technology. Robots may free hu-

Teleworking and Cottage Computing[6]

Computers can be an ominous Big Brother to office workers, or a liberating force, depending on how they are used. A much talked about application of office computers is their ability to allow employees to work at home on a terminal that connects them to their company headquarters.

Meet Jim, who manages a dozen professionals and one secretary. He begins his typical day at home, sitting down to his computer terminal with a cup of coffee in his hand. He calls up his calendar by typing "SHOW CALENDAR." His secretary has scheduled a teleconference meeting with a colleague and an appointment with his boss; his calendar also contains a reminder that tomorrow is his wedding anniversary.

With the command "SHOW MAIL," his terminal brings up a series of nine messages that have accumulated in recent hours. Jim sorts them into two piles on the basis of priority, and starts on the action items. While reading one of these electronic messages, his computer notifies Jim that one of his staff is trying to reach him. So he interrupts and converses with the employee via his terminal, then goes back to his electronic mail.

Later, after a mid-morning breakfast on his patio, Jim moves his terminal to poolside. He checks his subordinates' daily reports and sends a progress report to his boss, with copies to his staff. At 10 A.M., Jim connects to his colleague Bob in the Boston office. They are collaborating on writing a joint memo about a long-range forecast for the company. After the usual pleasantries—"How's the weather in Los Altos Hills this morning?" "Is it snowing in Cambridge?"—they place their individual outlines for the memo side-by-side on a shared screen and begin merging them into a single memo. They negotiate on their differences; at one point they decide to bring in a third-party expert from their firm via a three-way teleconference. Then they use their system's calculating power to project their sales estimates and print out a series of visual displays. Within an hour Jim and Bob have agreed on the main points of their joint project and break off their computer conversation to write up sections of the memo. Certain pages are delegated to subordinates to prepare in draft form. Later they will resume their teleconference in order to polish the final copy before it is transmitted to higher officials in the company.

That evening Jim takes his wife to a restaurant, the dinner reservation was made via his computer terminal, and gives her a necklace, ordered by teleshopping on his system. When they return home, Jim checks his computer "in-basket" to see if he has received any priority messages.

Such is a day in the office of the future at home. Among the advantages are that Jim saves an hour or two of commuting time. Of course once or twice a week Jim still has to go to his office to meet personally with his co-workers on a face-to-face basis. And one must keep in mind that at present only 1 or 2 percent of the U.S. workforce are teleworkers. Jim's wife complains that even though he is at home most of the time, she often has difficulty in getting his attention, and sometimes feels Jim is really married to his computer.

mans from performing monotonous and dangerous tasks on assembly lines, but unfortunately robots also put people out of work. Of course someone has to design, manufacture, and maintain the industrial robots. These tasks are information occupations—intellectual work that is replacing manual labor in the factory, just as office automation substitutes for typists and secretaries in white-collar occupations. The at-work applications of computers will replace large numbers of lower-skilled workers and create a demand for fewer, but more educated individuals.

The rapidity with which this social transformation is occurring is aptly called a revolution. Like all major social changes this one will benefit certain people, especially educated professionals in high-technology fields like microelectronics, and will harm many others, as the unemployed thousands in Detroit will attest.

Artificial intelligence is the ability of computers to think like humans. Considerable research is now devoted by university scholars and by R&D workers in certain high-technology firms to advance the field of artificial intelligence. Computers can consistently defeat the human chess player of average-to-expert ability. Other applications of computer intelligence are to teach mathematics, diagnose medical problems, serve as skilled chemical laboratory assistants, and to evaluate military tactics. These applications are primarily limited to an experimental basis at present. In the years ahead important breakthroughs are certain to occur in the uses of artificial intelligence and these may have even more impact on our society than the current concern about unemployment caused by office automation and robotics.

Microcomputers and Our Children

In no other area of daily life is the potential of the new communication technology having such a powerful impact as with children.

An estimated 25 million Americans are functionally illiterate. They cannot read a want ad or the label on a medicine bottle or a bus schedule. Another 34 million have only a minimum capacity for very simple reading. These two groups make up about one-quarter of the nation's population. They represent a major problem in a nation that is moving rapidly into becoming an information society. The ability to read and write is an even more essential individual skill in a world organized around computer terminals. Until voice recognition ability is much improved and becomes lower in cost, the main way to talk to a computer is through a keyboard.

Obviously the best way to raise the literacy levels of the U.S. population is to prevent additional millions of functional illiterates from being created by our currently ineffective educational system. Computers, especially microcomputers, can provide the means to revitalize our schools—the natural affinity of children for computers can be a powerful tool for teaching the information skills needed for life in an information society. An exciting revolution is now underway in U.S. schools and homes to harness the teaching/learning potential of microcomputers. However this revolution has a long way to go.

U.S. schools have 250,000 computers available to students for educational purposes. Little is known yet from scientific study about the introduction, acceptance, and implementation of computers in schools and the impacts of computers on teaching and learning by children in schools and in their homes.[7] But without doubt a kind of learning/teaching revolution is now underway, triggered by microcomputers.

Children learn about computers with much greater ease than adults. Most observers note that boys are attracted to computers more strongly than girls. If children's use of computers and video games teaches them useful skills for living in an information society, males are getting off to a faster start. In the U.S., girls have equal ability to boys in math and science until around age 12 (sixth grade), thereafter girls often develop a negative attitude toward these subjects and avoid them in high school, thus limiting their career opportunities. Perhaps microcomputers will provide a means of keeping girls interested in quantitative and scientific subjects. But this potential is not yet being realized, as boys presently outnumber girls 3 to 1 in learning to use computers.

Home computers are more accessible to socioeconomically advantaged children, thus serving to widen existing gaps between the "information-poor" and the "information-rich." A 1982 survey of grade school children in California illustrates this gap: 41 percent of the children in an upper middle-class school reported that they had a home computer, compared to less than 1 percent in a nearby Spanish-speaking, lower income school.[8]

The current generation of U.S. children will grow up with computers, much as the children of the 1950s grew up with television. What is different and special about computers is that they are interactive. It is this interactive nature of computers, and of related communication technologies based on computers, that marks a cultural turning point from the passivity of viewing television. Whether the instructional potential of the computer will be exploited by schools and teachers, or whether computers will just go the way of instructional television, programmed learning, and language laboratories, is yet to be determined.

Computers are a mass medium, but of a very special kind in that they are highly individualized due to their interactive nature. It is possible that the use of computers may affect how children think; some observers feel that children who grow up with computers will learn to be more logical and to think in linear sequences. We need to find out. Seymour Papert stated: "I believe that the computer presence will enable us to so modify the learning environment outside the classroom that much, if not all, the knowledge schools presently try to teach with such pain and expense and such limited success will be learned as the child learns to talk, painlessly, successfully, and without organized instruction. This obviously implies that schools as we know them today will have no place in the future."[9]

Nolan Bushnell: Electronic Pied Piper

In the 1960s Nolan Bushnell was an engineering student at the University of Utah in Salt Lake City, working summers as a pitchman in an amusement park. During all-night sessions on the university computer, Bushnell sometimes played Spacewar, a cult video game that had been invented at MIT. Bushnell sensed the addictive qualities of the game and realized that someone would become a quick millionaire if he could put a quarter coin slot on the computer. However that wasn't feasible on a mainframe computer costing $4 million.

After Bushnell moved to California and took an engineering job at Ampex, a Silicon Valley firm best known for making recording equipment and tapes, he didn't forget about computer games with coin slots. When he heard about microcomputer technology in the early 1970s, Bushnell knew it was time to make his entrepreneurial move. By day he worked for Ampex, and then commuted to his small tract home in Santa Clara at night to work on designing video games. He moved his younger daughter out of her bedroom, doubling her up with his other daughter, so as to have a workspace.[10] At four A.M. one morning in 1971 Bushnell finished designing his first game, Computer Space.[11]

It flopped. Only 2,000 were sold. Bushnell's engineering friends loved it, but beer drinkers in bars were baffled by the complexities of the game. Bushnell went back to the drawing board in his home workshop, seeking to come up with a simpler game. It was Pong, a kind of electronic ping-pong game. Bushnell installed it in Andy Capp's Tavern in Sunnyvale to see if anyone would play it. Two days later, he got a call that the game had broken down. It hadn't—the gallon-sized money container had just filled to overflowing. The quarters had backed up and Pong was drowning in money.[12] Very shortly its inventor would be too.

Bushnell resigned from his job at Ampex and invested $500 to launch his own company, Atari (named for the Japanese expression in the game of Go which means "I'm going to attack you"). Pong was an instant success. The first game was shipped in November 1972. The following year about 10,000 games were sold, each for around $1,200. Atari achieved sales of $3.5 million in 1973 and $15 million the following year.

Nolan Bushnell was called "Silicon Valley's Ted Turner" by *Life* magazine.[13] He is a 6'4" 40-year-old, who made $70 million by hypnotizing kids. He's a visionary who likes to question conventional thinking with a knack for knowing what kinds of entertainment America wants even before it knows it. Bushnell was raised a Mormon but abandoned the faith. He enjoys life and of course his wealth has helped make that easy to do. During his days at Atari, Bushnell ran a pretty loose ship. He had a "we're all brothers" attitude, greeting each new employee at Atari with a powerful handshake and a big grin. Standard dress at Atari was jeans and a t-shirt. Atari executives and design engineers would go off on two or three day retreats to Pajaro Dunes, a nearby vacation spot on the Pacific Coast. Some participants described those creative sessions as somewhat like fraternity house meetings, with plenty of beer and grass. Each promising idea for a new game was given a code name, usually that of a female employee at Atari. Bushnell said: "I remember Arlette the best. Boy, was she stacked and had the tiniest waist. I think she was Super-Pong."[14]

Bushnell's daily management of Atari left much to be desired.[15] Said Don Valentine, a local venture capitalist who had invested in Atari, "The state of the company in the mid-1970s was absolute chaos."[16] Certain of Bushnell's decisions were eccentric—for example, Atari tried to expand in Japan and quickly lost half a million dollars. But more money kept rolling in. In 1975 Atari started manufacturing a home television version of Pong, which was sold out even before it reached the stores. Sears agreed to buy all of the home versions of Pong that Atari could produce that year, around 100,000 video game cartridges.

However competitors were appearing and Atari needed some big capital to outgrow them. In 1976 Warner Communications, a media conglomerate, bought out Atari for $28 million. The sale was held up for several months when a photo of Bushnell appeared in a California newspaper showing the Atari founder in a hot tub with a lady friend. Bushnell's ex-wife brought a lawsuit questioning his clear title to his shares in the firm. She settled the suit and the sale to Warner went through, with Bushnell getting about $15 million for his half of Atari.[17] He continued with the firm for a while but soon quit and Warner brought in a professional manager to run Atari. Sales continued to grow to $2 billion by 1982. But the entrepreneurial craziness and the fun that went with it were gone. Three-piece suits replaced the jeans and t-shirts around Atari. Nolan Bushnell retired as a very youthful, albeit impatient, multimillionaire.

Atari received the supreme compliment of being widely imitated from the outset. In 1973 around 100,000 Pong-type games were produced, but only 10,000 were manufactured by Atari. The short, fast lifetime of the typical video game is a spur to continuous creativity in designing new games. Game designers are treated like rock music stars, the only problem, as one game designer wryly pointed out, is that their groupies are 13-to 14-year-old boys.[18] Most of the 30 to 40 game designers and the firms they work for are in Silicon Valley. Once Bushnell left Atari, many of the most creative designers started to drift away to launch new firms.

Nolan Bushnell not only created a company when he founded Atari, he launched a whole new industry. During 1982, 25 new video game companies were formed. Nevertheless Atari still dominated industry sales. Video game machines have an average weekly take of $109 per machine. The video arcade industry took in $8 billion in quarters in 1982, surpassing pop music (at $4 billion in sales per year) and Hollywood films ($3 billion). Those 32 billion arcade games played translate to 143 games for every man, woman, and child in America. A recent Atari survey showed that 86 percent of the U.S. population from 13 to 20 has played some kind of video game and an estimated 8 million U.S. homes have video games hooked up to the television set. Sales of home video games were $3.8 billion in 1982, approximately half that of video game arcades. During 1983, the video game industry showed signs of diminishing, though sales were about $5 billion.

One of Atari's big hits was Pac-Man, invented in 1980 by Toru Iwatani, then 26 years old and a video game designer for Namco Ltd. of Tokyo.[19] In 1982, under license from Namco, Atari marketed Pac-Man in the U.S. as a $35 cartridge for Atari's home video computer. Pac-Man derives its name from the Japanese word *paku* meaning "to eat." Pac-Man is a circle with a big mouth that eats dots in a maze, while four other mouths try to catch and eat Pac-Man. Pac-Man also eats quarters. The average game is over in only three minutes, it is a game of skill, and few who have played it can avoid its addictive appeal. Video arcades are generally dominated by adolescent boys—80 percent of arcade players are adolescents and 90 percent are males. Pac-Man was less violent than Asteroids, Raster Blaster, and its other predecessors.

It began to attract large numbers of females, especially a version of the game called Ms. Pac-Man. Another video game attractive to females is Centipede, created by Donna Taylor at Atari, who is one of the industry's few female designers.

After Pac-Man, an anti-video game movement developed in the U.S., growing out of parental concern that their kids were squandering their school lunch money. Game arcades were banned in several American cities (and in certain nations like Singapore). Despite public concern about the addictive and expensive habit formed by video games, there is appreciation that they teach hand and eye coordination and help overcome fear of computers.

After a short retirement Nolan Bushnell went back into business with a new venture, Pizza Time Theatre. He realized the need for an entertainment center that the whole family could enjoy. When Mom and Pop and the kids come to one of Bushnell's establishments (there are presently several hundred in the U.S. and more coming), they order pizza. During the twenty minutes it takes to bake, the kids use free tokens to play video games while the parents relax in an adjoining room, entertained by, perhaps, a buxom, piano-playing hippopotamus, a robot that sings oldies music. Then the pizza comes. As Bushnell stated: "No sane adult goes to a Pizza Time Theatre on a Saturday afternoon except under extreme duress from an eight-year-old."[20] Before they leave, the typical family has left behind about $20, and Nolan Bushnell smiles all the way to the bank.

Bushnell owns about half of Pizza Time Theatre plus a children's computer camp, a charter air service, a microwave components company, a restaurant, and Catalyst Technologies, an incubator for high-technology companies. One of these incubated ventures, Androbot, Inc., is now marketing household robots. In all Bushnell estimates he is now worth about $70 million, give or take a couple of million. He is so up-beat that his assistant is actually a "no-man" (the opposite of a yes-man), charged with the responsibility of throwing cold water on Bushnell's hot ideas.[21]

In the past decade Nolan Bushnell became a multimillionaire and multi-entrepreneur specializing in electronic entertainment. Thanks to him, the world will not be quite the same—nor will our children.

Hackers

The epitome of the new computer culture is the "hacker," a computer addict who sleeps by day and sits enthralled at a computer keyboard all night, feeding on junk food and the euphoria of computing. Hackers are social isolates who prefer interaction with a machine over talking to people. Hackers are often found in university computer centers. They may be only a few hundred students at a typical university, yet the significance of hackers lies not in their present numbers, but in their representation of a sub-culture that is rapidly expanding and becoming more influential.

A new generation of hackers is now being created in American homes, schools, and video arcades as vast numbers of children learn to use video games and microcomputers. Computing is "a priesthood of the young."[22] It will be only a few years until the several million school children of today who are becoming computer literates reach college age. Those most likely to become hackers are the extremely intelligent but socially inept. Indeed, it is the anti-social nature of hackers that is the basis for concern about them. Will the computer revolution turn large numbers of our youth into alienated hacker-nerds?

A character sketch of hackers is provided by Joseph Weizenbaum of MIT: "Bright young men of disheveled appearance, often with sunken glowing eyes."[23] Beside their computer terminal are stacks of printout, plastic Coke containers, styrofoam coffee cups, and evidence of their junk-food diets. They have rumpled clothes, unshaven faces, and uncombed hair. As one Stanford hacker pointed out: "The first thing to go is other academic interests .... The second ... is a normal living pattern. Eating and sleeping are completely rearranged to fit the addiction. The typical hacker thinks nothing of eating one meal a day, subsisting on junk food, and sleeping from four to noon almost every day of the week. ... The third thing to go is a balanced social life."[24]

Hackers will become more of a force in the future as America becomes more of an information society. Today's hackers will be writing the computer programs, creating new computer languages, and designing the new information systems to serve us in future decades. The hackers' strange ways may affect us all, as computers become more ubiquitous and the anti-social character of hackers, which seems weird today, may become common at some future time.

The hacker subculture began about a decade ago at certain high-technology universities, but now the phenomenon has diffused in varying degrees to many colleges, high schools, and junior high schools. Stanford's Low Overhead Time Sharing (LOTS) computer facility is acknowledged to be one of the national centers of the hacker subculture. A visit to LOTS during the very early morning hours is like stepping into a special world. Hackers are most likely to be concentrated at LOTS from two A.M. to ten A.M., when the computer service is free. About 4,000 of the Stanford student body of 13,000 use LOTS, as part of a computer science course, to compose a class paper, or to play games. Very few users become addicted, but some do.

A somewhat typical hacker is Mark Crispin, now an employee of the Stanford Computer Center. How did he become a hacker? "I was the typical bright kid stuck in a school system I hated. I was bored and burnt out. And I was the sort of kid who would contradict the teachers, which didn't set me off well with the other kids. . . . In those days, I got a lot of teasing and obscenities." Then Crispin met his first computer. "I began to like it more and more. The computer was neat and fun and didn't call me dirty names. The way I see it is that humans have basic needs and if they don't get them filled by society, they'll fill them elsewhere. And the computer seemed a better answer than drugs."[25]

Accessing the computer files on Stanford's LOTS can disclose a great deal about the hacker subculture. There is a certain kind of clever binary humor here. For example, one LOTS computer file contains titillating prose, some of it pornographic: an animated representation of the sex act, for instance, with a moving arrow and the letter "O," accompanied by appropriate sound effects. A HELP program provides directions to the nearest restrooms in the LOTS building and a list of pizza joints in Palo Alto. A SPY program allows the user to check on fellow hackers (identified by their computer names) and to "stare" at the programs they are using.

One computer file in LOTS that is most insightful about the hacker subculture is "The Hacker Papers," a series of exchanges begun in 1980 by "E.ERNEST" (real name: Ernest W. Adams). Adams, a senior at Stanford University, discovered the computer center as an unhappy 17-year-old freshman from Kentucky. "I became involved with LOTS to the exclusion of other things. I would come to drown my sorrows," said Adams. He soon learned the joys of programming: "It's a little like playing God." Thus Adams entered the world of computers. However after several quarters at Stanford, he began to reassess his life as a hacker. He had A's in his computer science courses, but had failed calculus because he virtually lived at LOTS. Adams began to wonder if his humanity was eroding, if he was becoming a machine.

Adams began "The Hacker Papers" on the LOTS computer, a free-wheeling exchange among Stanford hackers on the topic of their computer addiction. Adams began the dialogue by proposing a definition of hacker as "a computer addict, one who enjoys computing or being around computing machinery to the point that he sacrifices things most people consider important."[26]

Here are two selections taken from "The Hacker Papers." Each is identified with the hacker's computer name.

> "People have always found me strange. I have always worn my hair long because I felt it was more comfortable for me. I prefer clothes that are perhaps a bit scroungy. . . . Working with computers has been the only thing tolerable I have done in quite a while. . . . The problem is that the social structure of LOTS rewards people who hack well but don't interface well with people." (M.MCLURE, September 20, 1979).
>
> "I found some graffiti in the women's bathroom (here at the LOTS facility) which is actually relevant to the current discussion about hacking: 'Computers have no meaning themselves. They are a toolbox from which man can construct a universe of his own making. This is what makes them so powerful, so beautiful, so dangerous. It's what turns people into nerds—people fascinated by their own image within the screen.' " (Y.YDUJ, November 19, 1981).

"The Hacker Papers" in the LOTS computer continue to grow, as each generation of computer addicts comments on computerism.

Computer firms in Silicon Valley are eager to hire hackers, who ask only for flexible work hours, no dress code, and nontrivial assignments. "Our LOTS hackers of today will move on to Apple, Xerox, and H-P tomorrow," said Professor Ralph Gorin, the director of LOTS. Most of them will make "an obscene amount of money."[27] Their computer compulsiveness thus becomes a positive trait, and perhaps they will eventually rejoin the human race.[28]

Crime may be a next step for some hackers who create legendary images among fellow hackers by "crashing" a mainframe computer. Such hacker whimsy wipes out programs and data when the computer goes down. One way to crash a computer is to set in action numerous programs, each of which constantly fork into other programs, which bifurcate into yet more programs. Soon even a mainframe computer is brought to its knees.[29]

Paths Not Taken

Certain critics say that the technology coming out of Silicon Valley has a dysfunctional influence on society by heading us toward high-technology solutions to social problems. For instance, the utilization of computer-based technologies in medicine like the CAT scanner (each such machine costs about $1 million) may benefit individual patients, but it also leads to skyrocketing health costs.[30] Approximately 8 percent of the GNP now goes to pay the national health bill. Meanwhile more appropriate solutions to health problems are largely neglected. Preventive medicine receives little attention by medical doctors or by Silicon Valley's technologists. Improved diets, smoking cessation, and exercise offer direct and immediate health benefits to the public. Instead doctors and hospitals rush to purchase expensive medical electronics, status symbols which are profitable to the Silicon Valley firms that produce them. The unfettered pursuit of economic goals of high-tech firms can be disadvantageous to society.

There is a parallel in public education. During the 1980s schools displayed a mania for microcomputers. Many parents feel their children are shortchanged if their school does not have one or more microcomputers. But to date the potential of school computing has not been fully realized. Most computers are used for drill-and-practice exercises, as a kind of expensive set of flash cards. Software programs are needed that will enable teachers to utilize microcomputers in ways that make learning exciting, as gripping to school children as video games. At present they are still far from that objective. Microcomputers in schools are a classic case of a technological solution looking for a problem to solve. Unfortunately the relative high cost of purchasing computers can distort a school's budget, taking needed funds away from other educational programs. Undoubtedly computers have a great potential in learning and teaching, but today's school computers seem to be only a "technological fix."[31]

The power of the profit motive pulls us toward high-technology solutions to social problems. Computers are seductive status symbols and we often employ them in situations where alternative solutions might be superior. The appearance of microelectronics products as providing neat, effective solutions to problems creates a societal tendency to over-rely on sophisticated technologies; we become addicted to the technological fix. Instead society should carefully evaluate each technology-based solution to a social problem and judge it in relation to alternative approaches.

In addition to creating social problems, high-technology's close ties to military defense produce other kinds of problems. Weapons are among the biggest exports from Silicon Valley. Of the $104 billion in contracts awarded by the U.S. Department of Defense in 1982, $3.88 billion (3.7 percent) came to Santa Clara County. That year more than 500 companies in the county received defense contracts greater than $10,000 and hundreds of companies received subcontracts. Most of the defense money went to large aerospace and military equipment contractors such as Lockheed Missiles and Space, FMC, and Ford Aerospace for equipment such as missiles and armored vehicles. However a rapidly increasing proportion of the budget is going to the fast-growing field of electronic warfare.

Electronic systems, electronic counter measures, and what the jargon calls "C3I" (command, communications, control, and intelligence) all developed as a result of the increased sophistication of semiconductor technology. Most of these systems are designed to identify the radar of enemy missiles or aircraft, to track spy-in-the-sky satellites, and to transmit data from our own satellites and telemetry systems. The companies involved in electronic warfare contracts maintain a low profile and won't say much about their work. As George Hodder, marketing manager of ESL put it, "We don't do much of anything that isn't very sensitive." Not all defense dollars go to large industrial corporations. According to Pentagon data, Stanford University received research contracts worth over $23 million in 1982, making the University the fourteenth largest defense contractor in the county.

Many would argue that human welfare could be advanced tremendously if comparable sums to these huge military expenditures were invested in peaceful solutions to problems.

High-Technologists As Political Leaders

As a professional group, engineers have a "can-do" spirit, a feeling that they can improve the world, not just by their deeds, but also by their way of thinking; they have an understandable sense of superiority about their ability to apply the scientific method to practical problems.[32] This feeling of efficacy is an essential possession of the entrepreneur. If the entrepreneur is an engineer, he often finds himself doing more management and less engineering as the firm grows in size. In some cases, founding engineers in a start-up firm take quickly and easily to becoming managers, although engineers seldom have had any formal training in business skills. Bottom lines, spread sheets, and return on investment soon become familiar tools to the manager-engineer.

So now the middle-aged engineer-entrepreneur-manager has conquered technical problems, overcome business problems, and is admired by the community. A few of these entrepreneurial engineers then seek political office. They have the money, the connections, and the motivational drive. Today, several U.S. congressmen and senators have backgrounds as high-technology entrepreneurs. Following tradition, Silicon Valley entrepreneurs made money first, and are going after power now.

Typical of the new entrepreneur-politician is Ed Zschau (rhymes with "now"), 43, U.S. Congressman from California's 12th District, which includes Silicon Valley. When Zschau was president and CEO of System Industries (a computer disk memory company), he was frustrated by the lack of venture capital for small businesses. So he headed an American Electronics Association task force in 1978 that succeeded in rolling back the capital gains tax rate from 50 percent to 28 percent. That tax law change helped create a flood of venture capital in the U.S. It led to Zschau's election as a Republican to the House of Representatives in 1982; it also led to $600,000 in campaign contributions from Silicon Valley supporters (compared to only $15,000 for his opponent). Zschau, however, dismisses the notion that he "bought" the election: "If a candidate can't attract financing, it means that there aren't enough people out there who want to see him elected."[33]

On the morning after his victory, on November 3, 1982, Zschau addressed the Innovation 2 Conference in Palo Alto: "The role of government in encouraging innovation is to create an environment with the freedom to succeed or fail in business. Washington must provide incentives, like a favorable tax structure."[34] The statement expressed vintage Silicon Valley values. Congressman Zschau's speech received enthusiastic applause from the several hundred Silicon Valley executives in the audience.

One wonders what kind of national political leader a high-technologist would make. Likely the politician would be a conservative Republican with a strong belief in free market forces and faith in government policies that govern least. Most Silicon Valley tycoons are not concerned with issues of social inequality or injustice; to the entrepreneur, the poor and weak in society are poor and weak because they are inferior. It is the poor and the weak's fault that they are downtrodden, rather than the result of an unequal system. The engineer-entrepreneur believes in social evolution, the absolute correctness of competition, and in technological solutions to social problems. The engineer-politician lacks a liberal arts education, is suspicious of liberalism, and represents the ideology of hard-core conservative Republicanism.

As America moves forward as an information society, these values of competition, a faith in technology, and political conservatism are likely to become more widely shared and more strongly held by the public. The entrepreneurial game as it is now played in Silicon Valley will spread and be accepted elsewhere. Trends already advanced in Silicon Valley will gradually occur in the other "Silicon Valleys" being created around the nation. The process will take ten, fifteen, or twenty years, maybe less, and will be accompanied by increasing economic and political power for high-technology regions and for the entrepreneurs who lead them. That trend has already begun, and it can only speed up.

While most Silicon Valley captains of industry are conservative Republicans, a political movement recognizing the potential of high technology, entrepreneurship, and innovation for saving the U.S. economy has recently emerged among politicians and intellectuals associated with the Democratic Party. These leaders have been dubbed the "Atari Democrats." At present they are but a rump group within their party, which has traditionally represented labor, minorities, and the urban poor. Pointing toward the future, the Atari Democrats are proposing high technology as the route to revitalizing the ailing American economy, to providing future relief from unemployment, and to competing with the threats of Japanese trade and Russian military aggression.

The leaders of this high-tech movement are a set of thirty or so young, well-educated, and practical legislators in Washington: Senators Gary Hart, Bill Bradley, and Paul Tsongas, and Congressman Tim Wirth.[35] Also influential among the Atari Democrats are intellectuals like Lester Thurow, a 44-year-old MIT professor who wrote The Zero-Sum Society; Charles Peters, editor of the Washington Monthly; and his protégé, Michael Kinsky, only 30 and editor of Harper's. Felix Rohatyn, a financier who helped save New York City from bankruptcy in 1976, acts as a "Secretary of the Treasury" for the Atari Democrats.

The neoliberals' platform planks include compulsory national service (a Peace Corps-like voluntary service for youth), the negative income tax, and central economic planning, but none is more important than high-technology re-industrialization. That's why this emerging political movement is called the Atari Democrats. They believe that government policies should recognize that "sunset" industries are fading and that "sunrise" industries like microelectronics should get a special government boost. They want greater federal funding for R&D, tax incentives for more R&D by private firms, emphasis upon basic science, and more job retraining for unemployed workers. They propose setting up an Economic Cooperation Council in Washington, modeled after Japan's MITI. And they want much greater emphasis upon math and science education in the schools.

If the Atari Democrats become more powerful, their policies would not very easily or quickly turn the U.S. economy around, as the task is huge. Eight percent unemployment means 9 million people are out of work. The total high-tech workforce in Silicon Valley is less than half a million. Total employment in high technology in the U.S. is only 5 percent of all jobs. The 1982 general recession in the U.S. was felt even in Silicon Valley. High technology, while certainly the right way to go, is hardly an immediate or complete solution to basic economic problems in the U.S.

Nevertheless, the Atari Democrats have sensed the basic change in America from an industrial to an information society and they may be able to ride this wave to greater political power. Now they are a party within a party and one that doesn't fit too well with Democratic politics of the past. Could one imagine Mayor Daley or LBJ or their present-day followers championing microelectronics? Perhaps the high-tech political movement will someday break off from the Democratic Party, especially if that party is unresponsive to neoliberals' demands and they merge with "Atari Republicans" like Ed Zschau to form a high-tech third party.

Even President Ronald Reagan showed signs that he was getting "Atarized"; his 1983 State of the Union address recognized high technology as the hope for America's future. The following week, in January 1983, Reagan visited the Route 128 industries around Boston and told businessmen that he wanted to be "an apostle for your success story." He told the Massachusetts High-Technology Council that the federal government should take a more active role in promoting business recovery.[36] Even the President of the United States is now a booster for "Silicon Valley."

Silicon Valley represents a special kind of supercapitalism—it is a system resting on continuous technological innovation, entrepreneurial fever, and vigorous economic competition. The Silicon Valley game is played out by several thousand capitalist technologists involved in a myriad of deals, spin-offs, start-ups, successes, and failures. The role of the federal and state government is close to zero. Unfettered market forces pass final judgment on the boom or bust of firms and of individuals. Silicon Valley is high-technology capitalism run wild. There is nothing quite like it anywhere else in the world.

Quite understandably, Silican Valley's industry leaders take pride in the system they have created. Their industry has been good to them, making them millionaires. The microelectronics industry also has been good to the local area, with new jobs and taxes. The microelectronics companies did what the people in the local cities and counties wanted them to do: create new jobs. As the cornerstone of the information society, the microelectronics industry has been good for the nation, providing one of the economic bright spots in an otherwise dreary picture of obsolete, smokestack industries and undertrained workers.

But what about the future? Can such a record of success continue? Clearly the rate of job growth and facilities expansion must level off as the geographical and resource limitations of the Valley are reached. As yet there are no signs that Silicon Valley's spirit of innovation is slackening. Technical expertise and entrepreneurial spirit are firmly established in Santa Clara County, to a far more pervasive degree than elsewhere in the country, or the world.

Some observers claim that Silicon Valley's semiconductor industry has now entered a "second greening."[37] Not since the heady days of the late 1960s when semiconductor giants like Intel and National were born has there been such a surge of start-up companies. A booming future for high-tech is predicted. Although semiconductor manufacturing employment may peak in the mid-1980s and then level off, the application of semiconductors to new products will continue to boom. Venture capitalists are putting huge amounts of funding into start-ups. Jane Morris of *Venture Capital* magazine stated: "The amount of money out there is amazing."[38] Along with the riches, tax dollars, and good life created by the microelectronics industry are the problems:

pollution, housing shortage, traffic, and crime. For these reasons and others the microelectronics industry is expanding outside the limits of Silicon Valley. *But* it is not leaving the Valley. Even as high-technology firms expand outside of Santa Clara County, they add to employment there. Silicon Valley is still "where it's at." High-tech engineers/entrepreneurs want to be around people like themselves. Those who want to "go for it" need to rub shoulders with people who can help that happen. The network, that human chain of vital information, is there.

Silicon Valley today is more than ever the embodiment of the information society. The change can be seen in contemporary Silicon Valley start-ups. Twenty years ago, Silicon Valley began with the founding of companies that made objects, albeit small objects—miniature semiconductor chips. Today most start-up companies produce information—many are computer software firms. Certainly objects are involved, but in most cases the information is much more critical than the material objects.

We began this book with the Apple story, so it is fitting that Apple provides an illustration of the current transition. When Apple unveiled the Lisa computer in 1983 it was described as a "tool for the information age." Steve Jobs's pitch was that whereas factory production workers needed pliers and hammers and lathes, the information worker needs a terminal and a duplicating machine. In one sense, Apple doesn't manufacture a product. Apple doesn't make semiconductor chips, printed circuit boards, or disk drives. It buys those components from other manufacturers and assembles the parts. What Apple does own is information about how to make a computer. Apple, as a prototype information society corporation, controls the information that makes the components functional. Video game companies are also examples of information age companies. Imagic, Activision, and Atari creatively design new games, but their only involvement with a material object is to program the chips that they buy from semiconductor companies.

In the Middle Ages there was a famous quest for the philosophers' stone, a substance thought to turn base metals into gold. With time the notion of the philosophers' stone grew to include the idea of producing something valuable out of nothing. Inevitably the concept proved difficult to demonstrate and lost popular appeal. However the late twentieth century is seeing a resurgence of interest in the philosophers' stone. In Silicon Valley one can create value out of thin air: Information and innovation combine to produce economic value. Riches in excess of all the gold taken from California's mother lode come from Silicon Valley. Information is the Valley's resource.

Silicon Valley created and developed a system for producing something valuable from virtually nothing. Although it moves with fits and starts, the high-technology system works. If we nurture this system, it can thrive and be shared. When a system runs on information, there is an endless supply for everyone.

NOTES

Chapter 1

1. Theodor H. Nelson, *Computer Lib* (Chicago: Hugo's Book Service, 1974).

2. The Altair 8800, the first microcomputer to be sold, in December 1974, was produced by MITS (Micro Instrument and Technology Systems) of Albuquerque. The Altair was built around the Intel 8080A microprocessor. Ed Roberts, the principal at MITS, intended to sell 800 of the Altair 8800s during 1975, but after Les Solomon featured the machine on the cover of the January issue of *Popular Electronics,* MITS sold all that it could manufacture, about 2,000 in 1975. In 1977, MITS was acquired by Pertec for $6 million. Adam Osborne, *Running Wild; The Next Industrial Revolution* (Berkeley: Osborne/McGraw-Hill, 1979) pp. 28–30.

3. John V. Roach, "Personal Computers: The Newcomers—and the Old-timers" (Paper delivered at Personal Computer Forum, Lake Geneva, Wisconsin, 1981; published by *Rosen Electronics Letter*).

4. Steven Jobs, "The Personal Computer: A New Medium" (Paper delivered at Personal Computer Forum, Lake Geneva, Wisconsin, 1981; published by *Rosen Electronics Letter*).

5. Paul Ciotti, "Revenge of the Nerds," *California,* July 1982.

6. Ibid. Anyone with a microcomputer can copy a software program (perhaps purchased for $50, $275, or $450) from one floppy disk to another. If the software programmer put an encryption code on the disk to protect it, the pirate simply runs it on the Locksmith program, which breaks the encryption. Other piracy can be accomplished by simply dialing a phone number and downloading the program via a modem from a piracy service. While Jobs and Wozniak have gone easy on software pirates, they have cracked down hard on the 55 companies in Taiwan that manufacture counterfeit Apples. The look-alike Apple computers cost one-quarter the price of the real thing, and outsell the original four to one in Asia.

7. Cap'n Crunch is really John T. Draper. He holds the distinction of being the first

"phone phreak" (telephone/computer criminal) to go to jail. Today he is president of a software firm in Berkeley. *San Jose Mercury News,* 8 May 1983 .

8. Ciotti, "Revenge of the Nerds."

9. Ibid.

10. Ibid.

11. Harold Seneker, "The Forbes Four Hundred," *Forbes,* 13 September 1982.

12. *InfoWorld,* 8 March 1982.

13. Chuck Peddle is now the president of Victor Technologies, Inc., in Scotts Valley, California. He designed the 6502 microprocessor and the Commodore PET computer, and then started Sirius (which became Victor Technologies), which manufactures the Sirius and VICTOR 9000 microcomputers.

14. *InfoWorld,* 7 June 1982.

15. Ibid.

16. Ibid.

17. Ibid.

18. Adam Osborne in a speech at the Innovation 2 Conference on 2 November 1982 in Palo Alto said that "Steve Jobs was not just a lucky kid. He knew what he didn't know, and sought people who did. That was a very mature strategy."

19. *InfoWorld,* 8 March 1982.

20. Apple and the other microcomputer firms helped give rise to another sub-industry: computer magazines like *InfoWorld, Personal Computing,* and *Creative Computing.* The largest is *Byte* magazine, published by McGraw-Hill, presently second among all U.S. magazines in the number of pages of advertising sold per issue.

21. Steven Jobs (from a lecture at Stanford Conference on Entrepreneurship, Stanford, California, 3 April 1982).

22. Authors' interview with Boyd W. Wilson, Mountain View, California, 22 July 1982.

23. As Wozniak told it: "I tried to propose something similar to what became the Apple II—a $1,000 machine with 4K of RAM—to a lab manager [at Hewlett-Packard], and he lost a lot of sleep thinking about it, but it wasn't an H-P product. He said it was great for a start-up product, so I got a legal release to do the Apple." Thus both Wozniak's boss at Hewlett-Packard, as well as Jobs's, encouraged the start-up of the new firm. Wozniak has nothing but warm feelings for his former employer: "I love H-P. It's the best company I know of, period, and I hope Apple reaches that status someday." *InfoWorld,* 7 June 1982.

24. *Time,* 15 February 1982.

25. Jobs, Stanford lecture.

26. Ciotti, "Revenge of the Nerds."

27. Ibid.

28. Ibid.

29. Ibid.

30. Ibid.

31. Ibid.

32. Ibid.

33. Undoubtedly, the software program that contributed much to Apple's success is VisiCalc, for "visible calculator," designed in 1978 by a Harvard MBA student. VisiCalc is an electronic spreadsheet in which, if one variable changes, say, a salary, the computer immediately recalculates all other numbers that are affected. Over 250,000 copies of VisiCalc have been sold at $250 each, representing sales of $62 million. Early VisiCalcs ran only on the Apple II.

34. *Times* (London), 17 December 1980.

35. This book was written with WordStar on an Apple II microcomputer.

36. *InfoWorld,* 8 March 1982.

37. Ciotti, "Revenge of the Nerds."

38. Ibid.

39. Ibid.

40. About two years later Markkula resigned in favor of John Scully, who had been president of Pepsico. Scully is paid $1 million a year in salary and bonuses plus stock options, and was given a $1 million signing bonus.

41. Jobs, Stanford lecture.

42. *Time,* 3 January 1983.

43. *San Jose Mercury,* 19 January 1983.

44. Steven Jobs (from remarks at Apple annual meeting, Cupertino, California, 19 January 1983).
45. *San Jose News,* 21 July 1983.
46. Jobs, Stanford lecture.
47. Ibid.
48. *InfoWorld,* 8 March 1982.

Chapter 2

1. Hoefler credits Ralph Vaerst, then president of Ion Equipment, with suggesting the name "Silicon Valley" to him as a title for a series of feature articles that Hoefler wrote about the semiconductor industry for *Electronic News.* Hoefler's initial article was published on January 11, 1971, marking the first time that the name "Silicon Valley" was used in print. *San Jose Mercury News,* 28 June 1981.
2. *San Francisco Chronicle,* 23 September 1980.
3. This estimate of the number of millionaires in Silicon Valley was made for Thompson Tuckman Andersen Inc., by Data Marketing Inc., a Santa Clara-based market research firm. We have been unable to determine the exact methods of estimation that were utilized. *Peninsula Times Tribune,* 19 May 1982.
4. Gordon Brown, "Interview with Fred Terman" (Palo Alto: Hewlett-Packard Archives, 1973).
5. In 1977 William Hewlett and David Packard made a gift to Stanford University for the construction of the $9.2 million Frederick Emmons Terman Engineering Center. The $538 of assistance that Professor Terman had provided to his two protégés in 1938 had returned manifold.
6. Brown, "Interview with Fred Terman."
7. Ibid.
8. William Ouchi, *Theory Z: How American Business Can Meet the Japanese Challenge* (Reading, Mass.: Addison-Wesley, 1981).
9. Hewlett attributes the creation of the H-P management style to the facts that he and Dave Packard grew up in the Depression, seeing firsthand the meaning of unemployment; and to the slow early growth of their firm, which meant that they knew each of their employees personally, often going hunting or fishing with them. A fast-start firm, fueled with venture capital and forced into rapid growth by competitive pressures, will necessarily have greater social distance between its executives and their employees. Hewlett and Packard definitely did not want to own a "hire and fire" operation. Authors' interview with William Hewlett, Palo Alto, California, 30 August 1982.
10. Jeremy Main, "The Bull Market's Biggest Winners," *Fortune,* 8 August 1983.
11. For inclusion in *Venture's* list, a company must have been founded from scratch, rather than through a buyout or merger, and still be headed by the founder or founders. Dave Lindorff, "The *Venture* 100: No Limits to Growth," *Venture,* May 1982.
12. In recent years the name of the industrial estate was changed officially to the Stanford *Research* Park, in keeping with its high-technology nature. But it is still widely known by its old name.
13. Authors interview with Fred Terman, Palo Alto, California, 17 August 1982.
14. Brown, "Interview with Fred Terman."
15. These tended to be high-technology firms in the electronics industry because that was the field in which Terman had the most personal contacts, and where he thought the greatest growth potential existed, although he points out that it "wasn't as well-organized as that." Authors' interview with Fred Terman.
16. Ibid. The selling of leases in the Stanford Industrial Park in the mid-1950s is described by Terman: "We had a little system. The electronics industry was expanding around here, after World War II had shown what electronics could do. Dave Packard was on the Stanford University Board of Trustees, and his company was located in the Park. He turned up some prospective companies like Lockheed. Packard would send his prospects to me to hear about the advantages of being close to a center of brains. I would send company officials to Alf Brandin [business manager at Stanford], who would show them the campus-like qualities of the park. And sometimes Brandin would discover a prospect."

17. Further, the companies in the Stanford Research Park paid 30 percent of the property taxes in Palo Alto, a city of 100,000 population. Authors' interview with J.E. Wallace Sterling, Palo Alto, California, 7 October 1982.

18. One rental arrangement is the 60-acre Stanford Shopping Center, occupied by elite tenants like I. Magnin's, Saks Fifth Avenue, and Bullock's. Located at the other end of the campus from the Stanford Research Park, the shopping center earns about $3 million per year for the university.

19. Frederick E. Terman, "The Development of an Engineering College Program," *Journal of Engineering Education* 58 (1968).

20. Ernest Braun and Stuart MacDonald, *Revolution in Miniature: The History and Impact of Semiconductor Electronics* (New York: Cambridge University Press, 1978) p. 38.

21. Shockley tells the story of this important invention: "During the few months at the end of 1947 and early 1948 . . . the earliest and essential transistor inventions were made. . . . The details are . . . the failure of my field-effect transistor proposals of 1939 and again, independently, of 1945. . . . We put aside efforts to make a transistor. But the situation changed on 17 November 1947. Then Walter Brattain . . . did an experiment suggested that day by another member of the team. The result was evidence that the field-effect might be made to work. . . . The point-contact transistor of Bardeen and Brattain was born on 16 December 1947, less than one month after 17 November 1947. I invented the junction transistor about one month later. However, the junction transistor was not realized in a convincing form until early 1951. The stimulus of possible application in military uses was important in achieving its existence as early as that date." William Shockley, "Statement on Technology and Economic Growth before the Subcommittee on Economic Growth of the Joint Economic Committee, U.S. Congress" (Washington, D.C.: U.S. Government Printing Office, 1976).

22. Authors' interview with Fred Terman.

23. Dirk Hanson, *The New Alchemists: Silicon Valley and the Microelectronics Revolution* (Boston: Little, Brown & Co., 1982).

24. Intel's Bob Noyce said that he met William Shockley at the Electronics Devices Conference in Washington, D.C., in 1955. Shockley congratulated him on his paper. "When he was getting Shockley Semiconductor Laboratory going, he called me up. I was of course highly flattered. He was the great contributor to the field of transistors." Noyce had always wanted to move to the West Coast; his brother taught at Berkeley. "I had never been in California, but his letters were glowing about the West Coast, and the Bay Area in particular." So Noyce came west. Authors' interview with Robert N. Noyce, Santa Clara, California, October 4, 1982.

25. Authors' interview with Fred Terman.

26. Jim Gibbons, now a professor of electrical engineering at Stanford University, described working for Shockley in 1956–57 as the most exciting year of his life in terms of intellectual stimulation. But, he said, if it had lasted two years, he would have quit. Instead, he went to study in Europe. As Gibbons recalled: "Shockley was a brilliant man, with an incredible ability to attack scientific problems. He revolves a problem around in his head until he finds an entry point that looks promising. Often the solution just unfolds from this. Meanwhile, the rest of us are over there somewhere with our picks and hammers, trying to pound our way through a six-foot wall of obstacles." Authors' interview with James Gibbons, Palo Alto, California, 30 June 1982.

27. His father, George Fairchild, was one of the founders of IBM and Sherman Fairchild was IBM's largest individual stockholder until his death in 1971. He was an airplane builder who also owned other companies like Fairchild Camera and Instrument Corporation which provided funds for Fairchild Semiconductor.

28. All transistors had been made of germanium until Gordon Teal, formerly a Bell Labs colleague of Shockley's, was recruited by Texas Instruments in Dallas and pioneered the development of the first silicon transistors.

29. Shockley mentioned his entrepreneurial drive in testimony before a congressional subcommittee some years later: "In 1955, I attempted to start a transistor business in California. One of my motivations was that I had come to the conclusion that the most creative people were not adequately rewarded as employees in industry." William Shockley, "Statement on Technology and Economic Growth."

30. C.T. Lindner, "A Survey of the San Francisco Bay Area Electronics Industry," mimeographed (Stanford: Stanford University, 1963).

Chapter 3

1. There are two kinds of semiconductor companies: "merchant" producers like Intel, National Semiconductor, Texas Instruments, and others that sell semiconductors on the open market; and "captive" producers like IBM and Western Electric who manufacture chips for their own company to use.

2. Authors' interview with Dr. Lester Hogan, Mountain View, California, 15 November 1982.

3. Authors' interview with Nancy Henry, Head of Data-Processing, Fairchild Semiconductor, Mountain View, California, 6 August 1982.

4. A few years ago, Honeywell was considering acquiring Fairchild. Silicon Valley wags pointed out that the merger could be called Fairwell Honeychild.

5. Authors' interview with Howard Z. Bogert, Palo Alto, California, 20 July 1981.

6. *New York Times*, 7 March 1982.

7. Albert V. Bruno and Arnold C. Cooper, "Patterns of Development and Acquisitions for Silicon Valley Start-ups," *Technovation* 1 (1982).

8. Authors' interview with David Drennan, Sunnyvale, California, 20 September 1979.

9. Authors' interview with Mark Larsen, Palo Alto, California, 19 April 1982.

10. W.J. Sanders, III, "An Industry Overview Speech at the 1982 Semiconductor Forum," *Rosen Electronics Letter*. October 1982.

11. Les Hogan, who presided over Fairchild from 1968–1974, said, "One spin-off from Fairchild occurred because I fired the guy. That was Jerry Sanders, a brilliant marketing man. You know, Jerry would agree with me in my office, but then he'd go off and do what *he* wanted to do. So I finally got pissed off, and I fired him. Maybe Jerry succeeded just to prove that I was wrong!" Authors' interview with Lester Hogan. Sanders, however, recalls being demoted and then resigning. Authors' interview with Jerry Sanders, Sunnyvale, California, 25 August 1983.

12. Sanders, "An Industry Overview." Actually it took Arthur Rock 30 minutes to raise $2.5 million.

13. Authors' interview with Tom Skornia, former vice-president of AMD, San Jose, California, 18 August 1982.

14. Authors' interview with Les Hogan.

15. Authors' interview with Tom Skornia.

16. *Business Week*, "Executive Compensation Survey," 17 May 1982.

17. Katherine Davis Fishman, *The Computer Establishment* (New York: Harper and Row, 1981). In a speech at the Innovation 2 Conference in Palo Alto in 1982, Gene Amdahl described what happened: "IBM's response to Amdahl Corporation was to create as much fear, uncertainty, and doubt as they could. They largely succeeded."

18. Gene Amdahl obtained the financing for Trilogy through a complex arrangement called an "R&D limited partnership." It worked like this: 4,000 limited partners each put up a minimum of $10,000 to buy units in Trilogy Computer Development Partners, Ltd. This partnership contracted with Trilogy Systems to develop a mainframe computer, expected in 1984. Then Trilogy Systems would buy the computer from the partnership, either in cash or in shares of stock. In essence, the R&D limited partnership gives Gene Amdahl a big hunk of cash without his giving up ownership of Trilogy Systems.

19. "In the Chips," *Life*, March 1982.

20. *San Jose News*, 16 August 1982.

21. Adam Smith, "Silicon Valley Spirit," *Esquire*, November 1981.

22. Nolan Bushnell, "Entrepreneurial Engineering," (Speech delivered at National Engineers Week, Sunnyvale, California, 25 February 1983).

23. Schmieder identified 2,736 companies by searching through the municipal records of the 11 small cities in Silicon Valley and then contacting each firm so identified to determine whether it met his definition of an electronics manufacturing firm: "The companies must manufacture semiconductors; computers, computer software and services; peripherals; test and measurement instruments; capital equipment; telecommunications equipment and systems; word-processing and text-editing equipment; medical electronics equipment; military and/or aerospace equipment; process, production, and environment control instruments and systems; sound equipment; or R&D and other related industries." The characteristics of these firms, such as their size and location, were made available to us through the kindness of Dr. Schmieder.

24. Scott Mace and John Markoff, "Children Play Games to Learn Basic Skills at TLC," *InfoWorld,* 6 September 1982.

25. Authors' interview with Anne Piestrup, Portola Valley, California, 24 August 1982.

26. Authors' interview with Frona Kahn at TLC, Portola Valley, California, 2 August 1982.

27. Marcia Klein replaced Smythe as president of TLC in 1983.

28. Authors' interview with Frona Kahn.

Chapter 4

1. *Peninsula Times Tribune,* 10 April 1983. These estimates were made by Stanley Pratt, editor of *Venture Capital Journal.*

2. Ibid. The *Venture Capital Journal* estimated a total venture funding of $1,423 million in 1982. From 1970 to 1980 the number of individual venture capitalists in the U.S. increased from 41 to 460, a ten-fold growth, according to Dave Bellet, of Crown Associates, a venture capitalist firm, in a speech delivered at the Innovation 2 Conference, Palo Alto, November 3, 1982.

3. *San Francisco Chronicle,* 13 December 1982.

4. Western Association of Venture Capitalists, *Directory of Members* (Menlo Park, California: 1982).

5. Or, even easier, make a presentation at the annual get-together of venture capitalists who meet to hear from aspiring entrepreneurs. In March 1983, 100 different start-ups each made their pitch for funding to a crowd of 500 venture capitalists and investment portfolio managers in Monterey, California. *San Jose Mercury News,* 20 March 1983.

6. Jim Levy (speech delivered at the Innovation 2 Conference, Palo Alto, November 3, 1982).

7. Authors' interview with Franklin P. "Pitch" Johnson, Jr., Palo Alto, California, 30 July 1982.

8. Generally venture capitalists make further investments in one of their firms if it is making good earnings, but not always. Venture capitalists often say "we have deep pockets," implying there is more funding where the original investment came from. However, Ed Zschau, former president of System Industries, pointed out in a speech delivered at the Innovation 2 Conference (Palo Alto, November 3, 1982): "During the recession of 1974, our venture capitalists had deep pockets, but awfully short arms." As a result, Zschau's firm almost went belly up.

9. Compared to the venture capitalists, currently with $5 billion or so in finances, there are plenty of big spenders with more cautious leanings, who are ready to buy into a new firm once it goes public. Dave Bellet of Crown Associates estimated such funders of company growth presently have invested about $200 billion. But even this amount is dwarfed by the $1,000 billion of capital currently lent to established, mature companies like those on the *Fortune* 500 list. Why don't the big investment firms like banks, insurance companies, and pension funds put their money in high-technology start-ups and earn much higher average returns? Too risky, said Bellet. The more cautious investors want to see collateral, published reports about the firm by financial analysts, and so forth. They hold back until the new firm has a proven track record, and thus have to settle for a much lower return on investment. Bellet, speech at Innovation 2 Conference, 1982.

10. Peter Schille, *"Tal der Talente," Geo,* November 1981.

11. *San Jose Mercury,* 28 June 1981.

12. Ibid.

13. This account is based upon the authors' interview with Dr. Alice Ahlgren, Director of Communications at Cromemco, Mountain View, California, on August 17, 1982; a talk by Roger Melen, Cromemco's co-founder, at Stanford University, Stanford, California, on January 4, 1983; and Roger A. Mamis, "Cromemco's Never Taken a Dime From Anyone," *Inc.,* May 1981.

14. Mamis, "Cromemco's Never Taken a Dime."

15. Cromemco is very successful in China. This came about because a Chinese engineer in Palo Alto got hooked on a Cromemco computer, then introduced Harry Garland to his kinfolk in Peking and Garland was able to make some important connections. In the People's Republic of China, Cromemco's computers are now utilized to figure the optimal com-

bination of traditional Chinese herbs in various cures, an application that is a strange mixture of modernity and tradition. Cromemco also recently initiated sales outlets in Paris and Copenhagen and has high expectations for its European market. Authors' interview with Dr. Alice Ahlgren.

16. This section is based on the authors' interview with Frank G. Chambers, San Francisco, California, 4 August 1982.

17. *San Francisco Chronicle,* 23 September 1982.

18. Authors' interview with Pitch Johnson.

19. Our analysis of a dozen or so Silicon Valley venture capital firms shows that all of the principal actors are male. Venture capital, it seems, is a man's world, even more so than are other Silicon Valley activities.

20. *San Jose News,* 4 October 1982.

21. Peter Schille, *"Tal der Talente."*

Chapter 5

1. Authors' interview with Les Hogan, Mountain View, California, 15 November 1982.

2. Authors' interview with Howard Z. Bogert, Palo Alto, California, 20 July 1981.

3. Bill Grubb, (Speech delivered at the Innovation 2 Conference, Palo Alto, California, November 2, 1982).

4. Nolan Bushnell, "Entrepreneurial Engineering," (Speech delivered at National Engineers Week, Sunnyvale, California, February 25, 1983).

5. Dirk Hanson, *The New Alchemists: Silicon Valley and the Microelectronics Revolution* (Boston: Little, Brown & Co., 1982).

6. *Palo Alto Weekly,* 23 June 1982.

7. Ibid.

8. Ibid.

9. Authors' interview with "Karl Harrington," Sunnyvale, California, 8 March 1983.

10. Ernest Braun and Stuart MacDonald, *Revolution in Miniature: The History and Impact of Semiconductor Electronics* (New York: Cambridge University Press, 1978) p. 135.

11. Authors' interview with Howard Bogert.

12. Authors' interview with Hans Reiner, Stuttgart, W. Germany, 21 September 1982.

13. Jon Levine, "Living the Dream," *Venture,* Marck 1983.

14. Authors' interview with Gordon French, Stanford, California, 24 November 1982.

15. *InfoWorld,* 27 September 1982.

16. Ibid.

17. Ibid.

18. Colette Dowling, *The Techno/Peasant Survival Manual* (New York: Bantam Books, 1980) p. 92.

19. Thomas J. Murray, "Silicon Valley Faces Up to the 'People' Crunch," *Dun's Review* 18 (1981).

20. Authors' interview with "Paul Hess," San Jose, California, 23 August 1982.

21. *San Francisco Chronicle,* 23 September 1980.

22. Authors' interview with Stan Thomas, Sunnyvale, California, 6 January 1982.

23. Authors' interview with Sid Wilkins, Mountain View, California, 22 July 1982.

24. Ibid.

25. *San Francisco Chronicle,* 3 December, 1982.

26. *San Jose News,* 18 January 1982.

27. Authors' interview with Don Hoefler, Stanford, California, 12 February 1980.

28. Ibid.

29. Ibid.

30. Ibid.

31. Authors' interview with William Hewlett, Palo Alto, California, 30 August 1982.

32. Gene Bylinsky, "Intel's Biggest Shrinking Job Yet," *Fortune,* September 1982.

33. *New York Times,* 26 January 1983.

34. Eric von Hippel, "Appropriability of Innovation Benefits as a Predictor of the Functional Locus of Innovations" (Paper presented at International Conference on Technology Transfer, Berlin, 1980).

35. Authors' interview with Marcian E. ("Ted") Hoff, Santa Clara, California, 10 August 1982.

36. Von Hippel, "Appropriability of Innovation Benefits."

37. *San Jose Mercury News,* 9 January 1983. Quote is attributed to an article by Soichiro Tahara in the September 1982 issue of *Bungei Shunju,* a Japanese monthly magazine.

38. *Time,* 27 September 1982.

Chapter 6

1. *Newsweek,* 30 June 1980.

2. Authors' interview with Ted Hoff, Santa Clara, California, 10 August 1982.

3. Authors' interview with Robert Noyce, Santa Clara, California, 4 October 1982.

4. Robert N. Noyce, "Creativity by the Numbers," *Harvard Business Review* 58: (1980).

5. Certain parts of this section are based on the authors' interview with Robert N. Noyce.

6. Dirk Hanson, *The New Alchemists: Silicon Valley and the Microelectronics Revolution,* (Boston: Little, Brown & Co., 1982) pp. 91–92.

7. Ibid., p. 100.

8. Ibid., p. 98.

9. Les Hogan (authors' interview, Mountain View, California, 15 November 1982) provided insight into his celebrated move from Motorola to Fairchild Semiconductor: "I loved my work at Motorola, and was proud of our business success. Our 430 employees in Phoenix were shipping $20 million worth of semiconductors a month. And I had my arms around the whole operation; I knew every employee by first name. So I hated to leave. It wasn't because of the money, really. Certainly not the money alone. When Bob Noyce decided to leave Fairchild to start Intel, he flew down to see me in Phoenix and told me that I was his first choice to take his place. Sherman Fairchild took a liking to me, and he just kept upping the offer. It was a breathtaking offer. Fairchild was only about half the size of Motorola at that time. But Fairchild was the technology leader of the industry. So I decided to come to Silicon Valley."

10. Gene Bylinsky, "California's Great Breeding Ground for Industry," *Fortune,* June 1974.

11. Dave Lindorff, "The Venture 100: No Limits to Growth," *Venture,* May 1982. Co-founder Gordon Moore holds 9.8 percent of Intel's stock, worth $105.6 million.

12. Authors' interview with Robert N. Noyce.

13. Much of the material in this section is based on the authors' interview with Ted Hoff.

14. Gene Bylinsky, "Here Comes the Second Computer Revolution," *The Microelectronics Revolution,* ed. Tom Forester (Cambridge: MIT Press, 1981) p. 6.

15. Ibid., p. 6.

16. Ibid., p. 7.

17. Katherine Davis Fishman, *The Computer Establishment* (New York: Harper and Row, 1981).

18. Also involved in developing the Intel 8080 was Masatoshi Shima, who had worked on the 4004 while at Busicom. By 1973 he was working for Intel and today, Shima is director of Intel's design center in Tokyo.

19. *The Economist,* 25 January 1983.

20. William G. Oldham, "The Fabrication of Electronics Circuits," *The Microelectronics Revolution,* ed. Tom Forester (Cambridge: MIT Press, 1981).

Chapter 7

1. *San Jose News,* 28 December 1981.

2. Ibid.

3. *San Jose News,* 16 February 1982.

4. *San Jose News,* 30 November 1981.

5. *San Jose News,* 2 March 1983.

6. Authors' interview with Robert N. Noyce, Santa Clara, California, 4 October 1982.

7. Kathleen Wiegner, "The One That Almost Got Away," *Forbes,* 31 January 1983.

8. Authors' interview with "Jack," Los Altos, California, 1 March 1983.

9. *San Jose News,* 2 August 1982.

10. Authors' interview with "Herb" Sunnyvale, California, 4, March 1983.

11. Authors' interview with "Mike Nary," Palo Alto, California 12 March 1983.

12. Nolan Bushnell, "Entrepreneurial Engineering," (Speech delivered at National Engineers Week Banquet, Sunnyvale, California, February 25, 1983).

13. *Business Week,* 28 February 1983.

14. Authors' interview with "Kleis Bahmann," Palo Alto, California, 8 March 1983.

15. *San Jose News,* 22 February 1983.

16. *San Jose News,* 24 February 1983.

17. *San Jose News,* 23 February 1983.

18. Ibid.

19. *San Jose News,* 24 February 1983.

20. Bro Uttal, "A Computer Gadfly's Triumph," *Fortune,* February 1982.

21. *Business Week,* 22 February 1982.

22. *San Francisco Examiner,* 14 January 1983.

23. Uttal, "A Computer Gadfly's Triumph."

24. Mike Hogan, "The Wizard of Osborne," *California Business,* September 1982.

25. *San Jose News,* 13 January 1983.

26. *San Jose Mercury News,* 15 September 1983.

27. *San Jose Mercury News,* 17 February 1982.

28. *San Jose News,* 30 November 1981.

29. *San Jose Mercury News,* 11 April 1982.

30. *San Jose News,* 7 March 1983.

Chapter 8

1. *San Jose News,* 9 November 1981.

2. Authors' interview with "Karl Harrington," Sunnyvale, California, 12 July 1982.

3. *San Jose News,* 18 January 1982.

4. *San Jose News,* 9 November 1981.

5. *San Jose News,* 28 October 1981.

6. Authors' interview with Nick Larsen, Palo Alto, California, 9 December 1981.

7. Authors' interview with "Karl Harrington."

8. Lee Felsenstein, "Why Not Stay an Engineer?" (Speech delivered at meeting of IEEE, Sunnyvale, California, February 16, 1983).

9. Authors' interview with Dr. Alice Ahlgren, Mountain View, California, 17 August 1982.

10. Authors' interview with "Frank Vella," Palo Alto, California, 4 October 1982.

11. Authors' interview with "Kleis Bahmann," Sunnyvale, California, 10 February 1982.

12. Elizabeth Useem, *Education and High Technology Industry: The Case of Silicon Valley* (Boston: Northeastern University Institute for the Interdisciplinary Study of Education, 1981).

13. *New York Times,* 28 March 1982.

14. *Christian Science Monitor,* 6 October 1982.

15. James W. Botkin et al., *Global Stakes: The Future of High Technology in America* (Cambridge, Mass.: Ballinger Press, 1982).

16. *Peninsula Times Tribune,* 24 July 1980.

17. National Science Foundation, *Trends in Science and Engineering Degrees, 1950 through 1980* (Washington, D.C.: Science Resources Studies Highlights, October 7, 1981).

18. Betty M. Vetter, "Women Scientists and Engineers: Trends in Participation," *Science* 214 (18 December 1981).

19. Authors' interview with Ann Wells, Sunnyvale, California, 30 December 1981.

20. Authors' interview with "Frances," Mountain View, California, 1 March 1982.

21. Sandy Kurtzig, (Speech delivered at the Innovation 2 Conference, Palo Alto, California, November 3, 1982).

22. *Peninsula Times Tribune,* 8 December 1982.

23. Robert Howard, "Second Class in Silicon Valley," *Working Papers* 8 (1981).

24. *San Jose News,* 28 March 1982.
25. *San Jose News,* 19 April 1982.
26. *San Francisco Chronicle,* 25 February 1982.
27. Ibid.
28. Authors' interview with "Richard," Santa Clara, California, 25 January 1982.
29. Authors' interview with Eric Larsen, Palo Alto, California, 19 April 1982.
30. Charles Peddle (from remarks at the Student Entrepreneur Conference, Stanford University, Stanford, California, May 21, 1983).
31. Authors' interview with "Kleis Bahmann."

Chapter 9

1. *San Jose Mercury,* 28 June 1981.
2. Authors' interview with Barbara, Palo Alto, California, 11 January 1982.
3. *California Today,* 13 December 1981.
4. Authors' interview with Jim Wells, Mountain View, California, 26 February 1982.
5. Authors' interview with "Betsy," Cupertino, California, 4 May 1982.
6. Authors' interview with "Bev" and "Mike," Los Altos, California, 16 February 1982.
7. Authors' interview with "Marion," Sunnyvale, California, 20 January 1982.
8. Authors' interview with "Ann," Palo Alto, California, 13 April 1982.
9. Authors' interview with "Ellen," Los Altos, California, 19 February 1982.
10. *Peninsula Times Tribune,* 23 December 1981.
11. Authors' interview with "Ellen" and "Dennis," Palo Alto, California 6 January 1982.
12. Authors' interview with "Beth," Mountain View, California, 10 February 1982.
13. Authors' interview with "Connie," Saratoga, California, 22 January 1982.
14. Authors' interview with "Ken," Los Gatos, California, 15 May 1982.
15. Ibid.
16. Authors' interview with "Ellen."
17. Authors' interview with "Ken."
18. Authors' interview with Nick Larsen, Sunnyvale, California, 28 December 1982.
19. *San Jose News,* 16 February 1982.
20. Authors' interview with "Sue Rose," Santa Clara, California, 16 November 1982.
21. *Palo Alto Weekly,* 2 June 1982.
22. *San Jose News,* 25 January 1982.
23. *Sunnyvale* (Calif.) *Journal,* 7 October 1981.
24. *San Jose News,* 15 April 1982.
25. *San Jose Mercury News,* 23 May 1982.
26. *San Jose News,* 19 January 1982.
27. William H. Whyte Jr., *The Organization Man* (New York: Simon & Schuster, 1956).

Chapter 10

1. *San Jose News,* 3 February 1982.
2. Authors' interview with "John" and "Toni Manning," Santa Clara, California, 2 December 1981.
3. As per the *Marketing Economics Guide,* quoted in the *San Jose News,* 18 January 1982.
4. *San Jose Mercury News,* 9 May 1982.
5. *San Jose News,* 15 January 1983.
6. Authors' interview with Nick Larsen, Sunnyvale, California, 10 November 1982.
7. *San Jose News,* 7 December 1981.
8. *San Jose News,* 24 April 1982.
9. *San Jose News,* 13 August 1982.
10. *San Francisco Examiner,* 13 June 1982.
11. *San Jose Mercury News,* 28 March 1982.
12. Ibid.
13. *San Jose News,* 4 June 1982.

14. *San Jose Mercury, The Answer Book* (San Jose: *San Jose Mercury*, 1980.)

15. Annalee Saxenian, *Silicon Chips and Spatial Structure: The Industrial Basis of Urbanization in Santa Clara County, California* (Berkeley: University of California Institute of Urban and Regional Development, Working Paper 345, 1981).

16. *San Francisco Examiner*, 19 September 1980.

17. *San Jose Mercury*, 22 January 1980.

18. Saxenian, "Silicon Chips and Spatial Structure."

19. From a classified ad in the *San Jose Mercury*, 10 May 1980.

20. *San Jose News*, 31 August 1981.

21. *Palo Alto Weekly*, 9 December 1981; and *Peninsula Times Tribune*, 14 August 1983.

22. Authors' interview with Howard Z. Bogert, Santa Clara, California, 8 February 1982.

23. Authors' interview with "Karl Harrington," Sunnyvale, California, 12 July 1982.

24. Authors' interview with Mark Larsen, Santa Clara, California, 5 April 1982.

25. Authors' interview with Judy Wheeler, Santa Clara, California, 1 March 1982.

26. Authors' interview with Mark Larsen.

27. Authors' interview with Jim Wells, Mountain View, California, 26 February 1982.

28. Authors' interview with "Karl Harrington."

29. Authors' interview with Lester Hogan, Mountain View, California, 15 November 1982.

30. *San Jose News*, 1 September 1982.

31. *Peninsula Times Tribune*, 14 October 1980.

32. Authors' interview with Carol Bogert, Palo Alto, California, 5 April 1982.

33. *San Jose Mercury News*, 19 May 1982.

34. *San Jose News*, 18 January 1982.

35. *San Jose News*, 2 December 1981.

36. *San Jose News*, 11 October 1982.

37. Ibid.

38. Ibid.

39. *San Francisco Chronicle*, 10 March 1982.

40. *San Jose News*, 18 December 1981.

41. *San Jose News*, 29 November 1981.

42. *San Francisco Chronicle*, 18 April 1981.

43. *Peninsula Times Tribune*, 13 April 1982.

44. *Peninsula Times Tribune*, 6 April 1983.

45. *San Jose News*, 26 October 1981.

46. Ibid.

47. *San Jose News*, 25 February 1982.

Chapter 11

1. Authors' interview with Don Hoefler, Stanford, California, 12 February 1980.

2. *San Francisco Examiner*, 3 August 1980.

3. Susan Benner, "Storm Clouds Over Silicon Valley," *Inc.*, September 1982.

4. *Palo Alto Weekly*, 9 February 1983.

5. Benner, "Storm Clouds Over Silicon Valley."

6. Dirk Hanson, "Chips of War," *New West*, July 20, 1980, and *San Francisco Examiner*, 3 August 1980.

7. *New York Times*, 30 May 1982.

8. Ibid.

9. This account is based upon Bruce Entin, *San Jose News*, 14 December 1981.

10. *San Jose Mercury News*, and *Peninsula Times Tribune*, 12 June 1982.

11. *San Francisco Chronicle*, 6 January 1983.

12. *San Jose News*, 3 January 1983.

13. Robert Howard, "Second Class in Silicon Valley," *Working Papers* 8 (1981).

14. Lenny Siegel and Herb Borock, *Background Report on Silicon Valley* (Mountain View, Calif: Pacific Studies Center, Report to the U.S. Commission on Civil Rights, 1982).

15. Howard, "Second Class in Silicon Valley."

16. The hearing was held in the Santa Clara County Courthouse in San Jose on July 31, 1982.

17. Authors' interview with Robert N. Noyce, Santa Clara, California, 4 October 1982.

18. Authors' interview with Nancy Henry, Head of Data-Processing, Fairchild Semiconductor, Mountain View, California, 6 August 1982.

19. *San Jose Mercury,* 31 August 1980.

20. Ibid.

21. Ibid.

22. Ibid.

23. Ibid.

24. Lenny Siegel, "Microelectronics Does Little for the Third World," *Pacific Research* 10 (1979).

25. Authors' interview with Don Hoefler.

26. Wage estimates were obtained from the *Global Electronics Information Newsletter* 20 (1982): 2.

27. Howard, "Second Class in Silicon Valley."

28. Alan Bernstein and others, *Silicon Valley: Paradise or Paradox? The Impact of High Technology Industry on Santa Clara County* (Mountain View, California: Pacific Studies Center Report, 1977).

29. *San Jose News,* 3 January 1983.

30. *Peninsula Times Tribune,* 23 April 1982.

31. Certain details in the following account are based on Benner, "Storm Clouds Over Silicon Valley."

32. *Peninsula Times Tribune,* 2 February 1982.

33. *Peninsula Times Tribune,* 27 February 1982.

34. *Peninsula Times Tribune,* 8 March 1982.

35. *San Jose Mercury News,* 27 February 1983.

36. *San Francisco Chronicle,* 26 September 1980.

37. *San Jose News,* 4 January 1982.

38. A more detailed description may be found in Hardin, "The Tragedy of the Commons," and Garrett Hardin and John Baden, eds., *Managing the Commons* (San Francisco: Freeman, 1977).

39. Hardin, "The Tragedy of the Commons," *Science 162 (1968): 1243.*

Chapter 12

1. Alvin Toffler, *The Third Wave* (New York: William Morrow, 1980).

2. Elliot J. Schrage, *High Technology Trade Competition: The U.S.-Japan Trade Dispute in Integrated Circuits* (Cambridge: Harvard University Center for International Affairs, Program on U.S.-Japan Relations Report, 1981) p. 4.

3. Gene Bylinsky, "Japan's Ominous Chip Victory," *Fortune,* 14 December 1981.

4. Ibid.

5. Japanese firms had captured about 70 percent of 64K RAM production in 1981, then their share of the market dropped to 56 percent and will continue to drop in the immediate future. The true significance of Japan's success is that they got in early, reaped big profits, and now are moving on to production of the 256K RAM.

6. Benjamin Rosen, "64K RAMS at the Juncture," *Rosen Electronics Letter,* 26 March 1982.

7. Bylinsky, "Japan's Ominous Chip Victory."

8. *San Jose News,* 25 February 1982.

9. The Semiconductor Industry Association established a collaborative R&D program to which member firms are asked to contribute 2 percent of their R&D budget each year, as has the American Electronics Association. Further, eighteen U.S. companies have contributed to the funding of the Center for Integrated Systems at Stanford University.

10. William Ouchi, *Theory Z: How American Business Can Meet the Japanese Challenge* (Reading, Mass.: Addison-Wesley 1981).

11. As William Hewlett pointed out: "Professor Ouchi just called it Theory Z, and thus gave a name to what we were already doing." H-P was practicing their version of Theory Z since 1950, many years before the Palo Alto firm began to have direct contact with Japanese management style through its joint venture, Yokogawa-Hewlett-Packard, or Ouchi's book. Authors' interview with William Hewlett, Palo Alto, California, 30 August 1982.

12. *San Jose News,* 21 June 1982.

13. Ibid.

14. The economic power of certain of the *keiretsu* is considerable. For example, the Mitsubishi business group represents about 10 percent of Japan's GNP. Kenneth Beida, "The *Zaibatsu* and the *Keiretsu,*" in *Readings on Modern Japan: Culture, Politics, and Economics,* eds. D. Okimoto and Thomas P. Rohlen (New York: Aspen Institute for Humanistic Studies, 1979).

15. The five main Japanese semiconductor business companies are Nippon Electric Corporation (NEC), Hitachi, Toshiba, Matsushita, and Mitsubishi. These five semiconductor producers are also five of Japan's largest electronics manufacturers. The next five largest semiconductor firms in Japan are Sanyo, Fujitsu, Sony, Sharp, and Oki. Together these ten firms produce approximately 80 percent of Japanese semiconductors.

16. Chalmers Johnson, *MITI and the Japanese Miracle* (Palo Alto: Stanford University Press, 1982).

17. Kanichi Ohmae, *The Mind of the Strategist: The Art of Japanese Business* (New York: McGraw-Hill, 1982) p. 232.

18. Johnson, *MITI and the Japanese Miracle.*

19. Authors' interview with Yoshikazu Yamaguchi, Industrial Electronics Division, Machinery and Information Industries Bureau, MITI, Tokyo, 16 December 1982.

20. ICOT, *Outline of Research and Development Plans for Fifth Generation Computer Systems* (Tokyo: Japan Information Processing Development Center Report, 1982).

21. Bro Uttal, "Here Comes Computer Inc.," *Fortune,* 4 October 1982.

22. Authors' interview with Yoshikazu Yamaguchi.

23. The firms are Fujitsu, Hitachi, NEC, Mitsubishi, and Toshiba.

24. National Academy of Science, *The Competitive Status of the U.S. Auto Industry: A Study of the Influences of Technology in Determining International Industrial Competitive Advantage* (Washington, D.C.: National Academy Press, 1982).

25. Cost comparisons were made by James E. Harbour, an automotive industry consultant, whose analysis is cited by the U.S. Department of Transportation in an article by John Holusha, "General Motors: A Giant in Transition," *New York Times,* 14 November 1982.

26. Ibid.

27. Richard W. Anderson, "The Japanese Success Formula: Quality Equals the Competitive Edge," in *Quality Control: Japan's Key to High Productivity,* ed. Sydney S. Baron (Washington, D.C.: Electronics Industries Association of Japan, 25 March 1980).

28. Benjamin Rosen, "The Quality Goes In Before the (Japanese) Name Goes On," *Rosen Electronics Letter,* 31 March 1980.

29. Richard W. Anderson (from "A Summary of Remarks," Hewlett-Packard Systems Division, Cupertino, California, October 22, 1980).

30. Japan-U.S. differences in emphasis upon quality are illustrated by the standards used for the cleanrooms in which they produce semiconductor chips. American firms use a standard called "100"—meaning that up to 100 microns of dust per cubic foot per minute are allowed under the hood in which employees work, and "1,000" in the entire cleanroom. Japanese semiconductor firms allow a standard of "100" throughout the cleanroom and thus are cleaner by a factor of 10. Less dust translates directly into lower rejection rates for chips produced.

31. "I have lost $10 million contracts for semiconductors due to a one cent difference in price per device, when I knew my product was twice as high in quality. The customer just didn't care. But the customers did begin to care when the Japanese came in with semiconductors of high quality at about the same price," Les Hogan of Fairchild recalled. Authors' interview with Lester Hogan, Mountain View, California, 15 November 1982.

32. Perhaps the Japanese might equally label American establishments like the Intel Design Center in Tokyo or Yokogawa-Hewlett-Packard as "spyshops" too.

33. Authors' interview with Robert N. Noyce, Santa Clara, California, 4 October 1982.

34. Authors' personal interview with Dr. Michiyuki Oneohara, Director of Nippon Electric Corporation's Central Research Laboratories, Tokyo, 13 December 1980.

35. Authors' interview with Kaneshisa Enomoto, Manager of Engineering Administration, Toshiba Semiconductor Division, Tokyo, 17 July 1980.

36. *New York Times,* 8 March 1983.

37. Authors' interview with Tom Skornia, San Jose, California, 18 August 1982.

38. Allan Dodds Frank, "The U.S. Side of the Street," *Forbes*, 19 July 1982.

39. Kent E. Calder, "High-Technology Electronics Trade and the U.S.-Japan Relationship," *Fletcher Forum*, 1981. Calder shows that a somewhat similar concentration of microelectronics firms in a few Japanese prefectures has diminished the political power of the industry there as well.

40. As a response to the predicted shortage of 100,000 engineers needed in the near future by the microelectronics industry, the American Electronics Association created an engineering education foundation in 1982 to which its 1,800 members are asked to contribute an amount equal to 2 percent of their R&D budgets. The foundation seeks to increase faculty salaries and modernize laboratories at engineering schools.

41. Sabin Russell, "Intel, AMD Ink 10-Year 8086 Pact," *Electronic News*, 12 October 1981.

42. Ibid. Not to be outdone by Stanford, MIT established a Very Large Scale Integration Center in 1982, with $21 million donated by private firms (many located in Silicon Valley).

43. Authors' interview with John Linvill, Director, Center for Integrated Systems, Stanford, California, 23 June 1982.

Chapter 13

1. A research university engages both in enlarging the scientific knowledge base and in diffusing such knowledge into technological applications. Today there are about 50 to 75 such research universities in the United States. Robert M. Rozenzweig, *The Research Universities and Their Patrons* (Berkeley: University of California Press, 1982).

2. The importance of engineering in giving rise to a high-technology complex is not only due to the basis of microelectronics in electrical engineering, but also to the particular social class backgrounds of engineering students. Entrepreneurial activity is attractive to engineers, many of whom tend to come from working class backgrounds. We see this contrast at MIT versus Harvard—graduates of the latter university come from higher socioeconomic status parents and tend to enter professions such as law and medicine or to work for large corporations.

3. U.S. General Accounting Office, *Future University-Industry Collaboration Depends Upon Federal Support of University Research and Can Be Stimulated by Seed Funding* (Washington, D.C.: U.S. General Accounting Office Report, 1982).

4. Authors' interview with Robert N. Noyce, Santa Clara, California, 4 October 1982.

5. Ibid.

6. James F. Mahar and Dean C. Coddington, "The Scientific Complex: Proceed with Caution," *Harvard Business Review*, January–February 1965.

7. Christopher Rand, *Cambridge, U.S.A.: Hub of a New World* (New York: Oxford University Press, 1964) p. 9.

8. Authors' interview with Dr. Ed Roberts, Sloan School of Management, MIT, Cambridge, Massachusetts, 30 April 1982.

9. Georges ("The General") Doriot, a Harvard Business School professor, invested $70,000 in DEC, a 78 percent ownership of this start-up. DEC stands as one of the most profitable venture capital investments ever made on Route 128, and is its largest producer of minicomputers.

10. Paula Goldman Leventman, *Professionals Out of Work* (New York: Free Press, 1981).

11. The dominance of MIT does not mean it trained all the engineers who work in Route 128 firms. Northeastern University in Boston is a close second to MIT in producing engineers for Route 128 companies. Nancy Dorfman estimated that 92 percent of the electrical engineers who received their last degree in New England remained there to work, and few engineers are recruited from outside of the region. Route 128 is a relatively inbred complex, unlike Silicon Valley where immigrant engineers arrive in large numbers. Nancy S. Dorfman, *Massachusetts High Technology Boom in Perspective: An Investigation of Its Dimensions, Causes, and of the Role of New Firms* (Cambridge: MIT Center for Policy Alternatives, 1982).

12. Ibid.

13. Four MIT labs (Electronic Systems, Instrumentation, Lincoln, and the Research Lab for Electronics) were the parents of 105 spin-off firms on Route 128 as of the late 1960s,

and four MIT departments spawned 51 new firms. One private electronics firm (said to be Sylvania) had 39 spin-offs at that time. Edward B. Roberts, "A Basic Study of Innovations: How to Keep and Capitalize on Their Talents," *Research Management* 11 (1968).

14. Authors' correspondence with Ray Stata, Analog Devices, Norwood, Massachusetts, 2 July 1982.

15. Elizabeth Useem, *Education in a High-Technology World: The Case of Route 128* (Boston: Northeastern University, Institute for the Interdisciplinary Study of Education, 1982).

16. Half of the 1982 fiscal loss of $486 million in local government revenues was made up by additional state aid to local governments. Katherine L. Bradbury, "First Year Impacts of Proposition 2 1/2" (Boston: Federal Reserve Bank of Boston Economic Indicators, 1982).

17. Useem, *Education in a High-Technology World.*

18. Ibid., p. 22.

19. Ibid., p. 25.

20. Luther H. Hodges, *Businessman in the Statehouse* (Chapel Hill: University of North Carolina Press, 1962).

21. Ibid., and W. B. Hamilton, "The Research Triangle of North Carolina: A Study in Leadership for the Common Weal," *South Atlantic Quarterly* 65: (1966).

22. *Christian Science Monitor,* 15 June 1982.

23. Authors' interview with Mark L. Money, Director, University of Utah Research Park, Salt Lake City, 29 April 1982.

24. Authors' interview with Susan Mickelson, Manager of Administration, Evans and Sutherland Computer Corporation, Salt Lake City, Utah, 29 April 1982.

25. David Evans indirectly influenced Nolan Bushnell, founder of Atari, who indulged in nocturnal playing of Spacewar on Evans's mainframe computer when he was a student at The U.

26. Authors' interview with Mark Money.

27. *San Francisco Examiner-Chronicle,* 25 October 1981.

28. *San Jose News,* 12 July 1982.

29. *Peninsula Times Tribune,* 3 June 1981.

30. Ibid.

31. Authors' interview with Marcian E. "Ted" Hoff, Santa Clara, California, 10 August 1982.

32. Robert Noyce said: "Perhaps the entrepreneurial spirit will decay a bit. When Fairchild started, our average age was 30. When Intel started, the average age was 35. I see new start-ups today with a yet older age. However, maybe we have an aging of the semiconductor industry, but not of all entrepreneurial activities in Silicon Valley." Authors' interview with Robert Noyce.

Chapter 14

1. Paul J. Berman and Anthony G. Oettinger, *The Medium and the Telephone: The Politics of Information Resources* (Cambridge: Harvard University Program on Information Technologies and Public Policy, 1975).

2. Bro Utall, "What's Detaining the Office of the Future?" *Fortune,* 3 May 1982.

3. *USA Today,* 13 March 1980.

4. A national association of working women, "9 to 5," maintains that the automated office facilitates monitoring of employees. *New York Times,* 14 November 1982.

5. This scenario is adapted from Dan Mankin and others, "The Office of the Future: Prison or Paradise?" *The Futurist,* June 1982, pp. 33–36.

6. This example is based on N. Dean Meyer, "A Day in the Office of the Future: A Note on Office Automation," *Telecommunications Policy,* December 1979, pp. 314–19.

7. Most U.S. schools do not yet have enough computers to make an important educational impact. Ideally every school should have at least fifteen computers, so that a class of thirty students could use the equipment. At this time, the subjects most frequently taught with computers are math and computer programming.

8. These data come from an investigation on the effect of television viewing on chil-

dren's reading, directed by Donald Roberts of Stanford's Institute for Communication Research.

9. Seymour Papert, *Mindstorms: Children, Computers, and Powerful Ideas* (New York: Basic Books/Harper Colophon, 1980) p. 9.

10. Aaron Latham, "Video Games Star War," *New York Times Magazine,* 25 October 1981.

11. Bushnell's Computer Space was not the first video game. In 1966, three years before Bushnell created this game, Ralph Baer, an electrical engineer at Sanders Associates in Nashua, New Hampshire, had sold the idea for video games to Magnavox. Later Magnavox sold sublicenses to firms like Atari for the manufacturing of video games. Steve Bloom, *Video Invaders* (New York: Arco, 1982).

12. Latham, "Video Games Star War."

13. "In the Chips," *Life,* March 1982.

14. Peter W. Bernstein, "Atari and the Video-Game Explosion," *Fortune,* 27 July 1981.

15. Bushnell has said: "I'm not a great president on a day-to-day basis, worrying about all the problems. Atari was a really neat company that exemplified the best in high-growth, high-tech, go-go spirit in the early 1970s. In rapid growth, it's easy to lose control. Nevertheless, there was a magical group of technical talent; it was a lot of people with mutual respect, playing off each others' strengths, drinking beer together, raising hell, but working harder than they ever had before. Slowly it changed into a marketing-driven company, that had an awful lot of the characteristics of Proctor and Gamble, but not of Silicon Valley. I do not believe it is proper or intelligent to New York-ize a California high-technology company." Nolan Bushnell (speech delivered at National Engineers' Week Banquet, Sunnyvale, California, February 25, 1983).

16. Bernstein, "Atari and the Video-Game Explosion."

17. Ibid.

18. Game designers at Activision receive about 8,000 letters per week from their fans. Jim Levy (Speech at Innovation 2 Conference, Palo Alto, California, November 3, 1982).

19. In addition to Pac-Man, Japanese game designers also created the hit games Space Invaders and Donkey Kong.

20. Bushnell, speech at National Engineers' Banquet.

21. Ibid.

22. Levy, speech at Innovation 2 Conference.

23. Joseph Weizenbaum, *Computer Power and Human Reason: From Judgement to Calculation* (San Francisco: W. H. Freeman, 1976), p. 112.

24. Kenneth B. Peter, "The Hacker Papers," (Computer File on LOTS System, Stanford University, Palo Alto, California, 1979).

25. *San Jose Mercury News,* 16 May 1982.

26. Ibid.

27. Philip G. Zimbardo, "The Hacker Papers," *Psychology Today,* 14 October 1980, pp. 62–69.

28. Levy, speech at Innovation 2 Conference.

29. *InfoWorld,* 26 July 1982.

30. Alan Bernstein and others, *Silicon Valley: Paradise or Paradox? The Impact of High Technology on Santa Clara County* (Mountain View, Calif.: Pacific Studies Center, 1977).

31. Dorothy Nelkin, *Methadone Maintenance: A Technological Fix* (New York: George Braziller, 1973).

32. Levy, speech at Innovation 2 Conference.

33. *Peninsula Times Tribune,* 3 November 1982.

34. Ed Zschau (Speech at the Innovation 2 Conference, Palo Alto, California, November 3, 1982).

35. Randall Rothenberg, "The Neoliberal Club," *Esquire,* February 1982.

36. Jim Bartimo, "Reagan Lauds High-Tech Heartland," *Computerworld* 17 (31 January 1981).

37. *San Francisco Examiner-Chronicle,* 18 January 1981.

38. Ibid.

INDEX

ABC, 126–28
Activision, 66, 275
Acurex Corp., 14
Adams, Ernest W., 267
administrative guidance, 214
adolescent transition, 20–21, 47–50, 124–26, 130–31, 134, 135
Advanced Micro Devices (AMD), 27, 29, 48–52, 87, 91, 170, 182, 191, 209, 212, 220, 224, 226, 230, 245
affairs, 156–57
agglomeration, 148, 233, 234, 238
Ahlgren, Alice, 139
air pollution, 196–97
Allen, Paul, 17
Allied, 103
Altair, 3, 5, 71–72, 109
Altos Computer, 70
Amdahl, Carlton, 54, 135
Amdahl Corp., 53–54, 71, 180, 185, 221; capital problems, 53–54; competition with IBM, 54
Amdahl, Gene M., 53–54, 61, 71, 135
Amdahlization, 72
American Electronics Association, 28, 77–78, 141, 190, 224–25, 271

American Microsystems, Inc. (AMI), 46, 73, 91, 123–24, 144
American Research and Development Corp., 237
Ampex, 245, 261
Analog Devices, 238
Anderson, Reid, 125
Anderson, Richard W., 219
Anderson, Scott, 171
Anelco, 38
Ann Wells Personnel Services, 142
Apple Computer Inc., 3–24, 27, 34, 59, 60, 65, 69, 70, 73, 75, 77, 83, 86, 109, 169, 171, 179, 182, 212, 230, 268, 275; birth of, 8–11; disaster of Apple III, 19–21; as empire, 22–24; factors in success, 23–24; and IBM competition, 19; Lisa, 21–22; naming the new firm, 13–14; power supply for Apple II, 14–19; success, 18–19
Argabright, Keith, 72
Arizona State University, 249
art in Silicon Valley, 181–83
artificial intelligence (AI), 216, 257
ASK Computer Systems, 143–44
Asset Management Co., 62, 68, 75–76
Asteroids, 263

Atari, 4, 6, 8, 11, 12, 57, 60, 65, 66, 70, 80, 84,
    85–86, 93, 101, 111, 131–32, 160, 180, 181,
    261–64, 275
Atari Democrats, 272
Avantek, 14
Aweida, Jesse, 145

Bank of America, 13, 72, 136
bankruptcy, 122, 134–36, 170
Bardeen, John, 37
Bartel, Don, 171
BASIC, 17–18
Beavers, Jerry, 178
Beckman, Arnold O., 37
Beckman Instruments, 37
Bell Labs, 36–38, 103, 125
Bel Sale, Albert, 88
Bender, Lawrence, 182
Berg, Candace Linvill, 55
Bionic Valley, 242–43, 248
bits, 208
black market, 193–94
Bodo, Martin, 165
Boeing, 247
Bogert, Carol, 178
Bogert, Howard, 46, 91
Bohemian Club, 74
Boschert, Bob, 137
Boschert Electronics, 137
Boysel, Lee, 45
Bradley, Bill, 272
Brant, Ray, 138
Brattain, Walter, 37
Brown, Jerry, 226
Bruno, Albert, 47
Burkhalter, Edward A., Jr., 188
burnout, 152–54
Burroughs, 5
Bush, Vannevar, 31
Bushnell, Nolan, 4, 11, 12, 57, 65, 80, 84, 130,
    234, 260–64
Busicom, 104–107
business plan, 67
Byte Shop, 4, 9, 10–12

California Institute of Technology (Cal
    Tech), 37, 232
California Micro Devices, 164

California Microwave, 180
capital gains tax, 63, 271; and venture capi-
    tal, 63–64
Capital Management Services, 70
Cap'n Crunch, 6, 7
Capsco Sales, 164
career of a semiconductor engineer, 46
Casio, 97
casualties of Silicon Valley, 149–54
CAT scanner, 268–69
Catalyst Technologies, 57, 264
Cavett, Dick, 19
Center for Integrated Systems (CIS), 226–27
Centipede, 264
central processing unit (CPU), 105
Chambers, Frank, 73
cheap labor, 201–2
children and microcomputers, 258–60
Church, Frank, 225
CIA, 188
circuit board stuffing, 22
Clark, Candi, 7
clean room, 112–21
climate, 233–34, 248–49
Cohan, Kim, 171
Coherent, 14
Cole, Charles, 135
Colorado Springs, 245–46
Commodore, 5
communications technology, 253–54, 260
company secrecy policies, 79, 90
competition to collaboration, 226–29
Compton, Carl Taylor, 236
compunications, 253
computer addicts, 265–68
computer graphics, 243
Computer Kids, 4–8, 86, 87, 139
computer literates, 265
computer networks, 171–72
Computer Space, 261
computer stores, 10–11
computers, mainframe. See mainframe
    computers
Computer Terminals Corp., 106–107
Continental Capital Corp., 74
continuous technological innovation,
    96–97, 273
Control Data Corporation (CDC), 5, 247
Corrigan, Wilf, 45, 224
cottage computing, 257
Cow Girl Bar, 84, 162
Cox, Fred, 74
crime, 185–87
Crispin, Mark, 266

Cromemco, 4, 10, 47, 71–73, 86, 139
culture of high technology, 41

Daisy Systems, 145
Dallas, 244–45, 248
Data General, 5, 236–38, 243
Dataproducts, 73
Dataquest, 46, 83, 212
Datsun, 218
Davidson, Gordon, 81
Davis, Tommy, 77
Day, Lorraine, 197
Decathlon Club, 29
decentralization, 145–46
de Forest, Lee, 30
depression, 150
Desaigoudar, Chan, 164
design engineers, 88, 114–15, 175, 262
deskilling, 255
diffusion, 116
Digital Deli, 171
Digital Equipment Corp. (DEC), 5, 144, 236–38, 246, 247
divorces, 157–63
dopants, 116
Doriot, Georges, 237
Draper, Bill, 76
Drennan, David, 48
drinking problems of teenagers, 165–66
dropping off the edge, 153–54
Duke University, 231, 241, 248
Dwigans, Lynn, 89

Economist, 110
EEPROM (electrically erasable PROM), 114
EG&G, 236
Ehlers, Bryan, 182
Electronic Arrays, 220
Ellenby, John, 130
Electronic News, 107
electronics, birth of, 30–31
Electronics Industries Association of Japan, 219
employment, 255, 257, 272
ENIAC, 252
engineers, 240; a day in the life of, 148–49; and entrepreneurship, 60–61; and politics, 270–74

engineering shortage, 140–41
entrepreneurship, 38–39, 43–61, 134, 142, 229, 248–49, 250, 251, 272, 274; and the adolescent transition, 124–26; and Nolan Bushnell, 57; and engineering, 60–61; and immigrants, 144–45; inside 221–23; Mormon, 242–43; and politics, 270–74; and professors, 54–55; ratio to jobs created, 235; recycled, 53–54; and selective migration, 234; and Silicon Valley fever, 43–61; and "Silicon Valleys," 234–35, 247; and venture capital, 62–78
EPROM (erasable PROM), 114
Ericksen, Billye, 164
Evans, David, 243
Evans and Sutherland Computer Corp., 243
ESL, 270
executive search firms, 89
Exxon Enterprises, 170
Exxon Office Systems, 90

Fab 3, 82, 111–21
Faggin, Federico, 106–10
Fairchild, Sherman, 102
Fairchild Semiconductor, 14, 23, 26, 29, 38, 43–45, 46, 48, 50, 79, 84, 85, 91, 101, 102, 105, 112, 123, 135, 163, 177, 186, 190, 192, 194–95, 197–99, 224
father-child relations, 162–63
FBI, 94, 172, 188
Federal Bankruptcy Act, 136
Federal Telegraph Company, 30
Federman, Irwin, 186
feedthroughs, 16
Feinstein, Diane, 181
Felsenstein, Lee, 139
Fenwick, Stone, Davis and West, 81
Fifth Generation Computer Project, 216
Finegold, Aryeh, 145
first-round financing, 70
Fletcher, James, 242
Floating Point Systems, 246
floppy disks, 16
FMC, 269
Ford Aerospace, 246, 269
Four Phase Systems, 45
free market forces, 200–1, 224, 228, 271, 274
French, Gordon, 86
Fujitsu, 53, 124, 209, 219, 220, 228
Fulbright, J. William, 225

garages, 9, 32, 193–94
Garber, Steve, 172
Garland, Harry, 4, 47, 71–73
gatekeepers, 62
Gates, Bill, 4, 17, 61
Gelbach, Edward L., 107–9
Gelbach's Law, 109
gender inequality, 259–60
genealogy of semiconductor firms, 44
General Electric, 32, 239, 244
General Micro-Electronics, 46
General Motors, 218
General Technology Corp., 22
Glenmar Associates, 94
going public, 69
gold in the garbage, 174
goodies, 168–83
Gorin, Ralph, 268
Gould, Inc., 123–24
government-industry relationships in
    Japan, 215
Green Street, 187–88
grey market, 185–86
GRiD Systems, 54, 130–31
Grimm, Leslie, 60
Grove, Andrew, 99
Grubb, Bill, 80
gyosei shido, 214

hackers, 265–68
Hacker Papers, 267
Hambrecht, Bill, 69
Hanna, David, 131
Hardin, Garrett, 200
Hart, Gary, 272
Harvard University, 231
headhunting, 89–90, 151
health, 178–79
Heiser, Ted, 10
Helen Euphrat Gallery, 183
Hewlett, William, 14, 32–36, 66, 71, 145, 180,
    193, 234
Hewlett Foundation, 180
Hewlett-Packard, 6, 8, 9, 11, 12, 26, 32–36,
    52, 56, 66, 71, 82, 92, 97, 142, 143, 146, 157,
    175, 180, 191, 198, 211, 213, 219, 227, 228,
    230, 245, 246, 268; growth of, 33; history
    of, 32–34; management style of, 34; as a
    model, 71; success of, 34
high-tech entrepreneur, 166–67
high technology, 154; definition of, 29; and
    politics, 270–74

high-technology companies, 211, 225, 236;
    tension between R&D versus marketing,
    107
high voltage, 236
Hinkleman, Tom, 224
Hitachi, 94, 219, 220
Hitt, Joseph, 135
Hodges, Luther H., 240–41
Hodder, George, 270
Hoefler, Don C., 25, 92, 155, 185
Hoerni, Jean, 38, 112
Hoff, Marcian E. (Ted), 4, 81, 93, 98–111, 139,
    250
Hogan, Lester, 45, 79, 102, 177
Holt, Rod, 15, 139
Home Brew Computer Club, 9, 12, 86–87
homosexuality, 157
Honeywell, 246, 247
Hope, Bob, 218
Horley, Al, 83
Horley, Jeanette, 83
housing problems in Silicon Valley, 89, 100,
    173–74
house-sharing, 156
Hufstedler, Shirley, 142
Hunt, James B., Jr., 241
Hunting Gate Management Co., 168
Hwang, Kyupin Philip, 144–45

IBM, 5, 12, 19, 22, 52, 53, 92, 94, 95, 100, 125,
    136, 137, 144, 168, 180, 181, 206, 212, 213,
    215–16, 227, 241, 247; Adirondack, 94; and
    Japan, 215, 216, 217; sting, 94, 221
Imagic, 80, 275
immigrant entrepreneurs, 144–45
implementation problems, 255
inequality, 189–93, 271; and gender, 259–
    60
industry-university relationships, 231–32,
    236, 238
information, 276
information exchange, 79; and reciprocity,
    82
information revolution, 252
information-poor, 260
information-rich, 260
information society, 28, 154, 183, 189–93,
    205–6, 207, 232, 238, 251, 259, 265, 271, 273,
    275
Infoworld, 133
infrastructure, 232–33

Inmos, 246
inside entrepreneurs, 221–23
Institute for New Generation Computer Technology (ICOT), 216
integrated circuit, 101–2, 103
Intel, 4, 8, 13, 14, 27, 29, 38, 51, 68, 75, 80, 81, 84, 85, 86, 92, 96–21, 124, 131, 147, 150, 155, 176, 185, 186, 191, 198, 199, 205, 209, 212, 219, 220, 221, 224, 226, 227, 230, 233, 243, 245, 246, 247
interactivity, 253, 260
International Computer Modules, 46, 91
Intersil, 38
Introduction to Microcomputers, 133
ion implantation, 116, 120
Ionics, 236
Isuzu, 218
Iwatani, Toru, 223, 263

Jade Computer Products, 171
Japan as a blind spot, 228–29
Japanese competition, 92, 205–29; in autos, 217–18; in scaling-up, 129–30
Japan, Inc., 207, 213–17, 224
Japan lobby, 225
Japanese management, 92, 210–13
Japanese microelectronics industry, 95
Jaunich, Robert, 134
job mobility, 79, 87–88, 158, 159–60
Jobs, Steven P., 4–24, 65, 109, 145, 193, 234, 275
Johnson, Franklin P., Jr. (Pitch), 62, 68–70, 75–76

Kaypro, 134
keiretsu, 212–13
KGB, 188
Kilby, Jack, 101, 103
Kinsky, Michael, 272
Kleiner, Eugene, 38
Kleiner, Perkins, Caulfield and Byers, 57, 84
Kolff, William, 242
Kroos, David, 182
Kurtzig, Sandy, 143
Kvamme, Floyd, 83

Land, Ed, 232
Larsen, Mark, 50, 155, 176
Larsen, Nick, 137, 138, 170
Last, Jay, 38
layoffs, 150–52, 237
Learning Company, The (TLC), 58–60, 76
learning curve, 96–97, 109, 210
Lee, Richard, 126
Levy, Jim, 66
Life magazine, 261
lifestyles, 155–67
lifetime employment, 92, 147, 211
line operators, 119–21, 190–91, 192; training of, 120
Linvill, John, 54–55, 59, 61, 227
Lion and Compass Restaurant, 84
Lockheed Missiles and Space Co., 6, 39, 245, 269
Low, George M., 243
LSI (large scale integration), 108
LSI Logic, Inc., 221
luck, 154

Madden, Clifford, 54
Magna Power Tool Corp., 73
Magnuson Computer Systems, 134–36
Magnuson, Paul, 135
mainframe computers, 4, 109, 125, 135–36, 261, 268
Malone, Michael, 13
management assistance from venture capitalists, 69–70
management, Japanese, 92
management problems of Silicon Valley firms, 126–28
management team for a start-up, 66
management style in high-tech firms: Intel, 99; Tandem, 56–57; Theory Z, 212
Manatt, Charles, 225
market definition, 130–31
Markkula, Armas C., Jr., 13, 18, 20
Martin, Shirley, 144
Maruman Semiconductor, 221
masking process, 116
masks, 114–15
Massachusetts High-Technology Council, 141, 238–40, 273
Matsui, 213
Mayfield Fund, 77
Mazor, Stan, 105–108
McConnell, Vicky, 81

McCullough, Robert, 135
McKenna, Regis, 10, 12, 58
McLellan, Diana, 172
McMurty, Burt, 77
Measurex, 180
Medford, Sam, 179
Melchor, Jack, 60, 76–77, 133
Melchor Venture Management, 60, 76
Melen, Roger, 4, 71–73
Memorex, 46, 136, 137
meritocracy, 139, 154
Meter, Roberta, 165
Micro Mask, 246
Micro Smut, 172
Microsoft, 4
Micro Timesharing, 171
microcomputers, 5, 105, 109, 145, 247, 253, 265, 268–69; and children, 258–60
Microelectronics and Computer Technology Corp., 245
Microelectronics Center of North Carolina, 242
microelectronics industry, 36–39, 96, 99, 100, 140–41, 146, 189–93, 209, 241, 250, 274; and health, 195–99; and unemployment, 132; and venture capital, 69; Japanese, 95
microelectronics firms: agglomeration of, 148; size of, 58
Microelectronics News, 185
microprocessor, 5, 98, 250, 256; definition of, 105; invention of, 81, 103–11
military funding, 39, 237, 269–70
minicomputers, 105, 108, 238, 247
Minneapolis-St. Paul, 247, 249
MIT (Massachusetts Institute of Technology), 31–32, 231, 235–40, 243, 248, 261, 265
Ministry of International Trade and Industry, 206, 213–17, 221, 273
Mitsubishi, 94, 209, 213, 221
Money, Mark, 243
Monolithic Memories, 186–87
Monsanto, 113
Moore, Fred, 86–87
Moore, Gordon, 38, 97, 99, 102, 106, 199
Moore's Law, 97
Mormons, 242–43, 262
Morris, Jane, 273
MOS (metal oxide on silicon), 108
Mostek, 123, 219, 245, 246
Motorola, 49–50, 102, 209, 210, 220, 224, 245, 247
mouse, 21
Ms. Pac-Man, 264

Nakamura, Masaya, 222
Namco, Ltd., 222–23, 263
National Computer Conference, 139
National Enquirer, 198
National Semiconductor, 13, 52, 83, 131, 159, 164, 165, 177, 178, 186, 191, 205, 212, 224, 225, 247
NEC (Nippon Electronics Corp.), 209, 219, 220, 221, 222, 228
Nelson, Ted, 3, 4, 10
neoliberals, 272
nerds, 265, 267
networks, 79–95, 191
New York Times, 211
nondisclosure agreement, 90, 92
Norman, Bob, 46
North Carolina State University, 231, 241, 248
North County, 27, 189–93, 196
North Star Computer, 14, 86
Northrup, Malcolm, 126
Noyce, Robert, 38, 58, 61, 68, 96, 99, 101–5, 124, 155, 191, 205, 209, 221, 224, 233, 234
NTT (Nippon Telegraph and Telephone), 216

OEM (original equipment manufacturer), 143, 148
office automation, 254–56; effects on unemployment, 255; resistance to, 255
office of the future, 254, 256, 258
Olsen, Ken, 238
Olson, Richard, 22
Opel, J. R., 52
Optacon, 55
Orange County, 247, 249
Organization Man, The, 166–67
Osborne, Adam, 4, 133, 138
Osborne Computer Corp., 4, 76, 133–34, 138, 139
oscillator, 33
Ouchi, William G., 210

Packard, David, 14, 32–36, 66, 71, 145, 193, 234
pack investing, 65; by venture capitalists, 68
Packard Foundation, 181

Pac-Man, 132, 181, 223, 263
Paley, Maxwell, 95
Palo Alto Square, 80
paperless office, 253
patent, 93, 177
paths not taken, 268–70
Payne Associates, 95
Peat, Marwick, Mitchell, 89
Peddle, Charles, 8, 152
Peninsula Times Tribune, 141
Penisten, Glenn, 123
Penzias, Arno, 36
Peppermill, 84, 85
Peters, Charles, 272
Pfeiffer, Pat, 182
Pfotenhauer, Scott, 81
Philco Corp., 101
Phoenix, 247, 249
photolithography, 117
phreak, 6
physical fitness, 178–79
Piestrup, Ann, 59–61
Pizza Time Theatre, 264
planar process, 103, 112
Polaroid, 232, 239
Pong, 261, 262, 263
Poor, Victor, 106
Popular Electronics, 71
Popular Science, 103
Portland, 246–47, 249
potting, 94
price competition, 97, 132
Professional Secretaries International (PSI), 144
professor-entrepreneurs, 54–55
PROM (programmable read-only memory), 114
Proposition 2½. 239–40
pushes, 152–53

quality of life, 184; in Silicon Valley, 39; in "Silicon Valleys," 233–34, 248–49

Radio Shack, 245
RAM (random access memory), 97, 114, 207–10; definition, 208
Raster Blaster, 263
Raytheon, 49, 91, 190, 236, 239

RCA, 30
R&D, 99, 139, 143–44, 210, 215, 216, 217, 241, 246, 250, 251, 257, 273
Reagan, Ronald, 273
recession, 131–34, 170, 238, 247, 273
Reiner, Hans, 83
Rensselaer Technology Park, 244, 248
Rent-A-Computer, 171
Research Triangle, 230, 232, 240–42, 248
Research Triangle Park, 241
research university, 231–32, 247, 248–49
retail computer stores, 10–11
reverse engineering, 94
Rheem, 91
Richards, Evelyn, 134
Riley, Joe, 29
Roberts, Ed, 4, 71
Roberts, Shelton, 38
Robertson, Alice, 7
robots, 256–57, 264
Rock, Arthur, 18, 51, 74, 102
Rockwell, 46
Rogers, Michael, 43
rogue engineers, 91
Rohatyn, Felix, 272
Rolm, 69, 73, 76–77, 146–47, 179, 245, 246
ROM (read-only memory), 114
Rothschild, Unterberg, Towbin, 133
Route 128, 31, 231, 233–34, 235–40, 248
RPI (Rensselaer Polytechnic Institute), 230, 243–44, 248
Rozett, Marlene, 164
Rozett, Steve, 164
running, 178–79
Russia, 141, 185–88

Salt Lake City, 230, 232, 242–43, 248, 260
Sanders, Walter J., III (Jerry), 25, 49–52, 61, 87, 155, 170, 209, 212, 224
San Francisco Museum of Modern Art, 182
San Jose Black Theatre Workshop, 181
San Jose Mercury News, 13, 135, 197
San Jose Museum of Art, 181
San Jose News, 172, 179
Santa Clara County, 28, 169, 173, 184, 202, 231, 250, 269, 274, 275
scale-up problems, 129–31
Schlumberger, 45, 123
Schmieder, Richard, 58
schools and microcomputers, 258–60

Scott, Michael, 13, 18, 20
Seagate Technology, 62, 137, 168
Sears, John, 225
Seattle, 247, 249
second source, 49, 51, 106
seed financing, 67
semiconductor, 96–97, 186, 247, 250, 253, 275; complexity, 98; definition, 115; Japanese competition, 206, 214; production of, 111–21, 129–30; quality, 218–20; second source, 49; stages in life cycle, 48–50
semiconductor firms' genealogy, 44
semiconductor industry, 96, 142–43, 195; beginnings of, 36–39; and health, 195–99; invention of the transistor, 37; Japanese, 214
Semiconductor Industry Association (SIA), 224, 225
shake-out, 97, 132
Shell Oil, 133
Shockley Eight, 38, 101
Shockley Semiconductor Laboratories, 37, 101
Shockley, William, 37–39, 46
Shugart, Al, 62, 137–38, 168–69
Shugart Associates, 62, 137, 168
Signetics Corp., 14, 49, 176, 198
Silicon Desert, 247, 249
Siliconix, 46, 126, 180
Silicon Mountain, 245–46, 249
Silicon Prairie, 244–45, 248
Silicon Valley: art, 181–83; casualties of, 149–54; facilities, 145–47; father-child relationships, 162–63; future of, 250–51; goodies, 168–83; housing problems, 89; impact of, 252–76; infrastructure of, 147–48; kids, 164–66; lifestyles, 155–67; location of, 25–27; losing out in, 122–36; and luck, 39; military funding of, 39; naming it, 20; politicization of, 223–36; and recession, 131–34; rise of, 25–39; social problems, 184–202; spread of, 230–51; tomorrow of, 203–76; Third World women, 144; as an unhealthy place, 195–99; women in, 141–48; workstyles, 137–54
Silicon Valley East, 243–44, 248
Silicon Valley kids, 164–66
Silicon Valley North, 246–47, 249
size of microelectronics firms, 58
Skornia, Tom, 52, 224
Smith, Roger, 217
smog, 197
Smythe, Jack, 60
social evolution, 271

social problems, 268–69, 271; high-technology solutions, 269
socioeconomic gaps, 260
software, 17–18, 133–34, 177, 269, 275
software programmers, 17–18
Southard, Doug, 186
South County, 27, 189–93, 196
Spacewar, 261
Spectra Physics, 55, 170
Sperry, 247
spin-offs, 81, 213, 234, 245, 246, 247
Sporck, Charles, 52, 205, 224, 225
spy shops, 220
Standard Electrik Lorenz (SEL), 83
Stanford, Leland, 30, 36
Stanford Research Park, 26, 34, 36, 189, 232
Stanford Solar Systems, 164
Stanford University, 26, 30–36, 38, 39, 54, 66, 71, 75, 104, 143, 227, 238, 242, 243, 248, 265–68, 270
start-ups, 128–29, 130, 232, 236, 247; steps in the process of, 65–70
Stata, Ray, 238
State University of New York at Albany, 244, 248
Sterling, Wallace, 35
sting operation, 94
Storage Technology Corp., 145
Stratigos, Anthea, 81
Strip, The, 170–71
Strauch, Charles, 136
success factors for Silicon Valley, 231–35
Sunnyvale Community Center, 182
Super Computer Project, 216–17
supermoms, 163
Sutherland, Ivan E., 243
Suzuki, 218
sweatshops, 193–94
Syntex, 180
System Industries, 271

take-overs, 122–24
Tandem, 14, 34, 56–57, 67, 69, 84, 147, 164, 179, 228, 245; business plan, 67; people-oriented management, 56–57
Tandy Corp., 245
Taylor, Donna, 264
Taxachusetts, 239
Teatro de la Gente, 181
technological fix, 269
technology transfer: from universities, 231–32, 236; to Japan, 220–21

Technology Venture Investors, 77
technological innovation, 96–97, 223, 237, 272
Tektronix, 246
teleconference, 257, 258
Telesensory Systems, 55
teleshopping, 258
Televideo, 145
teleworking, 257
Terman, Frederick E., 25, 30–36, 38, 104, 230, 238, 242
Terrell, Paul, 10, 86
Texas Instruments, 48, 97, 101–102, 106, 108, 213, 219, 220, 244–45, 246
Theory Z, 210–13
thin film, 116–18
Third World: semiconductor assembly, 194–95; women, 144, 191, 194–95
Thomas, Stan, 88, 168
3000 Sand Hill Road, 64–65, 80
Thurow, Lester, 272
tilt-ups, 146
Toshiba, 209, 213, 221, 222, 228
Toyota Motors, 213, 218
trade secrets, 91, 94, 188
traffic problems, 196
tragedy of the commons, 199–201
transistor, 37–38, 104, 209
Treybig, James, 56, 84
Trilogy Systems, 54, 135
Triton Museum of Art, 181
TRW, 124
Tsongas, Paul, 272
Tunney, John, 225
two-career households, 164–65

under-capitalization, 128–29
unemployment, 255, 257, 272
Unicom, 46
Union Carbide Electronics, 38
unions, 119, 190–91, 241, 250
United Technologies, 123
United Way of Santa Clara County, 179–80
University of California at Irvine, 247
University of Minnesota, 249
University of North Carolina, 231, 241, 248
University of Texas at Austin, 245
University of Utah, 230, 232, 242–43, 248, 260

University of Utah Research Park, 230, 232, 242, 248
University of Washington, 249

Valentine, Don, 12, 70, 262
Varian Associates, 14, 35
venture capital, 13, 57, 62–78, 102, 127, 128, 142, 151, 233, 237, 242, 244, 247, 248–49, 262, 271, 274; definition of, 63; excessive, 64; management assistance, 69–70
Verbatim Corp., 14, 125–26, 182
vertical integration, 213
Vias, Thomas, 180
Victor Technologies, 152
video arcades, 263
video games, 132–33, 181, 222–23, 260–62, 269, 275; designers of, 263
VisiCorp, 233
Vitalink Communication Corp., 84
vulture capitalists, 63, 70

wafers, 111–21
Walker's Wagon Wheel Bar and Restaurant, 84
Walt Disney Studios, 33
Wang, An, 231
Wang Laboratories, 88, 231–32, 236
Warner Communications, 262
Warren, Jim, 86
Washington Post, 172
water pollution, 197–99
Weimers, Leigh, 172
Weizenbaum, Joseph, 265
Wells, Ann, 142
WESCON, 8
West Coast Computer Faire, 18
Wheeler, Judy, 176
Whitney, Tom, 60
Whyte, William H., Jr., 166
Wigger, Bob, 112
Wilkins, Sid, 89
Williams, Ray, 135
Wilson, Boyd W., 10, 86
Wilson, John, 81
Wilson, Pete, 226
Wilson, Sonsini, Goodrich and Rosati, 81
Winer's Living Bulletin Board, 172
Wirth, Tim, 272
women in Silicon Valley, 141–44
word-processing, 253, 254
WordStar, 17

work ethic, 140, 150, 188; Japanese, 207

workaholics, 163, 167, 176

working in Silicon Valley, 137–54

Wozniak, Stephan G., 4–24, 65, 86, 109, 193

Xerox, 268

Ylvisaker, William, 123

Young, John, 52

Zieber, Fred, 212

Zilog, 14

Zschau, Ed, 226, 271, 273

Zyvex Corp., 164